6 - IV, '22

Moin, Joy,
happy
reading.
gitta + yogi

FANATIC

A Novel by Norman Watt

Left page: Saint Eustace, Albrecht Dürer, 1501

1. Revised Edition December 2021

© 2021 by Norman Watt & Stoltenberg Institute for
German-American Forty-Eighter Studies, Flensburg & Northfield, MN
www.moin-moin.us • yogireppmann@gmail.com
ISBN 978-0-9912758-9-2
Layout by Jan-Reza Sadri

Print on Demand
www.lulu.com

Chapter 1

As usual, I was running a few minutes late. Hurrying from one shade tree to the next, I felt beads of sweat trickling down my forehead. Hochstraaten would be there, Charlotte had said. Maybe once I got to know him better . . .

Number 5 was a tidy red-brick bungalow set well back from the road like all the houses on Faculty Row. A black Mercedes 300D gleamed in the driveway; late '70s, I guessed, and in pristine condition. Charlotte Rossi was standing on the front stoop as I walked up the path.

"Well, here you are," she said. "I was starting to wonder."

"Sorry, got carried away unpacking."

"You might try setting your watch ahead a couple of minutes. Works for me."

"I don't own a watch, I just use my phone."

Charlotte gave me a skeptical look. "So come on in out of the heat."

"Nice Mercedes," I said as I climbed the front steps.

"It's not ours, if that's what you're thinking. We're Toyota folks."

She held the screen door open for me and I stepped into the welcoming chill. At the far end of the living room, Klaus Hochstraaten sat poker-straight in a rocking chair, looking as stern as an Old Testament prophet minus the beard. He fixed his eyes on me and rose a few inches from his seat.

"Guten Tag, Herr Ritter."

"Guten Tag, Herr Professor," I said with a nod, already feeling ill at ease. I followed Charlotte into the kitchen, where the appetizing aromas of basil and thyme filled the air.

"Colin, this is my husband Michael. He teaches art history here at the college, but today he's going to demonstrate his culinary skills."

Tall and gaunt, Michael Rossi hardly fit my image of a well-fed Italian chef. He stuck out an elbow for me to shake.

"Don't know how this will turn out," he said as he lifted the lid from a steaming pot on the stove. "I've made chicken cacciatore often enough, but I added a couple of new ingredients this time."

"Smells delicious," I said.

"We'll find out in a minute, it's just about ready."

"Something to drink?" Charlotte asked. "The rest of us are having pinot grigio."

"Perfect."

She ran a plump hand through her disorderly graying hair, poured me a glass from a bottle on the kitchen counter, then led the way back to the living room.

"Klaus is leaving for Argentina the day after tomorrow," she said as we sat down on the sofa. "He makes the trip every August to visit his father."

Argentina . . . I knew, of course, that many Germans had settled there, often under questionable circumstances. I'd have to be careful not to say anything that might put Hochstraaten on the spot. But he spoke before I had a chance to in any case.

"'Ein riter der gelêret was und ez an den buochen las . . .' That would be you, then, I assume?" he said with a smirk.

I forced a smile. Was he just punning on my last name as Germans sometimes liked to do, or was he trying to trip me up? My field was eighteenth century, but I knew enough of Middle High German literature to recognize the quote.

"Oh, I've read a book or two, but I'm not sure how 'gelêret' I am. And I certainly don't have the rank of a medieval knight. None of us with the name 'Ritter' do nowadays, of course."

Hochstraaten's mouth turned up at one corner. "You will not take it amiss, then, if I put you in the category of 'untitled'?"

I continued to smile. How about if I put you in the category of 'asshole,' I said to myself.

"Come off it, Klaus," Charlotte said, "you had a 'von' in your name yourself that you got rid of, so you told me."

"Ah, but only because it was cumbersome. People in this country have enough trouble as it is spelling my name. The 'von' is still present in the spirit."

Just as I was thinking 'double asshole,' Michael called from the kitchen that everything was ready.

Charlotte got up to help her husband carry the bowls of chicken and spaghetti into the dining room. As I followed Hochstraaten to the table, I noticed that he walked with a pronounced limp. Did he have some malady associated with aging? The man had to be seventy if he was a day.

"Welcome to Baumgartner Land," Michael said as we sat down.

"Baumgartner . . ."

"Lukas Baumgartner," Charlotte said, "the founder of the college. You'll see his mark on just about everything around here, the design of the buildings, the layout of the grounds . . . He was no doubt brilliant, if slightly loony."

"Now, Charlotte, you're exaggerating."

"I don't think so, Michael. How about those visions he supposedly had, and his last diary entry? Buried treasure or whatever."

Michael made a face. "That's not what he said. I don't quite remember how he put it, something like—"

". . . 'a certain *objet d'art* of inestimable value,' to be precise," Hochstraaten interjected.

"Yes, that's it. And then the diary entry ends with a cryptic poem. It amounts to a challenge to find whatever it is he's hidden."

Charlotte shook her head. "Right. If he actually *did* hide something."

"Well, I happen to believe he did."

Hochstraaten made a gesture as if shooing away a fly.

"Such nonsense. As Charlotte has indicated, it is a well-known fact that our unfortunate founder was of an unstable mind, especially in his final years. It would be sheer folly, if not utter madness, to waste one's time thinking about such an inane matter."

"Oh?" Michael raised an eyebrow. "For somebody who thinks it's inane, you have a surprisingly good command of his exact wording."

Hochstraaten shook his head. "This means nothing. It is simply that I have the gift—sometimes affliction—of what is akin to a photographic memory. Once I have read a passage, it remains in the recesses of my mind whether I like it or not."

"It *has* been over a hundred years now," Charlotte said, "and nobody's ever figured any of it out. Doesn't that tell you, Michael—"

"All it tells me is that, just as you said, nobody has figured any of it out."

"Have you ever tried?" I asked.

"Not a chance, I'm a purely visual kind of guy, not a wordsmith."

"So Baumgartner didn't say what the work of art was, I take it?"

"Not even a hint."

Charlotte turned to me. "Something for you to play with, Colin? Seems to me you said in your dossier that you liked to do crosswords and Sudokus."

I had to laugh. "Liking to do them isn't the same as doing them well. Mid-week New York Times crosswords are about my limit. Same goes for Sudokus."

"Baumgartner's puzzle isn't anything like those," Michael said. "It does involve a kind of word game, though. Have a look at that diary entry and you'll see what I mean."

"Maybe I will. As a registered art fanatic, I wouldn't mind winning his prize, whatever it is." I laughed again.

Hochstraaten stared at me. "I assume you are using the word 'fanatic' rather loosely, *Herr Ritter*?"

"To a degree, I suppose. It's what my college friends used to call me, because I worked whenever I could as a gallery guard at the Minneapolis Institute of Art—Thursday and Friday evenings, weekends, whatever. Had to quit in graduate school, I just didn't have the time."

"And how would you find the time now to pursue this ludicrous puzzle venture? I believe that you were hired to teach here, not to play games."

I bit my tongue and took a sip of wine. "You're right, it might not work out at all."

Charlotte passed me the salad bowl. "Say, what did you do to your hand?" she asked.

I felt my face flush. "Oh, I banged it against the car door when I was unloading yesterday. It's nothing, really." I didn't think my new colleagues needed to know that the sobriquet "Mr. Klutz" had appeared next to my high school yearbook picture.

"Well, I'm glad you were able to move down this early. You should have plenty of time to get your fall classes ready."

"I would think so. I'd like to research the Lessing paper I'm planning on writing, too."

"Lessing!" Hochstraaten shook his head with obvious distaste. "Famous for that preposterous play in which a wealthy Jew hoodwinks the powerful Sultan. . . ."

I gave him what I hoped would come across as a dirty look. "I wouldn't say he *hoodwinks* him, he simply convinces him through the power of reasoning of the value of religious tolerance."

"Reasoning can be ill-used. Lessing was in many instances far too limited by rationalist thinking."

"I suppose that's one valid viewpoint," I said, "but I happen to believe that rationalist thinking, as you put it, was a major strength of his."

Charlotte's eyes darted back and forth from Hochstraaten to me. "Lukas Baumgartner would have agreed with you there," she put in quickly. "Lessing as the bringer of enlightenment. Baumgartner even named our library after him."

Hochstraaten glanced at her out of the corner of his eye but said nothing. The conversation remained on the level of small talk as the meal continued. When we were finished with the main course, Charlotte brought in huge dishes of ice cream.

"Something to help us keep cool," she said. "July was a beast, even for Kentucky, and it doesn't look like August will be any better. I hope you don't have anything strenuous planned for the afternoon, Colin, like mowing the lawn."

"Oh, no. I thought I might stroll around campus, get to know the place a bit, check out the Dürer museum in particular. Must be pretty impressive, judging by the college website."

"*Pretty* impressive is an understatement," Michael said, "to say nothing of the castle where it's housed. You'll have to wait till tomorrow, though, the museum is only open two afternoons a week in the summer. I'd show you around, but Charlotte and I have a committee meeting that's likely to last most of the afternoon."

"How about you, Klaus," Charlotte said, "do you suppose—"

Hochstraaten frowned. "Yes, perhaps I could do this, though I will have little time. If you would come to the castle at two-thirty tomorrow."

"All right," I said, "I'll do that."

I was less than thrilled by the offer, but I didn't see how I could decline. I turned abruptly to the chef.

"Wonderful meal, Michael, thanks."

"Glad you could be here."

Hochstraaten seemed to avoid looking at me as Charlotte walked to the front door with us. "Two-thirty," he said. "Please be punctual."

"Yes, of course. Two-thirty, not a minute later."

He turned to me as he struggled down the front steps. "So, *Herr Ritter*, attempt your little game if you must. I'll wager you will find it one that you cannot win."

You're on, you son of a bitch, I said to myself.

Hochstraaten lifted his left leg with a grunt as he climbed into the Mercedes. I felt a distinct sense of relief as I watched him drive off.

"By the way, Charlotte," I said, "thanks for all the breakfast goodies you put in my fridge."

"Oh, it wasn't much, just enough to tide you over. I expect you'll be wanting to stop by the grocery store this afternoon."

"Right. Where would that be?"

"Well, there's not really any choice, Clyde's is the only one for miles." She pointed along the street. "You turn just past the last house on Faculty Row and drive down through the woods to Main Street. Once you're at the bottom of the hill it's not but half a mile or so to the town square. There's a bakery on the square, too, and a hardware store and a law office. Called Locke, Locke and Gates, of all things."

"No way, how funny is that!"

"Luke Baumgartner thought so too. At least the story goes he chose them over their competitor because of the name. There was only one 'Locke' at the time. I like to tell people they've had to beef up security since then."

"Not bad," I said.

Charlotte paused for a moment. "By the way, that business about Baumgartner's final diary entry . . ."

"Which you seemed to think was a crock."

"Oh, I just like to argue with my husband about it. Anyhow, if your puzzler's itch gets to you, you'll find the diaries on the third floor of the library, in the biography section."

"Hmm. Maybe I'll run over there before I go for my groceries."

"You know what else? You might want to have a chat with old Mr. Locke—that's Clay Locke III. He knows quite a bit about Luke Baumgartner. His father or grandfather, one, dealt with all of Luke's legal matters. Apparently his will contains some things that are just as strange as what he says in his diary."

"Oh? Now you've *really* piqued my curiosity."

"Don't let Mr. Locke's manner put you off, though. He can be kind of a cranky old cuss."

I said goodbye and walked back along Faculty Row to the house I was renting. Just what I need in my life, I thought, another cranky old cuss.

Chapter 2

Castle Arcadia, 18 November 1908

Twilight has come, and with it the conclusion of my diaries. I offer the fervent wish that those who read these volumes may discover something about themselves; certainly we can all learn from the study of other men's lives.

I wish also that one fine day there may happen along an uncommonly clever reader who, by discerning the true significance of my last words, seven in number, and by following the number three, may ultimately be led to a certain objet d'art of inestimable value.

One small hint (or two): the appropriate turn of mind and literary interests of the seeker may well prove helpful in the search.

What mystery may our great God
hold hidden where his books are stored,
reveal to one who finds that place
where pen is mightier than sword?

Such person, if I might advise,
may speed the pathway to success
by altering one certain word
to smooth my grammar's awkwardness.

So now, o sleuth, use well your time,
and fashion reason out of rhyme.

(Editor's note: Lukas Baumgartner died on the day after completing the third and final volume of his diaries with the enigmatic entry above.)

My God, where was he going with this? Every time I read through Baumgartner's poem, it retreated more and more into the distance until it became nothing more than a shadowy blur. The true significance of his last seven words . . . but which seven? From the end of his actual diary entry (*may well prove helpful in the search*), or the last seven of his poem (*time, and fashion reason out of rhyme*)? Or some other group of seven? And then the number three—how did that fit in? Hell and damnation, none of it made any sense!

Maybe Hochstraaten was right, that it would be ridiculous to spend any time thinking about this. On the other hand, his cocksure attitude was as good a reason as any to give it a shot. And maybe it would help me keep my mind off Annika.

Annika . . . no, no, I would not allow myself to think about her . . .

I hurried to the Xerox machine I had noticed on my way into the library and made a copy of the diary entry, then put the book back on its shelf and crossed the street to my rental house. What could be more convenient than to live a stone's throw away from campus? Even so, the short stretch of oppressive heat combined with Michael's substantial lunch told me that I was in need of a nap.

On my way up the stairs, Juniper, my black cat, raced past me and leapt onto the bed. I lay down next to her and stretched, musing about how uncomplicated the house rental had been. Walter Seifert had been so easy to work with; in a way, it was too bad that he was the one on sabbatical and not Herr *von* Hochstraaten. Screw you, Klaus, where do you get off trying to tell me what I can or can't do in my spare time? Forget about him, I told myself as I listened to the soft whoosh of the air conditioning . . .

I awoke with a start and glanced at the alarm clock. Just after three. Standing up unsteadily, I went into the bathroom to splash water on my face. Time to go looking for the grocery store. I gave Juniper a few strokes and headed on down the stairs.

The town square of the village of Arcadia was tiny, just big enough for a war memorial, two benches, a miniature clock tower, and a few shade trees. The parking lot next to Clyde's appeared to be full, so I parked on the street farther around the square. The store was icy cold inside; I pushed my cart along its four aisles, then headed for the lone cashier, a chubby boy who looked to be a high school student.

"Find ever'thing you were looking for, sir?" the boy asked.

"Pretty much. Plus a thing or two I wasn't."

"All right, then."

I carried my groceries to the car and stashed the perishable items in the cooler I had used on the trip down. On the far side of the square, the "Locke, Locke & Gates" sign adorned a narrow storefront. Why not, I said to myself. I crossed the street beyond the square, gazed at the gold lettering on the window for a moment, then pushed open the heavy oak door with its shiny brass letter slot.

The secretary's desk occupied a good part of the reception area. Monumental law books filled the shelves on three sides of the room; an ancient ceiling fan turned slowly overhead, creating at least a semblance of cooling. From behind her computer terminal, a smartly dressed middle-aged woman peered at me over the top of her reading glasses.

"Good day to you, sir, may I help you?"

"I hope so. I was wondering if I could speak with Mr. Clay Locke."

"Mr. Locke junior or senior, sir?"

"Oh . . . senior, I guess."

"Do you have an appointment?" she said soberly.

Why was she even asking—she knew very well I didn't.

"Well, no, I was just in the—"

"One moment, please. I'll see if Mr. Locke is free." She spoke into the intercom and a gravelly voice muttered something back. She gestured over her shoulder to a hallway that ran toward the back of the building.

"His office is the second door on the left."

I walked along the hallway, rapped on the door twice, and stepped inside. Several tinted lithographs, apparently of the town in its early days, filled the available wall space; the air was considerably cooler here. Behind a large mahogany desk sat an elderly man wearing rimless spectacles, a tan suit, and a flamboyant flowered tie. He glanced up as I entered the room.

"I don't necessarily have all the time in the world, you realize," he said with a slight drawl.

"I'm sorry. I just thought—"

"No need, no need. Have a seat." He reached over his desk and shook my hand. "I'm Clay Locke."

"Pleased to meet you, sir. My name is Colin Ritter."

Mr. Locke fiddled with the papers in front of him and ran his free hand through his shock of thick white hair. "So what can I do for you?"

"Well, I'm here to ask you a favor. And it might be something you won't be able to help me with."

Mr. Locke sat back in his chair and folded his arms. "Not exactly the best approach to getting a body to do somethin' you don't think they're going to want to do, now is it?"

I was tongue-tied for a moment. "No, I suppose it's not . . ."

"We always try to be as helpful as we can, of course. Southern hospitality, you know."

I grinned. "I guess my Minnesota accent must stick out like a sore thumb."

"Oh, 'tisn't as bad as all that." Mr. Locke leaned forward, then said in a confidential tone, "As a matter of fact, there are those who say that we Southerners are the ones with the accent. It shows a great deal of perception on your part to realize that it's *you* all, not us." He sat back in his chair again, his blue eyes sparkling.

"Well, I hope I have some perception about accents. I'm a language teacher, after all."

"Oh, is that right? Where, here at the college?"

"Yes, I'm a sabbatical replacement. I just arrived yesterday."

Mr. Locke stroked his chin. "So which language is it you teach? If I had to guess, I'd say German, given your last name."

"And you'd be right. My dad's parents were from Germany, and he spoke the language like a native. Sort of in my blood, I guess."

Mr. Locke nodded. "You know, now that I come to think of it, you're the feller Charlotte Rossi mentioned a while back. I see Charlotte every now and again."

"Oh, do you? She's a real gem. I'm lucky to be working in her department. She's the one who told me about your firm."

"Did she now? Well, we keep pluggin' along, my son and myself and Pearly. Paul Gates, that is, but we call him Pearly. Somebody gave him that nickname way back when, and he never could shake it. Pearly's been talkin' about retiring, but I can't figure why. The man's not but sixty-five years old! Can you imagine retiring at age sixty-five?"

I could, but didn't say so.

"Take me, for example—on the other side of eighty, and still goin' strong. Fit as a fiddle, the doctor says. And my mind is still pretty much all there, too. Leastways I think it is."

"I would say definitely so."

Mr. Locke leaned back in his chair and pointed to a print above his shoulder. "Now here's somethin' you'll recognize—Luke Baumgartner's castle up on the college campus."

"Well, barely. I only got a glimpse of it when I was here for my interview. My flight had been delayed, so—"

"It was originally his hunting lodge, you know, complete with a tiny little private chapel. Then over the years he built the whole campus around it. Ol' Luke, he was one of our clients. That is to say, he was a client of my granddaddy's. My father used to talk about him a lot. He'd come down to the office, Luke would—this was when Daddy was just a little tyke and the family lived in the back of the buildin' here—and he'd dandle him on his knee, and tell him stories and all. The wildest things you ever heard, I guess." Mr. Locke gazed up at the lithograph as if he were looking into the past, then turned back to me.

"So what exactly is it you think I won't be able to help you with?"

I had to crack a smile. "Well, . . . Baumgartner's will. I was wondering if there was any chance I could have a look at it."

Mr. Locke raised an eyebrow. "Intrigued by his diaries, are you?" He lowered his voice. "You know, I think he really might've hidden something."

"You do?"

"'Course, I realize how much he loved to fool people, too. Why, that man played so many tricks on my poor little daddy when he was a boy—" He paused for a moment. "But still. . . . Well, let's give you a look and you can see what you think."

He called the secretary on the intercom and asked her to bring the Baumgartner file from the vault.

"Say, thanks. I guess I was expecting you to say no."

"Oh, there's no problem with people looking at the will. Luke said it should be made available to anybody who asked. There've only been two in my lifetime. One feller came by just two, three years ago, a young prof from up at the college, probably about your age. Name of Fleisher, somethin' like that. Told me he'd figured out Baumgartner's last words."

"Really? Did he say how?"

"Oh no, he wasn't about to share that. He seemed pretty nervous about the whole business."

"But what happened then, why—"

"—why didn't he find what was hidden? I guess he didn't live long enough. He drowned in the creek under a footbridge down the hill from campus. Police chief said he must've been pushed, said it looked like he went over backwards and hit his head on a rock."

"So it was a robbery?"

"Hard to say. If he had a wallet on him at the time, it was never found. Turned out some of his students weren't too happy with him, but the police questioned everybody and they all had alibis."

"So they never figured out who did it?"

"Nossir, turned out to be a dead end. If you'll pardon the expression."

"In other words, the perpetrator's still at large."

"That would seem to be the case. But I wouldn't go worryin' a whole lot about it. Probably was what you young folks call a 'one-off' event."

"I suppose so. And maybe the guy wasn't even from around here."

"That's a distinct possibility."

I thought for a moment. "So you say someone else came by to look at the will, too?"

"That's right, long time ago. I don't remember much about him, he wasn't one for talkin'. Seems to me he taught German up at the college, like you." He paused before going on. "Can't quite put my finger on the name."

I frowned. "Not Klaus Hochstraaten?"

"That could have been it. Kinda tall, maybe forty-odd at the time. Sort of a broodin' type of man."

There was a knock on the door and the secretary stepped in with a file folder.

"Thanks, Elaine." Mr. Locke opened the folder and held the first page of the document up to his glasses.

"Last Will and Testament of Lukas Baumgartner . . . ," he muttered, then handed the next two pages to me.

> Be it known that I, Lukas Baumgartner, being of sound mind and without surviving blood relations, do hereby make the following bequests as my last will and testament:
>
> 1. the sum of $10,000 in cash to my faithful manservant Joseph Brown, residing at Castle Arcadia on the campus of St. Eustace College, Arcadia, Kentucky;
>
> 2. the equivalent sum of $10,000 in cash to my cook and housekeeper Nelly Brown, wife of Joseph Brown, in grateful recognition of her decades of unfailing service;
>
> 3. the sum of $50,000 to my personal physician and friend, Dr. J. Earl Davies, of Arcadia, Kentucky;
>
> 4. my personal library, and most especially my editions of Lessing, Goethe, and Schiller, to the library of St. Eustace College;
>
> 5. my collection of works of art by Albrecht Dürer to St. Eustace College, for the edification of future generations of its students;
>
> 6. the remainder of my estate, consisting of cash money, stock holdings, vehicles and equipment, valuables, and real property, to St. Eustace College, to be applied toward purposes of furthering the College and its mission as deemed appropriate by its board of trustees. All assets not useful to the College in their present form to be liquidated and invested.
>
> Addition A: In testimony of my abiding devotion to the above-mentioned collection of Dürer's works, my display room is to remain in precisely its present state, and this *in perpetuum*, or until further notice. To this end, a panel of five shall conduct a biannual inspection of the facility, said panel to consist of two trustees of the College and three additional members, each knowledgeable in the field of German art, to be appointed by the Governor of the Commonwealth of Kentucky.
>
> Addition B: The possibility of acquiring a certain *objet*

d'art of inestimable value is hereby offered to any party willing to undertake the search for same; a meagre suggestion as to how to begin said search will appear at the end of my personal diary. Significant progress along the way to be made known to the law firm of Locke and Gates.

Addition C: Aforesaid law firm is further entrusted with a certain locked container to which no one is to be granted access until such time as the situation shall clearly warrant.

(signed)

Lukas Baumgartner

Dr. J. Earl Davies

Arcadia, Kentucky, 28 October 1908

I looked up from the text. "Good grief."

"Kinda peculiar, all right."

"I'll say. And isn't it kind of short for a last will and testament?"

"Well, it's definitely not the way we would do it today. The story goes that Luke drew it up himself, brought it down to the law office, and pretty much demanded that my granddaddy approve and sign it. Said he didn't have time to fiddle with it, since he had this premonition that he would die soon. Well, he sure was right about that."

"Crazy. And speaking of crazy, what do you make of this nonsensical phrase in Addition A, '*in perpetuum*, or until further notice'? Seems to be a contradiction in terms, doesn't it?"

"Certainly does to me."

"And the container he mentions in Addition C—"

"It's just a flat little metal box, no bigger than half a sheet of paper—maybe eight inches by five. And locked, as it says in the will. Your guess is as good as mine as to where the key might be."

I glanced back at the date at the bottom of the will.

"His last diary entry was dated November 18th—I remember that because it's my birthday. So there were only three weeks between signing the will and the diary entry."

"That's right."

He leaned back in his chair and stroked his chin. "You know, there's one other peculiar matter that might be worth mentioning. I say this because it has to do with Dr. Davies, Luke's personal physician—you just saw his signature on the will there. Mabel, his only child, was a pal of mine. Sort of like an older sister, she was. Wonderful ol' gal. She's been dead for quite a spell now, twenty-odd years, I reckon."

"So what exactly . . . "

"Well, I wasn't but a little whippersnapper myself at the time. Mabel's father wasn't very old at all, sixty-some, and she would have only been in her teens herself. Her mother had died the year before that, and apparently Dr. Davies had been pretty despondent ever since. In any event he ended up committing suicide, and when his will was probated, there was this letter for Mabel that she was supposed to open on the fiftieth anniversary of his death—or leave to her heirs if she passed away herself. Turned out she never had any heirs—she stayed a maiden lady all her life. Anyway, just a few days before she was due to open the thing, somebody broke into her house and stole it. I shouldn't say *broke* in, really—she never locked her door, just like most folks in these parts."

"But why would anyone want to steal it?"

"See, that's what makes me think it might be related to the Baumgartner business. Maybe whoever swiped it thought it might contain some information about what he'd hidden; he and Dr. Davies were best friends, after all. And it was no secret that the letter existed in the first place—I think Mabel was actually kinda proud of being its custodian, you might say. And then the newspaper ran a big spread about it the week before it was supposed to be opened, 'cause it was such an oddity. Lots of folks, specially the older ones, were just burnin' with curiosity to know what it would say."

I scratched my chin. "I don't suppose his daughter might have opened it a little early, didn't like what it said, and got rid of it?"

"Mabel Davies? Not on your life! Why, Mabel was the straightest, most upright person you're ever like to meet on this earth. If she said the letter had up and disappeared, then that's what happened. And I don't place much stock in the other possibility people have suggested either, that she could have misplaced it. Why, Mabel's house was always as neat as a pin. Not only that, she even had a kind of shrine for the letter, right next to her father's picture on the piano, so she'd see it ever' time she walked by. Saw it on many an occasion myself."

I thought I'd heard all I needed to know, and more, for the moment. "Well, that's quite a story," I said, getting up from my chair. "Thanks so much for—"

"Don't mention it." Mr. Locke picked a business card off the stack on his desk and handed it to me. "In case you ever need to look me up again."

We walked out into the reception area together.

"So that colleague of mine looked at the will, too," I said, trying to sound casual.

"Yes, a good little while back it was. Twenty-five years ago? Maybe even longer. I tell you, when you get to be my age, it all kind of blends together. Good luck with the search—if that's what you end up doing."

I shrugged. "I wouldn't even know where to begin."

I shook Mr. Locke's hand and left the building. So Klaus Hochstraaten had examined the will, too. Klaus Hochstraaten, who had said that it would be ridiculous to take Baumgartner's final entry seriously.

Chapter 3

A withering blast of sultry air hit me in the face as I left the house at two o'clock; it was a full half-hour before my scheduled meeting with Hochstraaten, but I wanted to make sure I got there in plenty of time. The sky had become ominously black, and thunder rumbled in the distance. Skirting the library, I headed along a broad path lined with tall rhododendron bushes now denuded of the blossoms I'd seen in May. What a lavish display of reds and pinks they had presented—something a native Minnesotan could only dream of.

With every step, the stone structure in the distance loomed larger. I'd had the briefest of encounters with the castle on the day of my interview, due to the late spring snowstorm that had held up my flight in Minneapolis and reduced my time on campus to barely two hours. I knew from the map of the college grounds that the castle was positioned, hublike, in the very center, a few hundred yards from each of the academic buildings that stood on the periphery.

I was amazed once more to see the castle rise up before me, looking for all the world like it had been conjured straight out of southern Germany. Its crenelated walls were surrounded by a moat and extended from a massive square tower at one end to a tall round one at the other. Crossing a footbridge to the more imposing tower, I passed a granite slab bearing the inscription "St. Eustace Memorial Chapel." The first raindrops began to fall as I opened the heavy door and stepped inside. The door slammed shut behind me with a boom that reverberated from wall to wall.

Looking up, I surveyed the immense proportions of the tower. Illuminated by a single round chandelier suspended by a cable from the ceiling far above, the space felt clammy and had a musty smell to it. Two long tables, empty except for a few hymnals, stood on either side of open double doors that led into the chapel. An outsize facsimile of Dürer's engraving of St. Eustace, kneeling in wonder before a deer with a crucifix between its antlers, hung to the right of the doors.

My footsteps resounded as I crossed the stone floor and peered into the gloom. I was puzzled. Mr. Locke had mentioned a "tiny little" chapel, but this was a space that would hold two or three hundred people. The private chapel had to be located somewhere else in the building.

The rain was pelting down ferociously now and lashing against the entrance door. Suddenly it flew open and a pudgy figure came stumbling in, grasping the dripping cowl of his white cassock tightly around his head. Exhaling audibly, the spectral appearance pushed his hood back, then pulled out a red handkerchief and wiped his face and the front of his balding head.

"God be praised!" he exclaimed, gazing toward the ceiling. "Saved from peril and my own foolishness once again! Next time I will be sure to carry an umbrella." He paused to catch his breath. "I must confess that I am not fond of thunder and lightning, even though they are part of God's creation."

As if in response, a long, angry rumble sounded in the distance. The man raised his flashing, slit-like eyes heavenward for a moment and then turned to me.

"Forgive me," he said, "I don't believe we've met. I'm Pastor Rol—"

At that moment he was overcome by a sudden fit of coughing, turning the rest of his name into an extended series of hacks. Had he said Roulette? Or Rolex? The little man's face was perfectly round—as round as a roulette wheel or a watch. I covered my face with my hand to hide a smirk.

"My, my," he said, clearing his throat, "I really must get out of my wet things as soon as possible." He looked down and tried to brush the remaining water off his cassock. "As you may have guessed from my garb, I am, as one might say, the shepherd of St. Eustace College's flock—what remains of it, that is; it seems that our students have less and less interest in religion every year. In any case, I have been here for some time now—coming on for thirty-five years, to be exact."

"And your name again?"

"Roland—Martin Roland."

"Pleased to meet you," I said, extending my hand. "My name is Colin Ritter. I'll be teaching in the German Department this year."

"Ah, yes. As a sabbatical replacement for my dear friend Walter Seifert. Well, let me wish you all the best. May I be of assistance in any way?"

"I'm looking for the Dürer museum. I'm supposed to meet—"

"Ah, interested in art, are you? And in Dürer in particular?"

"Oh, yes. I had a graduate minor in art history. And as someone in the field of German—"

"Of course," the pastor said. "Well, I think you'll be quite taken by our little museum—it's our pride and joy, and mine in particular. You know about our founder's Dürer connection, I assume?"

"Only that he put together a large collection of his art."

"Ah, but there's more to it than that. Lukas Baumgartner hailed from the city of Nuremberg, as did Dürer, so he grew up with him, as it were, not quite four hundred years later. And he had, or maintained that he'd had, the same vision as St. Eustace, which Dürer captured so stunningly in his engraving."

"No way—the deer with the crucifix?"

"Yes indeed. And that vision became the basis for his founding of the college. But I should explain to you the presumed reason for his having identified with that particular saint. Are you by any chance familiar with the *Paumgartner Altarpiece*?"

"The nativity scene, yes. I saw it in the *Alte Pinakothek* when I was in Munich."

"Exactly. And do you recall the side panels?"

I rubbed my chin. "Can't say that I do. It's been a while."

"Surely. Well, the point is, several members of the Paumgartner family appear in the painting as patrons, each bearing a shield with the family coat of arms—a falcon and fleur-de-lys—and Baumgartner claimed to be a descendent of that very family. But what is even more intriguing is that the side panels depict the two sons of the family, each in the guise of a saint dressed in knight's armor. And the son named Lukas, of all things, is portrayed as . . ."

"Not St. Eustace, by any chance?" I smiled at the pastor. "Which would explain where the vision came from—or hallucination, or whatever it was."

"Precisely. You can read all about it in Volume III of his diaries. But now if you will come this way. . . ."

I followed him to a narrow corridor that ran alongside the chapel. A short distance past several Religion Department offices he stopped and pointed to a brass plaque on the wall that read "Albrecht Dürer Museum" in German script. A guard wearing a gray uniform and sidearm was standing inside the door studying a thermostat.

"How do, Reverend," the guard said, doffing his cap. "Gotta make sure this thang is puttin' out plenty of cold air today. Quite the hot spell we've been havin' lately." He smoothed back his few wisps of gray hair.

"We have indeed, Bobby," the pastor answered. "and I doubt that this rainstorm will help at all. I've brought along a new faculty member today. Professor Ritter—Bobby Franklin."

"Welcome to y', sir. If I can hep in any way, you lemme know."

We shook hands and Bobby took his seat next to the door. I turned and let my glance wander slowly along the picture-filled walls.

"Good Lord!" I whispered.

"Good Lord, indeed," the pastor agreed.

A few years back I'd seen an exhibition in Minneapolis of nine or ten Dürer prints. But here was a whole room full of Dürers! On the outside wall across from me, a good thirty to forty black-and-white pieces had been hung above and to either side of a large stone fireplace, some individually and others vertically in pairs. On the wall behind me there were at least as many again. The narrower side walls were covered with paintings of animals and nature scenes.

"Note how Baumgartner had the various pieces hung: engravings on one side, woodcuts on the other, and the small collection of watercolors at either end. Typical of the man's sense of balance and symmetry. And it will come as no surprise to you that the *St. Eustace* occupies center stage above the fireplace."

I walked slowly across the room to the engraving. Barely more than a foot in height, it was filled with profuse and delicate detail.

"It's a miracle of sorts, don't you think?" the pastor said over my shoulder, the smell of wetness emanating from his robe. "In addition to the subject matter, I mean. Just look at the precision of line. Baumgartner had his agents in Europe put an enormous amount of time and energy into finding the best prints available; money was no object, of course. As for Dürer's nature studies, it proved impossible to acquire any originals, money or not. All those you see here are copies, like the famous hare and the little owl over there to your right, and the *Three Linden Trees* at the opposite end of the room. Sixteenth or seventeenth century, mostly, and amazingly accurate, so I've been told."

I followed the pastor's gesture around the room, then turned again to the engraving of St. Eustace. In the foreground, a group of five dogs rested from the hunt; it was apparent that Dürer had lavished as much attention on them as he had on the miracle in progress a few feet behind them. This section of the engraving alone was a fascinating nature study in its own right.

At the sound of footsteps, the pastor and I looked toward the door. Professor Hochstraaten had just entered the room, dragging his leg and ignoring the guard as he dropped his umbrella into a stand by the door.

"I see that I need not have come," he said. "It seems you have already found a guide."

"Ah, Klaus, good day," the pastor said. "Were you to be this young man's docent today? Had I known that, I certainly would not have undertaken to—"

"I trust that you have been given an unbiased introduction to the museum, *Herr Ritter*? Not one prejudiced in any way?"

"Now, now, Klaus!" the pastor said with a waggish smile. "How can you suggest such a thing? In any case, I will be leaving our visitor in your care now; I must finally change out of my wet things. Professor Ritter, I was happy to make your acquaintance."

He shook my hand, then headed for the door. Hochstraaten looked after him, scowling.

"I happened to run into the pastor on the way in," I said. "We were looking at the *St. Eustace* here. It really is a remarkable piece. All that detail—the minuscule swans in the stream, the hint of a castle way off in the distance . . ."

"What?" Hochstraaten said. "But surely the castle can hardly be overlooked."

"No, no, I don't mean the one at the top of the hill. There's another one farther off." I stepped up to the engraving and pointed to an area at the extreme left.

"Ah, indeed," Hochstraaten said, leaning over and squinting. "You are very observant." He turned and pointed to the opposite side of the room. "The detail of the *St. Eustace* notwithstanding, I believe the *Apocalypse* woodcuts of 1498 to be the glory of the collection."

I crossed the room and scanned the double row of the much larger *Apocalypse* prints. The best-known of them, the *Four Horsemen*, hung in the top row. The terrifying riders galloped furiously across the scene, trampling everyone in their path as they sowed war and pestilence. Other woodcuts in the series depicted fiery stars falling from the heavens, angels embroiled in battle, and many-headed monsters. I glanced at Hochstraaten and found the expression on his face nothing short of ecstatic.

"Brilliant examples of the ultimate triumph of the Catholic faith, are they not?"

Lapsed Catholic that I was, I made a vague grunt and changed the subject. "How about the nature studies?" I asked. "What do you think of them?

"The watercolors, you mean. Copies, of course. Forgeries, in essence."

"Forgeries? But only if someone had claimed they were originals, which I doubt."

"You may well be right. But this still does not change the fact that they are nothing but copies. I would not have a copy of a work of art in my possession. Having said that, however, I will concede that these are quite well done. *Das große Rasenstück*, for example. What is it called in English . . . *The Large Piece of Turf*, I believe. Housed in the Albertina. You have been there?"

"I'm afraid not. I've spent very little time in Vienna."

"A pity. Their collection of pieces by Dürer is astounding." Hochstraaten pointed to another of the watercolors. "The *Three Linden Trees*, too, seems to be an accurate rendering. But I have not seen the original myself, only reproductions in art books. It belonged to the Kunsthalle in

Bremen, but it has been missing since the war. It and many other pieces were removed for safekeeping, and some were never returned."

"I haven't been there either, I'm sorry to say. In fact, the only art gallery I know really well is the one in Minneapolis I mentioned yesterday."

"Ah yes. And was there anything there that fueled your self-proclaimed fanaticism in particular?"

I decided to ignore his attempted dig. "Things too numerous to mention. The Institute's eighteenth-century collection, the earlier northern European pieces—and of course the Rembrandt *Lucretia*."

"Yes, who could not be impressed by that masterpiece? I have had the pleasure of contemplating it on only one occasion." He breathed a deep sigh and glanced at his watch. "I must leave you now, I still have some packing to do. But I think you will agree that this museum speaks for itself."

"Yes, it does, thank you for coming by. I hope everything goes well for you in Argentina."

Hochstraaten nodded. "I believe it will. My father is in reasonably good health, but at his age one does not know how long that will last. We will certainly spend as much time as possible visiting museums, since we are both impassioned art lovers."

It crossed my mind to ask if they weren't *fanatical* art lovers, but I kept the thought to myself. Without any further comment, Hochstraaten turned on his heel, picked his umbrella out of the stand, and limped out into the hallway. Well, I said to myself, that wasn't so terrible—but I don't think it's likely that we will become best friends.

I went back to the *Apocalypse* woodcuts and studied the fourteen prints one after the other. What a terrible view of humanity and the fate that, according to John, was awaiting it! Sister Agnes had constantly beat into our brains what would happen to us if we didn't improve our ways. By way of emphasizing her dire prophecy she showed us her favorite scenes from Dürer's *Apocalypse* from time to time—interestingly enough, leaving out the last one in the series, in which an angel shows John the new Jerusalem.

What could the message of these woodcuts be for Klaus Hochstraaten? Was it the terrible suffering that was portrayed in the great majority of them, or the luminous image of the future in the last one? I had no idea, nor did I have the least inclination to spend any time thinking about it. Concentrating on these mostly negative images had been depressing enough; I would save the rest of the museum for next Monday, when it would be open again. With a wave to Bobby, who had more or less dozed off, I headed for home.

Chapter 4

On the following morning I stuffed my few language-oriented books into my briefcase and carried them down Faculty Row to Riedenburg Hall, the foreign language building. Almost all of the fifteen houses along the "Row" were owned by faculty members; those who hadn't had the good fortune to buy (or rent, in my case) one of them lived either in the town of Arcadia or in the country. From Riedenburg Hall I could easily have waved to the Rossis, who lived right across the street.

We German faculty shared the third floor with the Classicists, while the Spanish, French, Russian, and Chinese Departments were located on the first and second, and the language lab had its home in the basement. Each language group had an anteroom plus three or four offices, depending. My office, next to those of Charlotte and Klaus Hochstraaten, was shaded by a giant tulip tree and I had a great view over the campus. The only negative was that Hochstraaten was my closest neighbor.

On my way home he still was in the back of my mind, but at least I knew that for a month I would have no further contact with him. Was I treating him unfairly? I didn't think so. Not only had he insulted me personally, he had cast aspersions on a writer who was a favorite of mine—one who was famed as a playwright, as a worthy opponent in matters of religious controversy, as a theater critic and a commentator on the art of earlier periods. The paper that I had in mind to write dealt with Lessing's essay on the origins of oil painting, and I hoped that recent research would help me to expand on his historical perspective. In his essay, Lessing was concerned with whether Jan van Eyck had invented the medium of oil painting, which was the prevailing view in the eighteenth century, or whether it went back to the early Middle Ages, which he thought he could prove.

Before the move from Minneapolis, I had considered buying the standard eight-volume Hanser edition of Lessing's works, but at 348 Euros—over $400—it was far beyond what I could afford. The only sensible solution now was to borrow the one volume I needed from the St. Eustace library; I would get a head start on the paper well before the November submission deadline and spend most of the month of August on my class preparations.

I crossed the street to the library through a spitting rain. The Lessing collection in the PT section filled two shelves; not bad for a college as small as St. Eustace. My eye was immediately drawn to an ornate folio-sized set in three volumes with green bindings worked in gold and black. Always a sucker for beautiful books, I took the first volume off the shelf and almost exclaimed out loud at the bookplate inside the front cover: Ex libris Lucani Baumgartneri. Well, of course, Baumgartner had stipulated in his will that his Lessing set, among others, was to go to the library.

After flipping through the book's lavishly illustrated pages, I replaced it on the shelf, since I had no choice but to use the standard scholarly edition on the shelf below. I pulled out Volume VI, Lessing's writings on aesthetics and art history, glanced at the table of contents and headed for the circulation desk, where a slender young woman with striking auburn hair was on duty. As I approached she put down the paperback she had been reading and I caught sight of the title: *The Nine Tailors*.

"Another Peter Wimsey fan, I see?"

She blushed slightly. "Yes, Dorothy Sayers is my escape reading. I've read three or four of her mysteries now. I think this one is going to be my favorite."

"It is mine. I've always loved church bells. Although in this story—"

"Now, don't go giving anything away."

"Wouldn't dream of it." I handed her the Lessing volume and my faculty I.D. card. "Could you check this out for me?"

"Sure thing." As she scanned the book she glanced at the dust jacket, where the author's full name was spelled out in large block letters: GOTTHOLD EPHRAIM LESSING.

"Hey, this is the guy the library's named after," she said.

"The very same."

"And you're . . . Professor Ritter! I'm signed up for your course this fall, Conversation and Composition. My name's Moira MacGregor."

"Well, Moira MacGregor, very nice to meet you."

Moira's hair hung in a single braid over her shoulder, its delicate golden and copper highlights glowing in the beams of light from a window behind her. I couldn't help but think of the beautiful woman who had appeared in several of Dante Gabriel Rossetti's paintings . . .

"If you don't mind me asking," she said, 'Ritter' means 'knight,' doesn't it?"

I snapped back to reality, wondering about all the interest in my name lately.

"Yes," I said. "I'm not a practicing one, though."

"I don't suppose. But maybe you're an aristocrat?"

I shook my head. "The German aristocracy was abolished after World War I."

"In other words—you're not entitled to a title?"

I laughed. "That's one way of putting it. Or you could just say that I'm . . . untitled."

"I like that better. Think of all the great works of art that are untitled."

"Very diplomatic of you to make that connection. Well, Moira, if you don't mind my saying so, your English has a lovely lilt to it. I couldn't identify what part of the South you're from, though."

She blushed again. "That's easy, I'm from just around the corner. The town of Arcadia, I mean."

"Really? I was down there yesterday for the first time. Seems like a nice enough little place."

"Oh, it's fine. Not much to do, like any small town, I guess."

"So you live at home, then?"

"I do now. Not during the school year, though—I wouldn't feel part of things if I didn't live on campus."

"I know what you mean, it was the same with me when I was a student. Well, I'd better be on my way. Have to start preparing that course for you."

Moira blushed yet again. "Okay. It was nice meeting you, Professor Ritter."

"You too."

Back at the house, I sat contemplating the lettering on the cover of the Lessing volume. GOTTHOLD EPHRAIM . . . How had the freethinker Lessing liked having such pious names, no doubt given to him by his Lutheran minister father? I could think of no other "Gottholds," although variants of the name had been frequent in that time period: Gotthelf, Helfgott, Gottlob, Gottlieb, Lobegott . . .

Quit daydreaming, I told myself. I opened the book to the essay on oil painting and started to read. The first few pages were smooth sailing, as Lessing's premises and conclusions followed one after the other with their characteristic logic. Three short quotations from the writings of a medieval monk slowed me down; my four years of parochial-school Latin plus two more years in college helped immensely, but the specialized vocabulary frequently sent me to my Latin-English dictionary. Just as I encountered a longer Latin passage I felt my stomach start to growl.

Down in the kitchen, I opened a can of soup and a made a ham and tomato sandwich. After lunch I sat on the sofa next to Juniper and massaged her neck, listening to the soft rumble of her purring. You've got it pretty good, I thought. But then working with Lessing wasn't so bad either. I mounted the stairs to the study again.

As I sat down, I glanced at the photocopy of Baumgartner's final diary entry that I had taped to the wall above the desk; maybe if I could figure out the poem, the business about the seven and the three would become apparent. Or maybe it wouldn't. I sat back in my chair and read through the poem again:

> *What mystery may our great God*
> *hold hidden where his books are stored,*
> *reveal to one who finds that place*
> *where pen is mightier than sword?*
>
> *Such person, if I might advise,*
> *may speed the pathway to success*
> *by altering one certain word*
> *to smooth my grammar's awkwardness.*
>
> *So now, o sleuth, use well your time,*
> *and fashion reason out of rhyme.*

Not bad as a poem, all things considered; the meter was perfect (iambic tetrameter), with only one structural hitch at the beginning of the third line, which could have been cleared up by adding "then" before "reveal." Baumgartner must have realized, though, that this would have messed up his metrical pattern.

If only the meaning were as straightforward as the formal elements! Well, some of it was. Where else, for example, could God be said to store his books but in the Bible? Assuming that "God's mystery" was actually Baumgartner's, could he have had a fancy old family Bible? But where in that Bible would I look, if it even still existed? Maybe the whole idea was bullshit.

The poem's second stanza was completely different in character, in that it offered a practical suggestion: to alter a word of Baumgartner's text. Which one, and to what end? Would the change possibly fix the structural problem in the first stanza? And how would that help?

My attempts at analysis were getting me nowhere, so I decided instead to read the whole poem out loud, a tactic that I knew could sometimes help to clarify a text's meaning. The double alliteration in the first and second lines ("great God / hold hidden") was curious, but did it have any particular function? If Baumgartner had wanted those particular words to stand out, I couldn't see why. He had me stymied again.

I leaned back in my chair. Nuts to this crap. With less than an hour remaining before my meeting with Hochstraaten, I decided to go back to what I had started that morning.

As I picked up the Lessing volume, the boldface name on the

cover seemed to leap out at me: GOTTHOLD EPHR— I looked at the beginning of the poem again: "great God / hold hidden" and did a double take. If "God" were changed into "Gott," the opening sentence would read: *What mystery may our great Gotthold, hidden where his books are stored, reveal to one who finds that place* . . . I took a deep breath. It was obvious where Lessing's books were stored.

I raced down the stairs, barely saving myself from falling by grabbing onto the railing, then trotted across the street to the library. I hurried past Moira, who was still at her position behind the front desk.

"Hello again, forgot something I wanted to check."

She smiled. "Aren't you too young to be the absent-minded professor?"

"Occupational hazard," I called back with a shrug.

Moments later I was standing before the Lessing edition that had belonged to Luke Baumgartner. Three volumes . . . "follow the three" . . . Could the third volume somehow contain what I was looking for?

The table of contents listed a hodge-podge of the author's critical essays, including several in the realm of art: *Laokoon*, a major work that sought to clarify the boundaries between the visual arts and literature; the short piece on the origins of oil painting that I had just begun to work on; and a treatise on the depiction of death in antique sculpture. Slowly I began to turn the pages. Almost every margin was filled with comments in German, some shorter and some longer, no doubt made by Luke Baumgartner himself; I scanned these for any marks or words that might have constituted a clue, but found nothing.

The treatise on the antique portrayal of death in particular was replete with marginal comments. I read through them carefully from beginning to end. Opposite the last page, an elaborate arabesque design marked the end of the volume. The space below was filled with several handwritten lines:

With gratitude to you, Herr Lessing, for what you have taught me in the preceding piece and in many other works of yours, I say farewell as I leave you to go down and pray in my little chapel. A quiet place which invites to contemplation, it has on many an occasion given me the repose that I seek. In doing this, it has aided me in achieving the leap to the lofty spheres above from this woeful world below. Soon I am to leave this world, as we all must, rich or poor, whether our sign be a simple huntsman's bow or a proud family escutcheon. Indeed, given my present condition, I would not be surprised if

I had but one more day to live, or at most two or three.
I hope that I may be granted the time to view once more
a site in the nearby woods that is of great importance
to me, inasmuch as it symbolizes the dual nature of our
lives: instability, in the rushing, uncontrollable stream,
and steadfastness, in the solid bridge high above,
fashioned of the most carefully hewn stones. In any
case, it will not be long until I will learn the ultimate
direction of my final path—whether up . . . or down . . .

Castle Arcadia
19 November 1908

Why had Baumgartner switched to English? His critical musings in the margins had all been in German. Then it dawned on me: though this paragraph might seem to express private thoughts, it had quite a different function. November 19th . . . one day after the date on the final diary entry, and the day on which he had died. Luke Baumgartner's last words were staring me in the face.

Barely able to contain my excitement, I made a photocopy of the page and hurried down the stairway, almost tripping again.

"Got it figured out, see you later," I said as I hurried past Moira.

"Glad to hear it," she said with a quizzical look.

Leaning forward in my desk chair, I read through the text several times, then continued to stare at the page dumbly until the words began to dance before my eyes. What could their "true significance" be? The chapel, the huntsman's bow, the family escutcheon . . . and that odd reference to the bridge with its precisely hewn stones. It, if anything in the whole passage, seemed to have been given the greatest emphasis.

The chapel was somewhere in the castle, according to what Mr. Locke had said. Would there be any point in my looking around inside? But what would I be looking for? And why the chapel? After all, Luke had only stated that *he himself* was going there; nothing in the text indicated that anyone else was invited to come along.

With a sigh, I taped my copy of Luke's last words onto the wall next to the text of the final entry. I would put the whole Baumgartner business aside for the time being; after all, I had my Lessing paper and hours of course preparations to think of. No doubt there would be enough time later on for me to 'play games,' as a certain colleague of mine had put it.

Chapter 5

The extreme humidity of the last couple of days had lessened somewhat. Even so, I noticed on my way to the castle that my usual walking pace had slowed down. The clammy coolness inside the entrance tower felt almost refreshing.

It was four o'clock when I stepped into the museum. I had pretty much lost myself in my work on the Lessing essay and the time had just flown by. There was barely an hour left till the museum closed, so that would have to do for this visit.

"Hi, Bobby," I said as I walked past the guard, "how's the air conditioning doing?"

"Hi, professor. Well, it's doin' a little better than last week. Because the air i'nt quite so humid anymore, y' see."

Not wanting to get into a conversation about the weather at the moment, I just nodded to Bobby and walked across the room to the fireplace. I had examined the hunting dogs already and wanted to focus this time on various other elements in the engraving. Back when I was a student, I had noticed a few things that struck me as odd: the great amount of space devoted to the horse; Eustace himself, who almost seemed to be levitating; the awkward positioning of the deer's rear legs. Or was I not seeing these things correctly? I put this aside for now and moved on to the engravings on the wall to the right of the fireplace.

A rustic *Birth of Christ* from 1504 was hanging right next to it. The simplicity of the scene reminded me of the earlier *Paumgartner Altarpiece* that Pastor Roland had mentioned. It most interesting aspect was the unusual wheel-and-pulley structure mounted above the well, which Joseph had used to pull up the bucket of water he was now emptying into a pitcher.To me, this section of the engraving seemed somehow more genuine than the crèche scene a few feet away, with Mary, the newborn baby, and a single adoring peasant.

Next along the wall were several images of the Madonna and Child, with a monkey, a pear, the fortress in Nuremberg, or with one or two angels, all of them in chronological order. I paid scant attention to a series of small renderings of saints that were of no great appeal to me, and then, just before the corner, I noticed a rectangle of a slightly darker color than the space surrounding it; a picture hook that must have supported an engraving at one time still protruded from the wall. What was missing here? Had one of the prints been lent out to another museum?

Next to the gap hung two engravings that I remembered well from one of my art history courses. In the first, an old man in monk's garb leaned over a small writing desk as sunlight flooded the walls and ceiling through bull's eye windows. The figure was St. Jerome, laboring over his translation of what later came to be known as the Latin Vulgate Bible.

The engraving next to the *St. Jerome* had fueled centuries of debate. Its title, *Melencolia I*, seemed to reflect the mood of the two figures who occupied the center area. One, a plump little putto, concentrated glumly on his writing, while the other, a winged woman of monumental proportions, held an architect's compass in one hand as she looked disconsolately off into space. Carpenter's accoutrements were strewn about everywhere and a ladder leaned against a wall in the background. Was this a building site? Possibly the whole thing was a metaphor of human endeavor, and the chief architect was not pleased with the way things were going. She was depicted as an angel—but why? And why was she a she?

A so-called "magic square" occupied a space just above the angel-architect's head. It was divided into sixteen smaller squares, each containing a number from one to sixteen in what appeared at first glance to be random order. By a sort of mathematical legerdemain, each row, column, and diagonal added up to thirty-four, as did the squares of numbers in each of the corners and the four squares in the center. It was almost like an early version of Sudoku, but with all the answers already given.

Glancing back at the empty space with the picture hook, I was pretty sure that I knew what the missing work of art was. Both the *St. Jerome* and the *Melencolia* bore the artist's monogram and the year 1514. But there had been a third engraving as well from about the same time, and I recalled having read that the three could be considered pendant pieces, each representing a different aspect of the human spirit.

"Say, Bobby," I called out, "would you know anything about the piece that's missing here?"

The guard got up from his chair and walked over to me.

"Not a whole lot. Somebody told me once it was a pitcher of a knight on a horse."

"That's exactly what I thought. It has to be the engraving called *Knight, Death, and Devil*."

"Yep, that shore sounds right, now that you say it."

"So it's been lent out, I suppose?"

"Oh, no. It got stoled way back when, before the college was founded. 'Course, they didn't have no 'lectronic surveillance or nothin' like that in them days. Somebody try to take a pitcher out of here today, why, bells would go off acrost the whole county. They never was able to figger out who took it, and that space there has been empty ever since. Seems like ol' Mr. Baumgartner didn't want to have nothin' there, 'less it was that engravin'—the very same one, I mean, not a different copy. 'Twern't a matter of the money, of course, the ol' guy was rollin' in it. Why, he coulda bought a dozen of 'em if he'd of had a mind to."

"Well, looks like I'll just have to go out and buy one myself, won't I."

"Yessir," Bobby replied, "a body might could do that, if he had three or four hunnerd thousand dollars layin' around."

"Really? That much?"

"I think so. I heard tell of a figure somethin' like that bein' mentioned a few years back. Don't rightly know what it would be worth by now. Even more, I reckon."

"No doubt. Guess I'll put that purchase on hold for a while. Thanks for all the information, Bobby."

"You're entirely welcome," he replied as I headed for the door, "come back."

I turned and looked at him uncertainly. "Goodbye," I said, wondering if that was the appropriate response.

I left the museum and walked the few steps to the round tower at the opposite end of the castle from where I had come in. A stone staircase with an iron railing spiraled its way up the wall for a good thirty feet, ending at a boarded-up opening in the ceiling. Light was provided by window slits that paralleled the course of the staircase, and, as in the front tower, by a chandelier that hung from the ceiling. It felt like I was in a dungeon. I walked past a small door on the right to the larger one that led outside.

The sky was a brilliant blue and not a cloud was to be seen. As I crossed the footbridge that spanned the moat at that point, Charlotte Rossi was waving to me from the rose beds on the other side.

"Hi, Colin. Been to the museum again?"

"You guessed it. It'll take me quite a while to study all those prints and watercolors. Luke Baumgartner must've been fabulously wealthy to have bought so many Dürers."

"Oh, he was. From managing the railroad in Louisville, first of all. And then he acquired I don't know how many square miles of forestland to the north of what's now the college campus and made tons of money off the timber. It's completely wild out there, off-limits to students."

"Is that where the Wicked Witch lives?"

"She might could. You'd better watch out if you're over that way. I'd stick to our South Woods if I were you. It runs along the hillside just past our backyards. It's right pretty in there, lots of crisscrossing trails, traces of Luke Baumgartner here and there. Nice time for taking a walk there now, late afternoon, if you're so inclined. There's a map of all the trails in the college catalogue."

"I might just do that."

We continued our stroll along the moat. "So the castle was originally Baumgartner's hunting lodge, I heard?"

"That's right. He and his wife would come for weekends whenever he could get away from his job. She died in childbirth, poor thing, and he moved into the top of the round tower you just came out of. I call it the Rapunzel tower—you know, like in the fairy tale. Sometimes when I walk by here I like to imagine Rapunzel letting down that ridiculously long blond braid of hers for the prince to climb up on. There's a fairy tale garden in the palace grounds in Ludwigsburg where that actually happens."

"I know, I've been there. Except she never lets it all the way down. Presumably because no one who passes by happens to be a prince."

Charlotte laughed. "I'd totally forgotten that. It was a good many years ago that I was there."

I couldn't prevent an image of Annika from flashing through my mind. She and I had traveled to Ludwigsburg together one summer so that I could meet her parents. While we were in the fairy tale garden I had teased her about her long blond hair and maintained that she would make a great Rapunzel. The four years we had lived together in Minneapolis had been exceptionally happy and seemingly stable. And then—God, how could I have been so stupid!

"You okay, Colin?" Charlotte asked. "You look like you're in another world."

I forced a smile. "Oh no," I said, "my mind was just wandering. You were saying that Baumgartner lived up in that tower . . ."

"Yes, even after the college was founded and he'd become president. I doubt that the students ever saw much of him, though, he'd turned into such a recluse. Apparently he'd only come down to pray in his private chapel. That's it just to the left of the tower."

I nodded. So that was where it was. The only evidence of the chapel was a bay-window-like apse that jutted out a few feet from the wall. Narrow windows, three in the middle and two on either side, rose to Gothic peaks just beneath the roof line. The little chapel was crowned with a slate roof, its ridge decorated with wrought-iron work.

"The main college chapel used to be Luke's Great Hall. This little one is kept locked up, hasn't been used since his death. I was lucky enough to have a peep inside once, during my last year as a student."

"Oh, I didn't know you were a St. Eustace alum."

"Sure am. Since those days I've spent most of my life here, in fact, except for a few years of graduate school in Virginia. Anyway, there were three or four of us girls who had always wondered what the little chapel was like inside, so we asked Pastor Roland, and he had a key to it. I remember it being right pretty, just like a miniature Gothic church, with beautiful stained glass windows."

Charlotte gestured toward one of several benches that dotted the gravel walkway across from the castle. As we sat down, a pair of swans came languorously gliding by.

"That's Max and Moritz," she said, "I'm not sure which generation anymore. There was a pair with those names in Baumgartner's day. Apparently they said back then that if they came swimming by and you whispered their names to them, it would bring good luck."

"Hang on a sec—Max and Moritz? Two males?"

"No, of course not. The females have always been called Max, it's become a tradition." She smiled. "But take a look now at the other side of the moat, in the bushes there."

Between the castle wall and the moat, I was able to pick out several brightly painted statues of dwarfs. One was digging with a spade, another was working the soil with a hoe, a third was stretched out taking a nap.

"So he had them shipped over from Germany, I suppose?"

"Oh no, he carved them himself. He had one of the stonecutters who was working on the castle give him some pointers, but mostly he just learned by trial and error."

I spotted a fourth dwarf and did a double take.

"Don't tell me . . . is that one really . . ."

"Yep, that's what he's doing, all right."

This particular dwarf, partially hidden behind a bush, was looking over his shoulder and frowning. He seemed to have just dropped his trousers, baring his plump behind. An uninterrupted stream of water spurted out from between his chubby legs.

"Luke was talented," Charlotte said, "but not always completely serious. Some kind of pipe mechanism connected to the moat keeps him going." She pointed to the castle roof. "There's one more up there, leaning on the wall."

I looked up toward the parapet, where another stone dwarf—this time a young woman—gesticulated wildly as she stared down aghast at the gardener who was relieving himself.

"She was an afterthought, apparently. Luke was already really old when he carved her, so I've heard. Guess he never lost his sense of humor."

"He must've been a man of many moods."

"No doubt about it. Have a look at his diaries sometime and you'll get a pretty good idea of what he was like. Speaking of which, have you had a chance to look at that final entry yet?"

"I have. I think I might even have made some progress. But I'm not quite ... "

"You don't need to tell me anything more. Same goes for a certain colleague of ours when he's back here at the end of August. You know, I have a feeling he's more interested in this business than he lets on."

I nodded. "I have the same impression."

"There's no telling with Klaus, there's much that he keeps to himself." She looked at her watch and stood up. "Sorry, Colin, I was supposed to pick up Michael in the Art Department ten minutes ago. See you later!"

She headed off along a path that apparently led to the art building. I stayed sitting on the bench for a while, watching as the two swans disappeared around the curve in the moat. I got up and headed for home to consult the college catalogue.

A detailed map of the South Woods showed two trails that led into the forest from different points on the edge of campus, and several others in the woods itself that ran roughly parallel to Faculty Row or zigzagged up and down the hillsides. I decided to take a shortcut and head straight into the woods from the end of my backyard, then trudge through the underbrush until I came to a trail, which would have to happen sooner or later.

Two or three minutes after setting out I began to wonder. The undergrowth was dense with ferns and brambles and shiny-leaved bushes I wasn't able to identify. Was I likely to encounter any animals today, beyond squirrels and rabbits? There had to be deer in the woods, but I was pretty sure that they usually grazed at dawn or in the evening.

The sound of laughter not far ahead made me stop in my tracks. Through the trees I caught sight of a patch of red, then blue, as two middle-aged women walked by about fifty feet away. Townies, I assumed, or possibly neighbors from somewhere along Faculty Row. What would they think if they saw someone lurking in the bushes not far off the beaten track? Feeling foolish, I stood stock-still behind the trunk of a long-needled pine until they were out of sight. Trudging on again through the underbrush, I reached the path they were on and turned in the opposite direction, picking burrs off my jeans as I went.

The air was fresh and invigorating. From far above came the call of a cardinal, interrupted by the raucous scolding of a bluejay. Every so often I noticed large yellow dots painted at chest-level on tree trunks at the edge of the trail. Soon I came to a signpost offering the choice of going straight or turning off to the left. The marker for the path I was on said "Yellow Trail: Amity House .6 mi." The other, pointing down the slope, read: "Blue Trail: Waterfall .2 mi. / Town .7 mi." Always a sucker for waterfalls, I took the left turn.

The angle of descent increased as I moved on. In a few minutes I heard the faint sound of rushing water. The path leveled out and led via several large stepping stones across a narrow creek. The gurgle gradually became almost a roar, and after one more winding the terrain dropped off sharply and I came to a stairway of split logs that had been built into the hillside. The stream was no more than two feet wide as it flowed over the edge, where it fell for seven or eight feet, loud enough to make the bird calls I'd been hearing all but inaudible. I climbed down the make-shift ladder to a wooden bench that stood near the bubbling pool at the bottom of the fall. I spread my jacket out on the damp boards, sat down, and leaned back with my legs crossed.

Only then did I see it. In a niche dug out of the hillside next to the waterfall, a miniature stone dwarf painted in bright colors sat on his own little bench. Holding a long-stemmed pipe in one hand and wearing a big grin, he looked over at me and seemed to be mimicking my relaxed pose. I laughed out loud—there really was no escaping Luke Baumgartner around here.

Sitting across from the rushing water, I couldn't help but think back to the wonderful May weekend when Annika and I had driven up to the North Shore and camped at Gooseberry Falls on a site high above Lake Superior. The next day we had continued along Highway 61 to the Baptism River and hiked in to the High Falls. What a perfect capstone that had been to our weekend up north.

Suddenly the vision was gone. How could this minuscule stream of water possibly have made me think of those majestic falls in northern Minnesota? Was there no end to the sights and sounds that would remind me of Annika? Grabbing my jacket, I continued down the hill in the direction of the town.

The trail soon led to a stone bridge over the creek that at this point rushed along in a gorge five or six feet below. Was this the bridge Baumgartner had referred to in his "last words" as being so important to him? And, coincidentally, the site of a murder? How ironic.

Standing at the waist-high wall, I gazed at the sparkling, gurgling water. Could it have been an accident? If a person were to slip and lose his balance . . . It didn't seem likely, but maybe it could have happened that way. Definitely a less distressing possibility than the alternative.

I crossed the bridge and continued down the slope. As the woods began to thin out, the Blue Trail joined the Red Trail, running parallel to the road from campus into town. Soon a row of small houses signaled the beginning of Main Street. Changing direction, I headed up the Red Trail. This way I would avoid the waterfall and, I hoped, keep my mind off Annika.

When I arrived home, a plaintive meowing greeted me as I

opened the front door.

"Good God, Juniper, I'm sorry," I said, "I forgot to put out your chow!"

I went into the kitchen and filled her food and water bowls while she waited impatiently. As she attacked her kibble, I sat down in a kitchen chair to watch her. I had managed not to think of Annika for a good half-hour.

Chapter 6

Time flies, as the platitude has it, and between my work on the Lessing article and my course preparations, August was over almost before it had begun. The challenge issued by Luke Baumgartner faded into the background; the two scraps of paper containing his final diary entry and his last words still hung above my desk where I had taped them, ignored but not forgotten. As I considered my fall schedule, I was pleased with its balance: two of my courses would meet on Mondays, Wednesdays, and Fridays for one hour each, and the third on Tuesdays and Thursdays for ninety minutes.

The first day of the semester fell on a Wednesday. The bell for my morning class rang at 9:40, just as I closed my office door and headed down the hallway. Blast it, I hated being late for class, especially on the first day. I raced along the hallway, trying not to trip over my own feet.

The dozen faces of my Conversation and Composition students looked up as I entered the room. Moira MacGregor, whom I'd occasionally seen in the library over the past month, was sitting in the front row. I began the class with my customary introduction.

"Guten Tag, liebe Studenten, ich heiße Colin Ritter."

A few of the class members tittered at being called 'dear students.' One, a guy with short blond hair and ragged black jeans, gave me a sour look from his seat at the back of the room. Was this because of what I had just said, or was it his general demeanor?

"Nun möchte ich wissen, wie Sie alle heißen, was für Interessen Sie haben und so weiter." I paused for a moment, my gaze drawn to Moira. *"Fangen wir mit dieser jungen Dame in der ersten Reihe an."*

Moira seemed pleased to have been called on first and returned my smile.

"Ich heiße Moira MacGregor und ich interessiere mich für Kunst. Und Deutsch, natürlich."

"Kunst und Deutsch, sehr gut, danke schön. Und wie schreibt sich Ihr Vorname?"

As Moira spelled out the five letters of her name, I wrote them on the blackboard in a vertical column. Next, I pointed to a male student sitting behind her.

"Und Sie, mein Herr?"

"Ick bin Brandon. Mein Interessen sind Sports und Kemie."

"Sport und Chemie—Basketball, vielleicht?"

"Ja, Basketball und Fußball."

Letter by letter, Brandon spelled his name, which I wrote parallel to Moira's, but a few inches to the right and slightly lower down. Two or three students began to whisper, probably wondering what this jerk of a teacher was up to.

"Und woher kommen Sie, Brandon? Aus Kentucky vielleicht?"

"Nein, ich bin von North Carolina."

"Ah, Sie kommen aus Nord-Carolina. Ich selber bin Minnesotaner. Waren Sie schon mal in Minnesota, junge Dame?"

I pointed to a woman student in the last row.

"Minnesota . . . nein, aber ich war im Wisconsin."

"Aha, in Wisconsin, da ist es im Winter auch sehr kalt. Und Sie heißen?"

"Ich heiße Ramona."

"Gut, Ramona, danke."

Using the 'r' in Moira as a point of connection, I wrote out the letters in Ramona's name in a horizontal line. Smiles began to spread over the students' faces. Continuing around the room, I had some of them ask questions of their neighbors. After everyone had spoken, all twelve names stood on the blackboard in a sort of zigzag square, each connected with two others like parts of a crossword puzzle. As I wrote out the final name, the students applauded and cheered.

For the remainder of the hour I had the class members form groups of three or four, then circulated around the room eliciting more information from them. Even Jason Miller, the student in raggedy clothes who seemed to have an attitude, participated reasonably well.

When the bell rang at 10:40 Moira was the last to pack up her things. I was right behind her as she walked through the doorway.

"Great class, Professor Ritter, I think this is going to be fun. I—" She put a hand over her mouth. "Oops, guess I shouldn't assume it's okay to speak English."

"Not a problem, Moira, as long as we're not in class. So you're back on campus again?"

"Yes, I'm in Amity House, just down the road from here." She paused for a moment. "This is your first year here, right?"

"Yes. Professor Seifert's on leave, so I'm replacing him."

"Of course, I should have figured that out."

We walked down the stairway to the main floor.

"Have you noticed any of the campus oddities yet?" she asked as we left the building.

"Don't know that I have. Or do you mean things like the garden dwarfs Baumgartner carved over by the castle?"

"That's one of them. There's another one just off the path be-

44

tween here and the library. Do you want me to show you?"

"Sure."

A short distance along the path she motioned to a large rectangular block of stone standing on a hillock.

"That's Mr. Baumgartner's grave marker. It's known as the monolith. His wife is buried there, too."

"Really? I've walked past it plenty of times, but I never gave it a second thought. A gravestone on a college campus—that's definitely an oddity."

"In a way. His wife died way before the college was founded, and he wanted to be buried next to her, of course. He carved some bas-reliefs on each side of the stone in the early 1900s. They're based on Dürer motifs."

"Hm. How is it you know so much about him?"

"I started giving campus tours last year, so I had to read up on the history of the college, the founder's life—that kind of stuff. I've read his diaries, too."

"Have you? I've only looked at his very last entry. About whatever it is he supposedly hid away somewhere."

"Yeah, isn't that the screwiest thing? Wonder if anybody will ever find it."

"So you don't think it's a total scam?"

"Oh, no, not at all. The impression I have from his diaries is that he was absolutely honest about everything. He just liked to jerk people around sometimes, is all. Speaking of strange things, you might want to have a look at the Garden of Time across from the castle. It has a life-sized statue that he carved, of an angel standing in a circle of columns. It's supposed to be his wife, and the circle represents a clock."

We had reached the library. Moira pointed to the lettering above the archway that led into the building's courtyard.

"GOTTHOLD EPHRAIM LESSING LIBRARY," I read aloud.

"The same as on the cover of that book you took out."

"Yes, exactly. Well, the name couldn't be more appropriate—Lessing was a librarian himself for the last several years of his life."

Directly below Lessing's name two angelic figures held up a stone banner bearing the inscription *Lux hominibus*.

"Mr. Baumgartner was fond of angels," Moira said.

"I'm getting that impression."

"Then there's his number thing. Do you know about the trees in the courtyard?"

"Not sure what there is to know. I sat under them often enough last summer whenever I wanted a break from what I was doing inside. Is there something special about them?"

"Something typical of Mr. Baumgartner, at least. If we go through the archway I can show you. He designed the whole space, like just about everything else on this campus."

Entering the courtyard was like stepping into the past. The library's upper stories were supported by an open arcade, creating a covered ambulatory on all sides. In the center, a three-tiered fountain played in a grassy circle. Neptune, his trident at his side, stood in the upper basin as water-spewing fish leapt all around him. Three majestic trees formed a triangle near the edges of the circle. Students sat on benches here and there, talking quietly with others or reading.

"Okay," Moira said, "first thing you have to know is that Mr. Baumgartner had a kind of fetish about the number three. He had nine buildings built along the road that runs around the campus—three times three. And he loved trees. He planted groups of three here and there, all kinds of different species. Three red oaks, three hickories, three whatever. You'll see markers everywhere. Seems to me the ones in the circle here are lindens."

She walked over to the closest tree and crouched down to read the marker.

"Yep, 'European linden—*Tilia europaea*,' or however it's pronounced."

I glanced around the courtyard again. "Everything here seems to have been perfectly planned. Baumgartner must have had quite the artistic sensibility."

"For sure. Speaking of which, I should be heading on over to Weiden now to work on my own."

"Weiden . . . ?"

"Weiden Hall, the art building, it's the next one around the circle. Except for the library, Mr. Baumgartner named all the academic buildings after German towns."

"Well, that's one I've never heard of. Same with Riedenburg, where we just had our class. They must have been places he was especially fond of."

"Maybe, but I think there's another reason. I checked on a map of Germany once, and the towns he chose form an almost perfect circle with the city of Nuremberg as the center. Just like the buildings themselves, with the castle at the center."

"No way! But I guess I shouldn't be surprised, considering all that I've heard about him. His love of order, and so on. So what is it you're going to be doing in 'Weiden'?"

"Well, I'm majoring in art—art and art history. I'll be mounting a photography show later this semester. Sometime in the middle of October, I don't know the exact date yet."

"Good luck with that, sounds like a lot of work."

"It's not so bad. I'm only taking two courses, Graphic Design and your German class, and then I'll be graduating in December. I overdid the electives in my first four years, so I'm staying on for an extra semester."

"Great. You know, I considered an art major myself when I was in college. Still make some drawings now and then. I have no talent, but I like doing it."

We walked under the archway to the front of the library again.

"You know what? I think I'll pay a visit to that Garden of Time you mentioned. How exactly do I get there?"

She pointed toward the center of campus. "Just go along this path and take a right when you get to the Promenade—that's what we call the gravel path that runs alongside the moat—and then take another right. You'll see a small sign on your left that points to the Garden. You have to look carefully, it's pretty much hidden in the rhododendron bushes."

"Okay, thanks. And thanks for the tour. See you in class on Friday?"

"Yes," she said with a snicker, "if you can find your way out of the Garden of Time."

"Beg pardon?"

"Don't worry, I think you'll be able to. Bye, now."

With a cheery wave, she headed across the lawn, leaving me to wonder what was in store for me.

A narrow opening had been cut through the rhododendrons, leading to a long, vine-covered arbor with a wooden bench in the distance that I could barely make out in the dappled sunlight. The gentle twittering of birds and the slight crunch of my footsteps lent an aura of tranquillity to the place. When I reached the bench, I found that the path had come to an abrupt end. What was going on here? There seemed to be nowhere to go but back the way I had come. As I sat down on the bench to consider the situation, a section of the latticework next to me sprang open. Beyond it, another arbored path led off at a ninety-degree angle.

Luke Baumgartner was apparently having some fun again. As I ducked through the opening, the latticework-gate swung shut behind me with a click. Feeling uneasy, I gave it a yank and was relieved to find that it opened easily.

I continued along the new path and soon was faced with a Baroque-style garden maze of neatly-trimmed hedges. Standing on tiptoe, I could see the head of a statue a short distance away, gleaming white in the late morning sun. I turned to the right and followed the twisting path, which, after two or three corners, came to a dead end at a wooden bench.

Retracing my steps, I tried a different route, one that left me at another dead end and another bench. After one more false start I took a different turn off the first path I'd followed and found myself in the inner sanctum, a circle about twenty feet in diameter that looked to have been modelled after a Roman rotunda. The periphery of the circle was punctuated with fluted marble columns, some no more than stumps, others supporting fragments of a frieze embellished with bas-reliefs of classical figures in dramatic poses. It was an artificial ruin, such as I had seen in gardens in Europe. Could Baumgartner have carved all this himself? If so, it was an amazing achievement.

I walked around the circle slowly, counting twelve columns in all—of course, the place was called the Garden of Time. On a pedestal in the center stood the statue whose head I had just barely been able to see above the maze, a life-sized winged woman dressed in a toga. The angelic figure's face was covered with a veil and her neck was bent as if she were lost in thought. In her left hand she held an inverted torch, the classical symbol of death. Her right arm was extended outward in what looked like a gesture of futility.

Climbing the three steps to the base of the angel's pedestal, I could see the castle in the distance, with the Rapunzel tower and the little chapel next to it partially visible above the bushes. Looking over this way from the tower where he had spent the final years of his life, Luke Baumgartner must have thought of his wife countless times. Carving the statue—creating this whole space, in fact—must have had therapeutic value for the old fellow.

As I fumbled my way back through the maze, making just as many false turns as I had on the way in, I smiled at what Moira had said. When I reached the Promenade, I turned off at the path to Riedenburg Hall and soon caught sight of Baumgartner's grave marker again. Cutting across the lawn, I climbed the small hillock where it stood and looked at the monument more carefully. A simple epitaph was engraved on one side:

Catharine Baumgartner
née Alexander
15 October 1844 - 19 November 1871

Lukas Baumgartner
3 March 1833 - 19 November 1908

Requiescant in pace

Baumgartner's wife had barely made it to her twenty-seventh birthday; he had lived almost three times that long. What an odd coincidence that both had died on the same date in different years.

Above the inscription was a bas-relief of a snake coiled around the branch of a tree and holding an apple in its mouth. It looked to me like a borrowing from Dürer's engraving of Adam and Eve. On the second side was a skull within an escutcheon, on the third a head of the crucified Christ, and on the last—to my great surprise—Dürer's magic square, the unusual sequence of numbers from the *Melencolia* engraving.

I walked slowly around the monolith again. The first three motifs, assuming I had looked at them in the intended order, seemed to form a chain of meaning: the Fall, the entrance of Death into the world as a result, and Christ's redeeming grace. But what about the magic square? Was it a reflection of Baumgartner's own sense of harmony and balance, or a symbol of humankind's attempts at creating order? Or perhaps this strange man had simply wanted to confound future viewers—which, given his final diary entry, didn't seem out of character.

My cell phone rang as I stepped down from the hillock. It was Charlotte Rossi.

"Colin, I have terrible news. Walter Seifert had a massive heart attack in the Princeton library and died on the spot. I got a call from Mildred just as I was walking into my office."

"Good God, she must be distraught!"

"Well, she was quite calm, actually. I've always known her to be a strong person, and she seems to be taking this remarkably well."

"So she'll be coming back here. I guess I'll have to—"

"No, no, she wanted me to tell you that the rental agreement still stands. She's going to move in with her sister in Lexington once things are settled out east. She wasn't sure what she'd do about the house, but for the time being everything will stay as is."

"Okay, thanks for letting me know. I'm heading back to the office now. If you can give me her address out there, I'd like to write her a note. What a shame. I barely even got to meet her husband."

"Yes, he was a fine man. I'll see you when you get here, then."

I looked up at the monolith one last time, shook my head, and walked across the lawn to Riedenburg Hall.

Chapter 7

My alarm startled me out of a sound sleep. I lay in bed thinking about my possibly changed situation at the college. The German Department would have to announce the position in the various academic journals, but given that my research specialty (the eighteenth century) was the same as Walter Seifert's, and since I already had my foot in the door, I might be at an advantage for getting a tenured position. I could only hope that my colleagues would give me positive evaluations over the next few months. Charlotte . . . and Hochstraaten.

A moment later I chided myself for thinking about such things when my colleague had just died. Even though the whole situation had fallen into my lap, I couldn't help feeling guilty.

The sun was shining as I left the house for my morning walk. Pausing at the Promenade, I looked across the moat to the little chapel's lancet windows, which seemed dull and colorless. How different they would look from the inside as the morning sun struck them.

I found the pastor sitting in his office behind the altar area of the main chapel.

"Ah, good morning, Professor Ritter. What a terrible thing, the passing of Walter Seifert—we all thought he would have many productive years ahead of him. Klaus Hochstraaten and I were talking yesterday about the wonderful discussion sessions we'd had with him over the years, typically once or twice a semester. We came to speak of ourselves as the *Tafelrunde*—not that a round table ever came into play, it was merely because one of our early topics concerned the Arthurian legends. Walter applied the term to our group ironically, and it stuck, even though Klaus, I believe, found it somewhat frivolous. At any rate, to make a long story short, we thought, or rather I thought, and suggested to Klaus, that you might be willing to take Walter's place as a discussant. It seems to me that this would be an especially appropriate way to commemorate him."

I was taken aback. "Oh . . . I don't know. He was a major scholar in his field. I'm just at the beginning of my career. Wouldn't it be presumptuous of me—"

"Not at all, we realize that you are a young man, a scholar in the bud, as it were. Furthermore, our discussions are really more conversations, you know, over a glass of cognac in one of our homes, all quite cordial and relaxed. Though on some occasions a considerable amount of heat has been generated, I must admit. Klaus, for example, is, as you probably know, an adamant Catholic, despite my efforts to convince him otherwise. But that, in the end, simply makes our conversations all the more interesting."

I thought back to my meeting with Hochstraaten in the Dürer museum and what he had said about the Apocalypse woodcuts—'a triumph of Catholicism.' I didn't exactly savor being part of a discussion group with him, but I couldn't think of an easy way out.

The pastor pursed his lips and went on. "I do hope you'll join us, Professor Ritter. With just the two of us . . . well, it simply wouldn't be the same."

I nodded slowly. "Did you have any particular day in mind?"

"Klaus will be very busy in the immediate future. He suggested Friday, October 3rd, at his house. The topic will be 'Dürer and religion.' It was my turn to choose this time."

I didn't feel comfortable telling the pastor that I probably wouldn't have much to say on the subject of religion, despite my parochial school upbringing. On the other hand, since I had worked on both Dürer and the Reformation during the past summer, there was a chance I might not make a complete fool of myself.

"Would you consider inviting Michael Rossi, too, to get an art historian's perspective?"

"Why, that's an excellent idea, I will certainly do that. I will pick you up, of course, and Michael, if he can make it. Klaus lives out in the country and his house is not easy to find."

"All right, I guess you've convinced me. And the date should be fine."

"Excellent, thank you for agreeing. The last time we met at Klaus's place the subject under discussion was also Dürer. I remember his saying how much he would love to own one of Dürer's woodcuts or engravings."

"Sure, I wouldn't mind having one myself."

"Well, but Klaus almost made it sound as if it were owed to him to possess a Dürer. He believes that he has a special facility for the appreciation of fine works of art, and I certainly can't gainsay him. It was an interesting evening out at his house. We had a guest participant on that occasion as well, a new appointee in the History Department and a most engaging young man. He had a brother in New York who was an art dealer, and he knew a great deal about German art himself. The poor devil died before the year was out. It seems he was murdered in the South Woods."

My ears perked up. "That must be the person I heard about last summer. I can't quite remember the name. . . ."

"This fellow's name was Fleishman, Ronald Fleishman—"

"Really? I knew a Ronald Fleishman who was studying history at the University of Minnesota. I think he went on to the University of Chicago after that. I lost track of him."

"The University of Chicago . . . that sounds right, now that you mention it."

"Hm. Do you know if your Fleishman played chess?"

"He certainly did. On the computer even, with several different opponents at the same time."

"That has to have been him! I was foolish enough to play him once. Beat me hands down."

"He was very clever indeed. Ronald and I had interesting theological discussions, he being a Jew, of course; one of them concerned Lessing's treatment of Jews in his dramas. Oddly enough, I had the impression that he and Klaus had become friends."

"Oh?"

"That is to say . . . and I probably should not say it . . . well, to be frank, Klaus has been known to make remarks that might be construed as anti-Semitic. Not that I intend to cast blame, none of us is perfect."

Why would Hochstraaten have made friends with Ronald Fleishman, I wondered? Could Ronald have told him that he had figured out Baumgartner's last words?

As I stood there pondering, it suddenly occurred to me why I had come to see Pastor Roland in the first place.

"Oh, Pastor Roland, I almost forgot: I was hoping to have a look at Luke Baumgartner's little chapel if that would be all right. Charlotte Rossi thought you would have the key."

The pastor was nonplussed. "You know, I did have one for many years. An oddly shaped thing—the end of it looked like the number one. You might check with the custodian, I believe I passed it on to him. I suspect he'll be in one of the classrooms cleaning blackboards at this early hour. His name is Ned, and he can be a bit brusque at times, but he'll help you out if he can."

I thanked the pastor and, with some misgivings, went in search of Ned.

The classrooms were located off the corridor from Pastor Roland's office, on the opposite side of the castle from the Dürer museum. In the first room I came to, a dark-skinned black man with close-cropped gray hair was washing the blackboards.

"Excuse me," I said, "would you be Ned?"

The custodian glanced over his shoulder. "That's me."

"My name's Colin Ritter, I'm new in the German Department. I was wondering if I could have a look at the private chapel. Pastor Roland thought you might have the key."

Ned continued wiping the board. "Had it at one time, s'pose I still do. It'll take some lookin', though."

"Of course, if this is a bad time, I could—"

"No worse'n any other." Ned deposited the rag he was using in his bucket of water and walked toward the corridor. I stood there looking after him.

"You comin'?" Ned said over his shoulder.

Feeling foolish, I followed him through the entrance tower and along the corridor on the other side of the castle. Ned's utility room, long and narrow and lit by a single window, was between the Religion Department offices and the museum. Near the door were a sink and several shelves full of cleaning materials and utensils. At the far end a dilapidated old desk stood under the window, with a pile of sheet music stacked neatly on one corner. Ned rummaged around in the top drawer and pulled out a ring of large iron keys.

"Might be one of these," he said. "Most all the locks in the buildin' been changed since these were made, though."

"The pastor said that the end was shaped like the number one."

Ned nodded and detached a key from the ring. "Must be this one, then."

We walked along the corridor to the Rapunzel tower, where Ned stopped at a small door and inserted the key. After several unsuccessful attempts at turning it, the bolt finally disengaged with a screech of protest.

"Sounds like it's been a while since this door was last unlocked," I said.

"Oh, yeah," Ned said. "Somethin' like twenty, twenty-five years, I'd say. "First and last time I ever opened it, till now."

"Really? Who was it wanted to see the chapel back then?"

Ned scratched his stubbly beard. "Don't rightly know who it was. Looked like a professor, but I don't think he ever said his name. Had some kinda foreign accent. I don't remember ever seein' him again after that."

I frowned. Well, fine—Hochstraaten was certainly as interested in art as I was. Or had he had other reasons?

Ned turned the key back and forth a few more times in the squeaky lock, then pulled the door open.

"Well, thanks a lot," I said. "Should I let you know when I leave?"

"Yeah, so I can come back and lock up." He walked off to resume his work.

A musty odor of damp stone and stale air came wafting toward me as I stepped through the doorway. On my left, a life-sized wooden statue of St. Eustace, its paint faded and chipped, stared at me. He was dressed in armor and carried a banner bearing his deer's-head symbol; cobwebs trailed down beardlike from his chin to the hilt of his sword. Glancing around the chapel, I was struck by the same sense of anachronism I always felt on entering the library courtyard. Charlotte's description had been accurate: the chapel was like a miniature Gothic church—or a playhouse for a monk's child, I thought irreverently.

Two pairs of saints sculpted in bas-relief stood in separate niches against the back wall. They looked oddly familiar, but something seemed not quite right about them. Suddenly it dawned on me: they were copies of a sort, of two late oils by Dürer known collectively as the *Four Apostles*. I went down on one knee to read the inscription carved in the lowermost stone: 'Lukas Baumgartner fecit 1885.' Amazing. When had he found the time to do all his stone carving? The transference from one medium to the other had worked surprisingly well, even though the figures had lost something of their expressive power in the process. Dürer had presented his paintings to the city of Nuremberg shortly after the city fathers had declared themselves for Martin Luther. It made sense that Baumgartner had wanted a version of these holy men in his own little Lutheran chapel.

Behind the altar at the opposite end, brilliant sunlight poured in through the lancet windows, spreading a myriad of colors over the marble surface of the altar table. The tiny nave was divided by a center aisle, with three rows of pews on either side, each barely long enough to seat four or five people. Piers ran up the side walls to a vaulted ceiling at least twenty feet above. Several small clerestory windows were the chapel's only other source of natural light. Apparently the place had never been wired for electricity; sconces with candles were mounted in each of the piers, and a cobweb-draped candelabra stood in the center of the altar table.

Shielding my eyes from the glare with one hand, I climbed the three steps to the altar and examined the windows. The central panes contained depictions of Jesus walking on water, Jesus changing water to wine, and Jesus and Lazarus, while the others showed a hodge-podge of scenes. On the far left a young man wearing a crown sat playing a harp—King David, maybe? Alongside him Jonah grimaced at the prospect of being swallowed up by a diminutive smiling whale. A mournful-looking female saint bearing the stigmata stood on the right side. Catherine of Siena, I remembered from some high school religion class. Next to her, a triumphant St. George had just run his lance through a silly-looking blue dragon with bright red eyes. Luke must have had a hand in these designs. Some of them, at any rate, seemed more likely to tickle the fancy of the viewer than to inspire feelings of reverence.

Below each of the lancet windows and separated from them by

narrow stone blocks were small square panes containing a variety of designs. In the left-hand corner I spotted the Baumgartner family's falcon and fleur-de-lys. I remembered having seen similar stained glass coats of arms in two churches in Nuremberg; Luke had simply transplanted this tradition, as he had so many others, to his adopted soil.

Stepping down from the altar, I sat in the front pew and let the repose of the place and the play of colored light wash over me. Suddenly a feeling of desolation struck me, as it had at the waterfall. Annika and I had visited countless Gothic cathedrals throughout Germany together. And now. . . .

I leaned forward, my head in my hands. What had gone wrong with our relationship? Well, it was pretty obvious, wasn't it? We had both become encapsulated in our individual worlds—in my case, the job at Macalester College and the demands of teaching and publication; in Annika's, the massive amount of research necessary to preparing a doctoral dissertation and all the tension it engendered. We had both been victims of situations that were, once we had bought into the system, beyond our control.

I sat up again and forced myself to stare into the brilliant light as it flowed in through the windows. Who was I trying to kid? It hadn't been that way at all. Had there ever been a weekend evening when I hadn't taken the time to go out with Annika for a beer, or to go to a movie? And had Annika ever been closed off to me? Not in the least. She had always had time for me, had discussed my new course ideas, asked my advice on possible dissertation topics, massaged my neck muscles at the end of a long work day. Yes, life with her had become routine in some ways. But didn't everyone need routine in their lives? Routine did not have to mean drudgery, it simply was part of life. Damn it to hell, how had I ever gotten involved with Nina in the first place? Her lackadaisical view of the world and her unpredictability tended in the direction of chaos. Who, in his right mind, would not choose a degree of routine over chaos?

I walked past the statue of St. Eustace, then stepped out into the mustiness of the Rapunzel tower. Finding Ned mopping the floor in the adjacent corridor, I motioned to him, mouthed the word 'thanks,' and left the building.

The swans seemed to have just snatched up the last bread crumbs a student had thrown to them. As they swam on past, I bent over and resisted the temptation to whisper something to them.

I sat down on a bench and looked across to Luke's garden dwarfs, finding them at the moment not at all amusing. I debated back and forth whether I should call Annika before finally pulling out my cell phone and scrolling down to her number.

"Hello?"

"Hello, Annika . . ."

"Colin, is that you? I didn't recognize your number."

"I've only had it for a short time. Look, Annika, I wasn't sure if I should call or not. I thought you might not want to talk to me again."

There was a moment's silence. "How brilliant of you to think of that possibility."

"All right, I deserved that. Look, if you'll just listen for a minute. I wanted you to know that . . . that I'm sorry how it all ended."

"How it all ended. You mean, how *you* ended it. Are you not willing to take responsibility, Colin?"

"Yes, yes, of course I am, I shouldn't have put it that way. It was my doing, and I treated you terribly. I should have been more considerate of your feelings."

"*More* considerate? Do you think you were at all considerate?"

I took a deep breath. "I guess not, seeing you don't seem to think so. Look, I know I'm really botching this . . . let me try to say it a different way. What I did was stupid, inconsiderate, and a bad idea—as I found out soon enough. I don't know where my head was. It was like I had gone crazy."

"I see. Well, you're not the first to have fallen for Nina's charms—and to have been disappointed."

"I suppose not. But how do you know that?"

"Our community is small—one hears things. That your relationship with Nina ended several months ago, for example. Perhaps if you had called me then we would have had something to talk about."

"I was afraid to, Annika. I couldn't imagine that you'd want to talk after what I'd put you through. And then there was all the job hunting business, which was depressing enough in itself."

"I heard that you were looking. You were quite happy at Macalester, I thought?"

"I was. But there were no prospects there for a third year."

"You knew about this before . . . before the break-up?"

"It looked likely then. I didn't tell you because I didn't want you to worry."

There was another silence before Annika spoke again. "So have you been able to find a position?"

"Yes, at a small college in Kentucky called St. Eustace, in the middle of nowhere. The job is a sabbatical replacement. But how are you doing? You've decided on a dissertation topic, I assume?"

"Oh yes, long ago. I've made quite good progress, in fact. Just now I'm walking to Folwell Hall. I find I work better in the German library there than at home."

"What exactly are you writing on? Did you decide to stick with Neidhart?"

"Yes, of course. The title is 'Ethical Questions in the Poetry of Neidhart von Reuental.'"

"Great topic. He's one of my favorite poets of the period."

"I remember that. From the class on Middle High German poetry we took together."

"Yes. That seems so long ago."

"It does. Well, I'm almost at Folwell Hall now."

"I'll let you go, then. Would it . . . be all right if I called again?"

"I don't know, Colin. For now, I think I will say no."

'For now'—what did that really mean? 'Never darken my door-step again'? I didn't want to know.

"All right. Well, best of luck with the dissertation."

"Thank you. Goodbye, Colin."

"Goodbye."

I got up from the bench and started to walk along the moat. Why had I called Annika? Just to hear her voice again? Had I hoped that some sort of reconciliation might be possible? How ridiculous was that. How stupid of me to think that I could explain my way out of what I had done. And even if she had been mollified to a degree, how would that have helped? We were separated by almost a thousand miles, for God's sake. I was convinced that my call had done more harm than good. I continued walking around aimlessly for awhile, then headed back to my office to run off the syllabus for my course on German cultural history.

The first meeting went reasonably well, or so I supposed. Frankly, I was in no state to be able to judge, since my mind had been on Annika as much as on the course materials. Since it was the first day of class, I let the students go after forty minutes. I had done the crossword puzzle thing again, so I was reasonably sure that I would remember at least some of the students' names next time.

Without really thinking about it, I left Riedenburg Hall, walked along the path to the library and climbed up to the second floor. I needed to escape into someone else's world for a while.

Pulling out Luke Baumgartner's Volume I, *Memories of a Youth in Germany*, I went over to the windows that overlooked the courtyard and sat down in a study carrel. Neptune stood below among his water-spouting fish and seemed to contemplate the endless ripples that expanded slowly in concentric circles around him. At my eye level, the branches of the three giant linden trees that framed the fountain moved almost imperceptibly in the breeze. Maroon and lavender chrysanthemums stood out in their beds in the late afternoon sunlight. Tearing myself away from the mesmerizing scene, I opened the book and began to read. A brief editor's preface indicated that there would, in fact, be no preface at all, since Mr. Baumgartner had maintained that any necessary or interesting details concerning his life would best be expressed by the diarist himself.

Young Hare, 1502

The Little Owl, 1506

The Large Piece of Turf, 1503

The Three Lindens, 1494

Chapter 8

I translated the first two of the three volumes of my diaries from the original German in the weeks after the turn of the new century. Preceding the dated entries are three recollections of my earliest days, rendered as faithfully as memory has permitted through the mists of time. The events described in the first two of these may be considered prescient vis-à-vis a certain experience which I was to have much later in life.

My very earliest recollection is as brief as it is poignant to me. It has as its setting my father's summer house in the countryside near Nuremberg, to which our family made many a carefree excursion; the year would have been 1836, though at the time I had no notion of such things. In the foreground am I myself, at first frolicking about gaily, as a child of three years is wont to do. All at once I sit stock-still and look up at a most unexpected visitor: a majestic stag, which, a moment later, begins to lick my forehead with its warm tongue. Then, as quickly as it had come, the stately beast vanishes again, and the curtain falls on this first memorable moment of my life.

Let us now leap ahead to my sixth year and an event which can be characterized as my first loss of an ideal. The scene is the estate of an elderly count who was a friend and business associate, I believe, of my father's. The count had invited my parents of a Sunday afternoon, and, as there would be other children present, my brother Stefan and I were permitted to be part of the company.

The count's residence was awe-inspiring enough, but the park at its back contained numerous flower gardens and a hedge-lined maze, the likes of which I had never seen before. We children were permitted to run about its intricate turnings to our hearts' content, and I especially enjoyed hiding from my brother, three years my junior, then calling his name in a somber voice and pouncing on him like a ferocious lion as soon as he came into view. Each time he squealed with delight, and I ran off to seek yet another point of vantage. This early version of hide-and-seek, I am sure, set the tone for my propensity, even as an adult, to carry on in this fashion.

Yes, the count's park was a paradise for small children, certainly. But I was soon to be reminded, in a most unpleasant way, that my father had not entirely outgrown his own fondness for tomfoolery.

Following our noon meal, he announced to us children that we would now go out-of-doors, where, as he proclaimed, he had something unheard of to show us. At the foot of the stairway which led down to the gardens, he pointed to a stag's head mounted on the adjacent wall. Bidding me stand directly opposite it, he told me that if I closed my eyes as tightly as I could and recited a certain magical incantation over and over again, the creature would speak to me. He whispered the incantation in my ear and then, putting a finger aside his nose to indicate that quiet was of the essence, drew the other children a few paces back so that I might perform my recitation unhindered.

And I, trusting unquestioningly as I did in my father – I stood there, eyes tightly shut, and said in as ceremonious a voice as I was able:

> Edler Hirsch,
> Sei nicht unwirsch;
> Liebes Tier,
> O sprich zu mir!
>
> Edler Hirsch,
> Sei nicht unwirsch . . . *

Suddenly it felt as if my face were being pierced by countless sharply-pointed icicles. I opened my eyes in terror and found myself dripping wet from head to waist. Gasping for breath, I retreated, and, as the other children, led by my brother, proceeded to break out into gales of laughter, I began to cry. I cried until my mother, hearing my miserable lamentation, came running down the stairway and swept me into her arms, at the same time scolding my father for playing such a wretched trick on an innocent and sensitive child. He, slightly repentant, sought to appease me by telling me that no less than an archbishop had had such a device installed at his palace near Salzburg for the amusement of his guests. I for my part was not amused, however, and – much worse – was forced to see this my image of absolute trust come crashing to the ground.

The above occurrence – I eventually forgave my father, but never fully trusted in him again – was in its way the precursor of a process which was set in motion six years later, a process which was to require yet a few more years before its ultimate influence upon my development came to the fore. The final result was the dissolution of my ties to my parental home.

* Noble deer, / Do not be gruff; / Dear animal, / Oh speak to me!

It was in 1845 that Herr Georg came into our house as the fourth of the private teachers I came to know during my few remaining years in Germany. My father found each of these to be unsatisfactory, and each was told sooner or later that he might seek employment elsewhere. This Herr Georg, a fiery-tempered young man who wrote poems, was to continue the instruction begun by my previous teachers in German, Latin, French, history, geography, mathematics, and other sciences of the spirit then deemed worthy of being imparted to the sons of well-to-do fathers. Aside from the excellence of his instruction, I will never forget Herr Georg's outbursts of rage, which were directed precisely against men like my father. It was he and his upper class accomplices, I was told, who daily exploited the working classes and held them in bondage.

It was not long before Herr Georg's political views became known to my father – more than likely through my brother's tattling – with the result that, to my great disappointment, he was given his walking papers within the year.

To Herr Georg I will be eternally grateful for two things: for instilling in me a love of the bitter-sweet poetry of Heinrich Heine, and for planting the first seeds of class consciousness in my fertile mind.

After Herr Georg's departure, my father took on the task of educating my brother and me himself. As a well-to-do banker, he assumed that I too would be interested in this area of endeavor. Though much of what he taught me was sheer drudgery at the time, I must confess that it has provided me with a sound background in business matters which has been helpful in my subsequent life. As for the remainder of my childhood education, its nature will become clear in the pages that follow.

Nuremberg, 3 March 1847
Having entered manhood on this day, I propose to keep a journal, with the sincere hope that I will write something, be it ever so brief, each day. The gifts I received were a splendid edition of Goethe's works and some fine drawing pencils and paper. It is impossible for me to say which of these delights me more.

Nuremberg, 4 March 1847
I passed most of the day in drawing and in reading a good portion of 'The Sorrows of Young Werther'. This Werther possesses great sensitivity and artistic talent, but he does not enjoy the company of those he considers stiff and respectable. I think that I am quite similar to him. I, too, am fond of drawing, though I know, alas, that I am nothing in comparison with that great son of our city, Albrecht Dürer.

Nuremberg, 12 April 1847

It has been over a month now since I have written in my journal. I see that I will not be able to keep my pledge to write every day, not because I do not have the will to do so, but because there is in my life so little that is worth writing about.

Nuremberg, 14 September 1847

Uncle Wilhelm, my father's brother, has moved here from Berlin to become our new tutor. Stefan, by nature obedient and industrious, has done well under his tutelage. By contrast, Uncle Wilhelm finds my preferred activities, drawing and reading works of literature, to be a waste of time. I complete my lessons as best I can under the threat of his stick, but I do not like him, nor do I believe that the good Werther would have.

Nuremberg, 25 December 1847

Our family Christmas celebration was as joyous as ever, and even Uncle Wilhelm seemed to make the effort to be less harsh than usual. The service in our Sebaldkirche was beautiful and uplifting, and the choir sang with great feeling. I must admit that I am not fond of hymns, but Christmas songs are quite a different matter.

Nuremberg, 18 January 1848

There has been nothing in the New Year worthy of being put down on paper. The daily lessons of my uncle continue to bore me, but I must pretend that I find them interesting and do as he instructs me. If I resist at any moment, I am immediately reminded of his readiness to use the stick. And my father, whenever he speaks of him, finds him a "man of great principle in every respect"!

Nuremberg, 28 February 1848

Today I was given permission to venture beyond the walls of our house – a rare boon which is granted me only when I perform exceptionally well. While I was in the old town, I overheard several people speaking of fighting in the streets of Paris, that many had been killed, and that the French king had been forced to flee. Since I had earlier heard my Uncle Wilhelm praise him, I know that this can only be a good thing.

Nuremberg, 3 March 1848

For my birthday my mother gave me two beautiful books that contain the dramas of Goethe and Schiller. We did not have an elaborate celebration, since Uncle Wilhelm finds such things foolish and because my father agrees with him for the most part. This afternoon I read Schiller's "Robbers", though I will not mention having done this to either of them.

Nuremberg, 30 March 1848

During our morning hour of instruction I learned a good deal of forbidden knowledge, as my dear uncle ranted and raved concerning recent uprisings of the people in Baden, Vienna, and Berlin. He inveighed against anyone who would institute certain freedoms for the lower classes, as if they were the equals of those placed by the will of God above them. Oh, Uncle Wilhelm! If only you realized that every word you utter in this regard convinces me ever more of the opposite!

Nuremberg, 19 April 1848

Today Uncle commenced to tell me of an evil book he had heard of during his recent travels abroad – a book which, as he says, preaches the overthrow of the existing God-given order of society by the ignorant masses, who themselves are subsequently to become rulers over all. This book was written by a renegade German, but published in England, since no German censor would ever allow such rubbish to sully our lands. I made a pretense of agreeing with Uncle Wilhelm in order to avoid the rod, and asked him innocently who the author might be. (For in all truth I must say that I felt an instant craving to devour this book.) But this he would not tell me.

Nuremberg, 22 May 1848

Recent events have left Uncle Wilhelm full of wrath. Alas, he laments, we are surrounded by republicans on all sides. In Austria they have established a parliament, and in Frankfurt a so-called national assembly has been convened. Soon our beloved rulers will themselves be ruled by men without the tradition of centuries behind them!

How can he not see that all men are equal in the spirit, that those of us who are "higher born" should do all that we can to further this equality in the world around us? But no, this I am sure he will never understand . . .

Venice, 3 July 1848

My parents and I have arrived for a stay of three weeks in this astounding city – without Uncle Wilhelm, I am pleased to say, who has been in ill health of late. To think that my beloved Albrecht Dürer himself was here so many centuries ago, and that I may, on occasion, tread in his very footsteps! Our accommodations are but a few paces from the expanse of the Piazza San Marco and are lavish to say the least. I cannot *claim that I do not enjoy this, although it makes me feel all the more the poverty I see everywhere.*

Venice, 21 July 1848
    Alas, our stay in this magical place draws to a close, and I have written nothing in my diary! I have, however, made several drawings, though I am afraid that I would not impress the city of Venice with my art as Master Albrecht did in his day. Yet the act of drawing gives me pleasure, and that, my dear mother assures me, is what is most important.

Nuremberg, 15 August 1848
    How long it is since those glorious days spent in Venice! Uncle Wilhelm has regained his health, and once again I must toil under his brooding eye. If I cry out when I am caned, it is only to convince him that he is teaching me a true lesson. Strike away, Uncle Wilhelm, strike away!

Nuremberg, 28 September 1848
    I have learned that the people of Baden have once more risen up against their oppressors – only to be beaten down again immediately. Will there never be justice?

Nuremberg, 9 October 1848
    The brave Viennese have gone to the barricades again, and Kaiser Ferdinand has been forced to flee. Hurrah!

Nuremberg, 6 December 1848
    Franz Joseph has become emperor of Austria. Unlike his predecessor, he is young and vigorous. I believe now that the Austrians will never succeed in overthrowing the shackles of their monarchy.

Nuremberg, 1 January 1849
    I have not yet given up hope. If any of the German peoples can win a victory over their soulless monarchs, I believe that it will be our neighbors to the west, the brave folk of Baden. They have not lost their fighting spirit and will certainly make still another attempt to break their centuries-old yoke of enslavement. And at the first sign of such a hopeful beginning, I pledge that I will leave this Nuremberg, this bastion of the wealthy, and join them in their brave endeavour. I am tall and strong enough, and not lacking in courage, and if asked I will gladly add a year or two to my actual age.

Nuremberg, 12 February 1849

I have met together secretly with two brothers, one 17, the other 19, who live in a neighboring house. They too are the sons of an old patrician family, and they too share my ideals. We have spoken at length of the justification – or lack thereof – of taking part in an armed uprising against the established powers. Martin Luther condemned such an action during the peasant revolts of 1524, but was <u>his</u> action, which led to the death and continued suppression of countless peasants, justified? And here we are, more than 300 years later, and little has changed. Can the present situation be allowed to continue?

Nuremberg, 3 March 1849

I am now sixteen years of age. Old enough, in my opinion, to become involved in the important events of our day. I am more and more pleased every day to have two like-minded "brothers" in our neighborhood.

Mother's birthday present was a small, but very beautiful edition of Lessing's dramas. Instead of reading them in chronological order, I began today with his best-known work, "Nathan the Wise".

Nuremberg, 8 April 1849

The King of Prussia has declared himself willing to become "Emperor of the Germans," but only if the other German princes agree. Why should it be they who decide? And why should we be ruled by an emperor? Are not kings, dukes, prince-bishops and the like bad enough?

Nuremberg, 19 May 1849

Word has come from Baden that soldiers in Karlsruhe and in the nearby fortress at Rastatt have mutinied. This is the news that my friends and I have been waiting for. We will leave as soon as possible to join the battle for freedom. Sadly, I will have to leave Stefan behind. It was difficult to convince him that he could not come along; I could not, of course, tell him that a twelve-year-old boy would be of little use. But he quickly accepted the necessity of his staying at home when I explained that someone had to do so to watch after our parents. At that, I could almost see the dear little fellow's chest swell with pride. Stefan will keep my secret. I know this. He is completely loyal to me.

Nuremberg, 22 May 1849

Tomorrow, in the dead of night, I and my two friends will begin our westward march, taking along whatever provisions we can. The brothers and I have each written notes to our parents, to the effect that we will go to Vienna to help prepare the overthrow of Franz Joseph. By *the time they have read those words, we will be miles down the road in the opposite direction.*

Künzelsau, 28 May 1849

Our journey has been difficult indeed. But for the friendliness of the occasional farmers along the way, who allowed us to ride on their carts, we might well have become discouraged. But when we crossed into the Kingdom of Württemberg yesterday, we knew that we had made good progress. People have been friendly to us everywhere, allowing us to do menial tasks for them and thus earn a loaf of bread or a few eggs – enough to sustain us on our way.

Carlsruhe, 3 June 1849

We have reached the goal of our journey. How good it is to be in the Grand Duchy of Baden, especially as we have been told that the Grand Duke, in the cowardly fashion of aristocrats, has fled for his life. The city vibrates with "revolution fever," as one calls it here.

My two fellow travelers and I have been welcomed by the citizenry with open arms, and during our short time here we have spoken with countless republicans from many a distant place – from France, Poland, Hungary – each filled with unbounded enthusiasm for the cause of freedom for all of Europe. Most remarkable among those we have met is one François, a Negro who was once the servant of the Marquis of B. . . in Paris. A young man of perhaps twenty-five, he had left his lord to fight in the February revolution of a year and a half ago in that city, and has now made the long journey to Baden in order to join the German cause. His few scraps of our language hardly suffice for what can be called true conversation, but we are able to communicate quite well through a mixture of badly maimed German, even worse French on my part, and vigorous gestures. Tall and powerfully built, he will no doubt be courageous in battle. How can we thank him enough for having joined our cause!

Carlsruhe, 5 June 1849

My brothers and I enlisted yesterday in the Freikorps of Carlsruhe. We have been given as good as no training, but we believe that our courage will be enough to make up for this lack. Tomorrow, we have been told, we will be despatched north by railway to reinforce the troops who have skirmished with the Hessians near Mannheim. We are prepared to do whatever honor demands of us.

Mannheim, 13 June 1849

The fighting had subsided by the time we arrived here, and things have been quiet since then. But now, we are told, a vast Prussian army is on the march toward the city. Will we be prepared to meet its assault? Though our numbers be relatively small, we feel that, with God's help, we shall prevail.

Heidelberg, 16 June 1849

Several thousands of our soldiers marched this evening into Heidelberg, where we were greeted with loud singing and the flames of hundreds of torches in celebration of our victory. We have pushed back the mighty forces of the Prussians and their allies, and I must try to be joyful at this turn of events. But, alas, our victory was dearly paid for – I must lament the loss of my brave comrade-in-arms François, who became separated from me as we charged the enemy at Schriesheim and was set upon by three Prussians, who dealt with him with the utmost brutality. Having been wounded in the leg myself, I had managed to crawl to a clump of bushes, whence I could but watch in horror as the soldiers thrust their sabres into him repeatedly. Never will I forget your cries of pain, my dear François, and the contortions of your face as you expired. Know that you will be with me always, providing me with constant inspiration to meet the enemy bravely on whatever occasion this should be required of me. I shall not fail you! I shall not fail the cause of freedom!

Heidelberg, 22 June 1849

The wound in my leg proved to be not severe and I was soon on my feet again. Then came the fateful encounter with the enemy to the south of this city. Alas, "all is lost" is the cry most commonly heard now. The city of Heidelberg, a few days ago so resplendent, now seems desolate to me. Where ever will I find beauty in the world again?

Already rumours say that we shall soon march south to the fortress at Rastatt. But what are we to do there? Fortresses can be encircled, and the unlucky ones within made to starve. If the decision were mine, I would say: let us stay here and hold our ground and die like men, not like rats in a trap. But the decision is not mine, and I will do as I am commanded.

Zürich, 26 October 1849

Having been in a state of spiritual anguish for some time, I have not found it possible until now to take pen in hand and write of the developments of the last weeks. Suffice it to say, the retreat from Rastatt toward the Swiss border was the most discouraging occasion in which I have ever participated. For it was apparent that we were retreating not with the intention of forming our battle lines elsewhere, but only to save our skins. Yes, some were heartened again by talk of continuing the war, but I was no longer among them. What would have been the result of this? Simply the needless loss of more lives.

And now I sit in the security of this lovely city nestled against the hills above Lake Zürich – safe from the monarchist troops, safe from my father and Uncle Wilhelm, who, I am certain, would gladly arrange for my execution were he able to do so. What shall I do now? Many comrades here say that the tide will turn, that the next uprising in German lands will bring victory to the revolutionaries. Others speak of beginning a new life in America. It may be that I will join them, for here there is no future for a renegade from Germany. Nor can it be much more difficult to learn the English language than the dreadful Schwyzerdütsch that passes here for German.

Ah, is my sense of humor perhaps returning? This is indeed a hopeful sign. I have managed to save a good portion of the Franken which I have earned in the past weeks as a street laborer, and will continue to do so. When I adjudge that I have accumulated enough to see me on my way, I will depart for France. And from there to America? This I cannot say, only the Fates know – and they are keeping their own counsel.

Le Havre, 22 April 1851

It is time for me to resume my long-neglected diary. Having scrimped and saved for well over a year now, I finally have something worthy of recording.

I have since trekked across a good part of France, having written to my parents beforehand to inform them of my intention. I gave no details, however, since these, I fear, might be used against me. Perhaps one day, in more settled times, our awkward familial situation may take a turn for the better.

After crossing the Rhine into France at Basel, I decided to pursue an easterly route via Nancy, Reims and Amiens in order to avoid passing through Paris, which, as I had been told, could be an inhospitable place for a German. My path – and I say "path," because I traveled on foot for virtually the entire distance – took me to Orléans and thence to Chartres, with its magnificent cathedral overlooking the town from on high. Which, as I was made to understand, is as it should be in this eminently Catholic country.

My journey then led through several small towns until I reached Rouen, where I managed to gain employment as a jack-of-all-trades on a barge sailing downstream along the twisting Seine to Le Havre. There luck was with me once again. I have been working now as a laborer in one of the city's shipyards for several months.

As my facility with the French language continues to improve, I begin to wonder whether it will be my lot to remain for the rest of my days in this country, which, unlike the several German states, has been a republic for some time now. The men with whom I work tease me about my strangely accented French, but they are convivial enough. So we shall see.

Le Havre, 16 January 1852
Events are taking place in this strange country which I do not understand. A new constitution has been declared, permitting Louis-Napoléon to hold the office of President for nothing less than ten years. Ten years! What can this lead to, if not dictatorship?

Le Havre, 2 December 1852
France is an empire again. Louis-Napoléon is its emperor, and his office will be hereditary. Ah, but surely this is better than the situation in the German states – for is not an emperor loftier than a king, a duke, or a mere count? The die is cast. I must save what I can, take it ever so long, and depart for America.

Le Havre, 12 October 1853
My savings grow apace. I believe that I now have approximately half the amount that I will need to book passage for that new, and freer, world across the sea.

Le Havre, 1 March 1854
I leave for New York on the St. Denis in one week's time. I can barely contain the excitement that I feel at this prospect, and the hope that I may fare better in the new world than in the old!

The Four Horsemen, 1498

The Seven-Headed Dragon, 1498

The Devil Cast into the Abyss / The New Jerusalem, 1498

Chapter 9

I stayed at my window seat for a while, staring down at Neptune and his fish. Luke's life had been amazing, from the time he reached the 'age of manhood' at fourteen until almost his twenty-first birthday, which he was about to celebrate on the open sea. Had it been an extremely courageous life, or one characterized by foolhardiness? At any rate it had been an adventurous one.

I went back to the stacks and replaced Volume I in its place, then headed back to Riedenburg Hall. As I stepped into the German Department anteroom, Klaus Hochstraaten was standing next to Charlotte at her office door.

"Hi, Colin," she said, "have you seen the beautiful ring Klaus acquired when he was in Argentina this summer?"

With apparent reluctance, Hochstraaten held out his hand.

"I have never before worn a ring," he said. "This belonged to my father, who viewed it as a sort of talisman, one that had meant a great deal to him in his younger years. He said that he wanted to pass it on to me before he died. His health had deteriorated considerably by the time I left."

"That's an emerald, isn't it? Must be pretty valuable."

"For me it is of purely sentimental value."

"Yes, of course, I didn't mean to imply—"

"I have much to do." Hochstraaten turned and walked to his office at the far end of the anteroom without another word.

Charlotte shrugged. "He's a little touchy on the subject of his father. So what have you been up to, Colin? Haven't had a chance to talk to you in a while."

"Well, I finally got around to reading the first volume of Baumgartner's diaries. The way he ran off to fight in the revolution and all that . . ."

"He fought in the Civil War over here, too—he tells about it in the second volume. Got a serious head wound in one of the major battles. It ended up changing his life." She lowered her voice. "Been working on Baumgartner's puzzle at all?"

"Oh, a bit. I have a hunch that his private chapel might be involved. Or it might not be."

Charlotte chuckled. "Now there's a definitive statement if I ever heard one! Maybe I should do a Tarot reading to help you work it out."

"Tarot? Do you believe in that esoteric stuff?"

Charlotte grinned. "You never know." She peered at my face for a moment. "A classic Knight of Cups, I'd say."

"Beg pardon?"

"You're not an adept, I see. Well, maybe some special occasion will present itself. I don't do readings just any old time." She checked her watch. "Better be getting on home to see what Michael's cooking for dinner."

"Okay, have a nice evening."

"You too."

As I stepped into my office, I heard Hochstraaten's door closing quietly. Had he been standing there listening the whole time? Fortunately, I hadn't said anything of great significance. Or had I? Feeling my forehead wrinkle into a frown, I packed my briefcase and left the building.

As the semester wore on, Conversation and Composition continued to be my most lively class, not least because of Moira MacGregor's infectious enthusiasm. Jason Miller's work, by contrast, remained inconsistent. Jason had some reasonably good days interspersed with an occasional bad one. On those days he said next to nothing in the conversation groups and seemed to be looking out the window the whole time. One Friday after class I had him come into my office to sound him out.

"You doing okay, Jason?" I asked. "Sometimes you don't seem to be quite with it in class."

Jason ran his hand over his short brush of blond hair. "I'm fine." He looked out the window and hugged his chest, as if trying to conceal the Iron Cross tattoo on his left forearm and the two lightning bolts on his right.

"Your written work is pretty good on the whole, but you need to pay more attention to grammar. The conversation groups, though—it's like you're just not connecting a lot of the time."

Jason nodded vaguely, still looking out the window.

"You know, if you don't feel like talking to me about things, there's a whole network of counselors on campus to help students."

Flashing a hostile glance my way, Jason muttered, "I've seen enough counselors in my life." He looked away again. "How come you're always late to class?" he said.

"I'm not always late to class." I could feel my face start to burn.

"You're late half the time, at least. My uncle docks his students if they're late."

"Your uncle . . ."

"He's a professor too."

"Oh? Where does he teach?"

"Here."

"Really? What does he—"

"Look, can I go? I have to be somewhere."

"This was just a little conference, it's not a prison cell."

Jason got out of his chair and picked up his backpack, then headed for the door.

"Stop by any time," I called after him.

I couldn't read his expression when he turned around and looked over his shoulder at me.

On the following Monday and Wednesday Jason failed to show up for class. Did he have a legitimate excuse? Had he caught some bug? I had my doubts. On Wednesday afternoon, as I was walking across campus to check my mail at the post office boxes in Bamberg Hall, I ran into him on the Promenade. He stopped in his tracks and hung his head.

"I know, I know," he said, "I've been cutting class."

"Thanks for not making up a story. Can we talk?"

We sat down on a bench next to the rose beds that bordered the moat. Jason was wearing his usual heavy-metal black T-shirt and black jeans with holes in the knees.

"Look, I'm not going to lecture you, but I really am getting concerned. Once you get behind in a foreign language class it's almost impossible to catch up. Do you think a tutor might help, just to keep you going?"

Jason sat hunched over clenching his fists. "I don't want any special treatment."

"I wouldn't call it special, it's just—"

"That's all I've ever had, is special treatment," he said, clasping his close-cropped head. "'You've got one of the best therapists in Boston,' my father says. How many of the best goddamn shrinks have I been to? If people just wouldn't bug me . . ."

I almost expected him to jump up and run off. But he stayed put and kept talking.

"Look, I know you're trying to help, but *I'm* the one that's gotta do it. I've gotta stop letting things get me down."

"Well, start coming to class again, all right? You still have plenty of time to get back on top of things. It's going to take some work, though."

"It doesn't help any having Moira there."

"Moira? You don't need to be comparing yourself with her—"

Jason shook his head. "I don't mean that. It's just that—I can't concentrate when I'm around her. Even when I'm *not* around her."

"Oh, I get it. Yeah, she's a good-looking girl. I don't blame you."

"She doesn't even know I exist." He glanced at me, then turned

75

away. "She's too busy looking at you."

"Me? Well, I am the teacher, of course. Where else should she be looking?"

"It's not that kind of look. It's . . . different."

"Could be, students often get crushes on their profs. It passes. Anyway, I really hope to see you in class next time."

Jason stood up. "I don't know," he said, and walked off.

My wayward student did in fact show up for class on Friday, but seemed completely distracted. Was Moira the problem again? There wasn't a thing I could do about that. She herself was lacking her usual energy and hurried out of the room as soon as the bell rang. I wondered for a moment if I should send her an email to see if something was wrong. But that would put her on the spot, and besides, there was no way I should be prying into my students' private lives.

My Beginning German class met Mondays, Wednesdays, and Fridays at 1:10. As I walked along the hall I was looking forward to what I thought would be an interesting session. I truly love to teach beginners, especially those who have never encountered a foreign language before, to spark their interest in thought patterns and manners of expression that are different from English usage. There was one such pattern coming up in the chapter on sports and hobbies today, and I could almost predict how most of my students would react to it.

I began the new lesson by asking one of the class members about her leisure activities.

"So, Melanie, was machst du heute Nachmittag? Spielst du Tennis? Oder gehst du vielleicht schwimmen?"

"Ich spiele Tennis heute Nachmittag," she answered.

"Ich spiele heute Nachmittag Tennis," I corrected.

Melanie had made the type of word-order error that I had expected. But that was fine, as I had pointed out on many another occasion—mistakes were necessary little detours on the road to mastering a language. Melanie, however, looked disgruntled.

"I don't get it," she said. "Why does Tennis go last? I mean, that's like saying 'I'm playing this afternoon tennis.'"

She had broken the 'no-English-in-class' rule, but I allowed this to happen occasionally if the situation warranted.

"Well, it's bound to sound funny to you at first. English and German have different word order rules. German often puts the most significant piece of information at the very end of a sentence; we tend to put it earlier. In that particular sentence, 'Tennis' is what you're highlighting."

Melanie was not satisfied. "That seems crazy," she said. "Why should the most significant thing be the last word? Doesn't make any sense."

"Well, the last word—" I stopped in mid-sentence. Somewhere in my brain, relays started clicking. "I'm sorry, Melanie," I went on, "my mind was wandering. What was it you said?"

"I was asking how the most significant part of a sentence can be the last word. It seems completely illogical."

I stared at Melanie for a moment, struggling to focus on the sense of her words and not on the words themselves.

"You know, there are different theories about this—" I paused again for a moment, trying to concentrate. "I don't think they're very helpful for our purposes, though. You don't really need to know *why*, you just have to do it. Eighty million Germans can't be wrong."

Including Luke Baumgartner, I added to myself. Damn, could it be this simple?

The rest of the hour dragged by. When the bell finally rang, I followed a cluster of exceptionally slow-moving students down to the main floor, then sprinted all the way home and raced up the stairs to my study. Tearing the photocopy of Luke's last words off the wall, I read through the text again, underlining the last word of each sentence.

With gratitude to you, Herr Lessing, for what you have taught me in the preceding piece and in many other works of yours, I say farewell as I leave you to go down and pray in my little <u>chapel</u>. A quiet place which invites to contemplation, it has on many an occasion given me the repose that I <u>seek</u>. In doing this, it has aided me in achieving the leap to the lofty spheres above from this woeful world <u>below</u>. Soon I am to leave this world, as we all must, rich or poor, whether our sign be a simple huntsman's bow or a proud family <u>escutcheon</u>. Indeed, given my present condition, I would not be surprised if I had but one more day to live, or at most two or <u>three</u>. I hope that I may be granted the time to view once more a site in the South Woods of great importance to me, inasmuch as it symbolizes the dual nature of our lives: instability, in the rushing, uncontrollable stream, and steadfastness, in the solid bridge high above, fashioned of the most carefully hewn <u>stones</u>. In any case, I will soon know the ultimate direction of my final path— whether up . . . or <u>down</u> . . .

Seven sentences, seven words. I double-checked to make sure I hadn't missed any sentence breaks, then repeated the words out loud: chapel – seek – below – escutcheon – three – stones – down; *chapel – seek – below – escutcheon – three – stones – down!* This couldn't be a coincidence. The presence of the 'three' made it seem all the more likely, and Luke had said that his last words numbered seven. The elaborate stone bridge sentence had been nothing but a red herring—he'd needed it only for the word 'stones' at the end!

If I hurried, I might be able to catch Ned before he left for the day. When I was almost out the door, it occurred to me to grab my sketch pad. I left the house in such a rush that I forgot to lock the door.

It was two forty-five by the time I reached the castle. Outside Ned's utility room I heard the faint sounds of a saxophone. The music stopped when I knocked on the door. A moment later Ned appeared, instrument in hand.

"Sorry to bother you, Ned. Looks like I picked a bad time."

"Oh, not so bad," he said, looking down at his instrument. "Got a gig comin' up tonight with some of the students."

"I didn't know you were part of that. I've been seeing posters around campus for some time now."

"Yeah, the kids are lettin' me play with them. You need me to do somethin' for you?"

"Well, I was going to see if you could let me into the little chapel again." Feeling foolish, I held out my sketch pad. "I'm sort of an amateur artist—ever since I was in the chapel last time I've been itching to go back and do some drawing."

Nodding slightly, Ned walked to the end of the room and laid his saxophone on the desk, then reached into the drawer and pulled out the key to the chapel. Brushing past me, he headed along the corridor toward the Rapunzel tower, with me falling in step behind him.

This time the key turned with only minor screeches; Ned had apparently oiled the lock in the meantime. I thanked him, stepped inside, and pulled the door shut. Glancing at the statue of St. Eustace, I tossed my sketch pad onto one of the pews and climbed the three steps to the altar. The late afternoon sun was on the other side of the building now and the colored reflections were more subdued than when I had been there last. *Below – escutcheon – three – stones – down*, I recited to myself. I dropped to one knee in front of the Baumgartner coat-of-arms in the separate pane to the left of the altar. The third stone down rested directly on the floor. Now what? Do I push it, or is there a hidden catch somewhere? Is this *The Name of the Rose*, or what?

I rapped on the stone with my knuckles and thought I heard a hollow sound. Going down on all fours, I scrutinized the joints for any telltale cracks. There were none, but I noticed that the mortar around the stone was of a slightly different color than elsewhere.

Suddenly I heard a heavy thumping noise coming from the wall to my left. Jumping to my feet, I walked quickly to the door and stood there for a moment holding my breath. There was another thump, followed by the muffled sound of voices. Nothing to worry about, just students entering and leaving the building through the tower.

Hurrying back to the window, I took my Swiss Army knife out of my jacket pocket and began chipping away at the vertical strip of mortar on the left side of the stone. When I'd penetrated to a depth of about a quarter of an inch, the knife blade thrust through into emptiness, slashing my index finger in the process.

"Son of a *bitch*!" I shouted, then jerked my head around as if someone might have heard me. All was quiet. I grabbed my handkerchief out of my pants pocket and wrapped it around the wound to staunch the flow of blood. Holding the makeshift bandage in place as best I could, I continued to hack away. Once the entire side was free, I used the same procedure on the right side. Finally I tackled the much longer strip of mortar above the stone. At the center point the blade struck something hard and metallic. What was going on here? Puzzled, I decided to work toward the middle from the opposite corner. Another few minutes later, with less than an inch left to be chipped out, the point of my blade snapped off.

I dropped the knife with a clatter and swore to myself. What to do now? The thin strip of mortar along the floor was still in place. Re-wrapping my bloody handkerchief, I grasped the right side of the stone and applied as much pressure as I could. Nothing doing. Next I tried stretching out on my back and kicking at it with the heel of my shoe. At the fourth or fifth kick I felt something give—the left side of the stone had moved inward a fraction of an inch, and the right side was now projecting outward. At the next kick the stone moved a good two inches, spraying fragments of mortar over the floor.

I knelt next to the wall again and ran a finger along the top of the stone. It appeared to have been set in place with a vertical pin running through its center to allow it to turn on its axis. Luke, you clever bastard! Grasping it on the right side, I succeeded with some effort in moving it until it was almost perpendicular to the wall. Through the gaps on either side I could see only blackness. Why didn't I have my penlight along? It had to be in my other jacket. Slowly, gingerly, I slipped my good hand through the opening on the left side, hoping that I wouldn't end up with a rodent bite. A few inches in I felt something with my fingertips—something that moved slightly. Startled, I drew my hand back, but whatever it was hadn't bitten me. I put my ear to the opening, half-expecting to hear the patter of tiny feet. Slowly I stuck my hand back into the hole. This time I grabbed one end of the object and pulled.

It was a flat horizontal package about nine inches long and six inches wide—just narrow enough to fit through the hole when tilted diagonally. The dusty black-oilcloth covering was held together by a piece of frayed white ribbon tied in a neat bow. I stared at the package, feeling almost like a grave-robber, like someone exhuming a past that might better be left in peace. Don't be stupid, I said—it was Baumgartner, after all, who had gone to the trouble of stashing the package here in the first place.

It was almost four o'clock now. Using the back of my hand, I brushed the fragments of mortar into the hole and turned the stone back to its original position. Feeling a slight rush of anxiety mixed with an almost pleasant tingling, I re-wrapped my wound again, then concealed my find under my sketch pad and walked past St. Eustace to the chapel door. Hadn't I closed it properly when I came in? I was sure that I had. As I pulled it shut, Ned entered the tower from the outside carrying what appeared to be a bag lunch.

"How'd the drawin' go?" he asked.

"Oh, fine. Thanks for letting me in again." I sensed a slight tremor in my voice. "The concert's at eight?"

"That's right. In the theater in Bamberg Hall."

"Great. Well, I'll see you then."

"Okay. I'll go get the key and lock up."

As I crossed the tower to the outside door, I saw that my left jacket sleeve was covered with dust and tiny chips of mortar. Had Ned noticed? It almost seemed like he had given me a funny look. Shaking my head, I pushed the heavy door open and stepped out into the warm air. A familiar figure dressed in black glanced over his shoulder near the end of the footbridge, then began trotting along the Promenade. Was it a coincidence that he had just been in the castle? I almost called out, but at the moment my only interest was in the small package hidden under my sketch pad. Breaking into a trot myself, I was home within five minutes.

Knight, Death and the Devil, 1513

St. Jerome, 1514

Melencolia I, 1514

Chapter 10

Luckily for me, the Seiferts' bathroom was well-equipped with medical supplies. The wound was a good inch-and-a-half long but didn't appear to be very deep. I washed it out and applied first-aid cream and a bandaid, then sat down at my desk and undid the package. Under the layers of oilcloth were several sheets of yellowed stationery, with a hand-written date at the top of the first one—the same date I had seen at the end of Baumgartner's last words in the Lessing volume, and also on the monolith. Could the old man have written the pages I was about to read on the day he died? The ink had faded in places, but the handwriting was still easily legible.

Castle Arcadia, 19 November 1908
Greetings and salutations to you, fellow admirer of the noble poet Lessing – for you would hardly have found your way here with-out having deciphered a certain passage which I appended to the final volume of his writings. How long have I had to wait for your arrival? Weeks? Months? Centuries? Be that as it may, I sense your presence, that you are reading my words at this moment.

In order to establish a trusting relationship with you, I feel com-pelled to tell you the true story of my sudden departure. Surely anyone, your illustrious self included, who had the interest and occasion to pe-ruse my diaries, will have been not a little surprised to learn that my death occurred on the very day after the completion of the last of those pages. Many will no doubt have wondered: how could the poor fellow have sensed that his death was so near? Had his physician given him, perhaps, a prognosis to that effect? Well, if the truth be known, his shuf-fling-off to that much talked-of, though undiscovered country had been planned for some time prior to the actual event.

Having by natural transition arrived in the third person, let me remain there; indeed, with what justification should I say "I," since "I" no longer exist in the corporeal sense? From this point on, then, any further use of that pronoun would seem to indicate the presence of some observer or other who has wandered onto the scene.

As you will have concluded from his diaries, the man of whom we speak had a relationship to "reality", as we call it, which was un-usual to say the least. On most days he was as much a part of the world as his fellows, but on others he was likely to fly off into realms known only to him. It is true that the task which occupied him for the last few months of his life gave him a great deal of pleasure. This, of course, was the <u>mise en scène</u> of the elaborate project in which you yourself have now become involved.

But there were also days on which he grew depressed, especially when his thoughts turned to his beloved wife and the wonderful days they had spent together so many years before. Thus, he mused, having reached the age of seventy-five and no longer in the best of health, what better day on which to join her in that other, better world than on the anniversary of her passing? His trusted doctor and long-time friend proved willing to administer a sleeping powder which would despatch him quickly and painlessly. And who would ask questions in the case of a man of so many years?

If his doctor-accomplice has executed his task as agreed – executed his patient, one might say, were not such a witticism in exceedingly bad taste on the occasion of a man's demise – if, then, this event has taken place, only a few hours will have passed between the secreting of these pages and his peaceful crossing-over on this fateful day.

But let us finally get to the point. Since you have now deciphered our dearly departed's "last words", your immediate task at hand will be to follow three steps of a more pointed nature. Why three? Well, can it be surprising that a person born on the third day of the third month of the year 1833 has always seen a certain significance in that number? Be that as it may, the steps in question will be in the form of riddling clues; the first will lead you to the second, the second to the third. Upon the completion of this final step, you will be tantalizingly close to your goal. Be but patient!

And now, without further ado, on to the first clue. May you have good luck in your quest!

> Sitting in a night of light,
> a little angel, halo gleaming;
> he seems to be about to write
> or is, mayhap, he only dreaming?
>
> Were he to do as I advise
> and look about, his eyes new-seeing
> would spy a ladder, and he'd rise
> to reach a state of higher being.
>
> Anon he'd see a little maid,
> who points quite clearly toward the goal;
> but <u>how</u> she does this, I'm afraid,
> is not, perhaps, so clear at all!

The angel's eyes are falling shut,
'tis you must climb, then, in his stead;
seek one and two to crack the nut,
then look afar from head to head.

And next, sir, you must tell the time!
Is't one, is't two, or three, or four?
Be led by stony pantomime
and there will be but one step more.

Time stands not still, as well we know;
the hour at hand must therefore turn,
advancing in its clockwise flow;
this hour, my friend, is your concern.

I leaned back in my chair and drew a deep breath. Crosswords and Sudokus were one thing—but this weirdo poem?

My finger was throbbing. I frowned at it, imagining the scar I had produced; it would be almost parallel to one from a cut I had inflicted on my middle finger several years earlier. I checked the bandage for seepage, then turned back to the poem.

Was the reference in the first stanza to a *picture* of an angel, or had Luke sculpted one somewhere on campus? No, that couldn't be it, sculpture couldn't create a whole ambiance like "a night of light" the way a painting or a drawing could. So wouldn't the Dürer museum be the most likely place to look? Problem was, it was closed now and would be until Monday. Which didn't matter, since there was no way I would be able to spend any significant amount of time there for at least another week; in addition to my usual classes, I had scheduled individual oral exams from Monday through Friday.

As for the rest of the poem, I read through it quickly again and decided that everything hinged on finding the "little angel" and then going on from there. The jazz concert would be starting in less than forty-five minutes, and I had as much as promised Ned that I would be there. I stashed the pages in my desk drawer, then went down to the kitchen to rustle up some bacon and eggs. I wolfed the food down, washed the dishes, and gave my teeth a perfunctory brushing. As I headed for the front door, Juniper came slinking into the kitchen and lapped at her water dish.

"See you later, cat," I said. "Maybe the solution will come to me while I'm sitting in the theater listening to jazz."

Did I really believe that? No way. As soon as the concert began, I would be so absorbed by the music that all other thoughts would leave my mind. This always happened to me at jazz concerts, and—Baumgartner or no Baumgartner—it would happen this time too.

Juniper seemed to sense this. As I glanced at her over my shoulder, I could have sworn that she had a sardonic smile on her face.

The Four Apostles, 1526

The Rest during the flight to Egypt, 1504 - 1505

Chapter 11

I trotted around the moat to the other side of the castle and took the path to Bamberg Hall. A large poster outside the entrance to the theater announced the concert. The band called itself *Eusless Blues* and consisted of three student performers, on piano, bass, and percussion, with Ned Avery as special guest on alto sax.

The band was setting up when I arrived. Most of the seats had been taken, but I was lucky enough to find one near the front. Looking around, I spotted three or four colleagues I recognized and a few students from my classes. Ned was sitting on a folding chair at the back of the stage and seemed ready to go.

The question of the little angel wouldn't leave me alone. The most likely possibility I could think of was Dürer's woodcut of the *Rest on the Flight into Egypt*. The piece contained lots of little angels, though I was pretty sure they were helping Joseph with his carpentry; plus, it seemed unlikely in that setting that any of them would be writing. It seemed like a long shot, but I would check in one of my Dürer books when I got back from the concert.

All four musicians were on stage by now and began playing without any introduction. The opening piece was "Laura," one of my favorites. Ned's tone and his expressivity were amazing—this was clearly a first-rate performer. After the piece was over, the piano player, a student who wore his hair in corn rows, spoke into a microphone at the front of the stage.

"Hi, my name is Shawn. Thanks for comin' out to hear our band. We're very pleased that Mr. Ned Avery has agreed to play with us this evening"—there was a round of applause from the audience as Ned rose from his chair and then sat down again—"and we hope he will again. You all just heard what a fantabulous musician he is. We're going to go on to some livelier pieces now. Thanks for coming."

The band played two fast bebop tunes, allowing the performers to shine in turn as they went through their riffs. The remainder of the concert was a mixture of blues and faster pieces; the band's last number, "Lester Leaps In," amounted to one long, rapid-fire saxophone riff. After the final notes sounded, the audience broke out in cheers and whistles. Ned smiled faintly as he took a bow with the others, then turned and headed for a door at the rear of the stage. Glancing back just in time to see me give him a thumbs-up, he smiled again and nodded before stepping through the doorway.

I walked up to the edge of the stage and mouthed a "thank you" to the drummer and bass player, who were busy taking down the drum set. Shawn was kneeling near the front disconnecting speaker cables.

"Thanks, Shawn, great performance."

Shawn looked up. "Glad you liked it. Wasn't too bad, I guess."

"To say the least. You sounded pretty much like the real McCoy to me—I mean the *real* McCoy. Especially that long part you had in the Coltrane number."

Shawn laughed. "'Bessie's Blues'? I still got a long ways to go till I'm anywhere near McCoy Tyner. If I ever get there."

"Hey, you're young. Keep working at it. Ned was really amazing too, wish I'd had a chance to talk to him. Is he okay? He seemed to be in a hurry to leave."

"Oh, that's just 'cause he wanted to get back to his wife and kids as soon as possible. Ned's a real family man."

"Well, he has an amazing talent—if he just could get a start somewhere."

"He might could do that, if he lived in a big city. But he and his wife don't want to do that."

"I don't blame them. Well, thank him for me if you see him, okay? My name's Colin Ritter, I teach German here."

"Okay. And thanks for comin' to the concert."

Outside, there was hardly a star to be seen and only an occasional hint of the moon behind swiftly moving clouds. A chill, cutting breeze had picked up, and I was not surprised to find few people out and about. As I came to the Promenade, I noticed the figure of a solitary woman walking slowly in my direction, her head down and her braid dangling over one shoulder.

"Moira?" I said, when she was a few feet away.

She looked up, startled.

"Oh, hi." she gave me a half-smile.

"Is it safe for you to be out alone like this? It's pitch-dark tonight."

"Like I care," Moira answered sullenly.

I didn't respond.

"It *is* dark, isn't it," she added, looking around as if she were noticing it for the first time.

"Moira, what's wrong?"

"Nothing," she said, sounding like she was on the verge of tears.

"Let me at least walk you to wherever you're going. I really don't think it's good for you to be out here alone."

"All right," she said, sniffling. "I wasn't going anywhere, really—just walking. I had to get away from the dorm for a while."

"Well, which way, then?"

"I don't know. We can go the way you were going."

"I was heading home after the jazz concert."

"Oh, yeah. I kind of forgot about it, I guess."

We turned in at the path that led to the library. As we rounded the corner a figure dressed in black was coming our way. None other than Jason Miller.

"Evening, Jason," I said.

Moira glanced in his direction. "Hi," she said tonelessly.

Jason nodded and kept on walking. I had the creepy feeling that he was looking back over his shoulder at us.

"Do you know him very well?" I asked when we were out of earshot.

"No, not really. He's got problems, I think. He has this huge chip on his shoulder. He really had it in for one of our German profs a couple of years ago. The one who was murdered."

"Really?"

"All I can say is, I heard Jason talking about him with some other guys after class one day. They were saying he was conceited and a blowhard, stuff like that. Me, I thought he was just smart. When I heard about what had happened, I almost had to wonder. . . ."

"But everyone was cleared, from what I heard."

"So they said."

"I actually knew Ronald Fleishman back when we were students. Hard to believe that anyone would want to murder him. I wonder what the motive could have been."

"Guess we'll never know."

"Well . . ."

Moira gave me a sly smile. "Are you thinking of pulling a Lord Peter?"

I smiled back. "I just might. There could still be clues all over the place, if we only knew where to look."

Moira grew silent again as we walked on.

"You know," I said, "I'm a pretty good listener if there's anything you want to talk about."

"Oh, it's nothing. Just feeling sorry for myself."

"We all do that sometimes. That's exactly where I was until I found the St. Eustace job."

She looked up at me. "You're glad you came here, then?"

"Yes, I am. I'm feeling more at home all the time. Despite being a Yankee."

Moira gave a hint of a smile, then put her head down again. We were silent until we rounded the library and came to Faculty Row.

"Just about to my place now," I said. "How about if I walk you to your dorm? You're just down the road in Amity House, right?"

Moira sighed. "I really don't want to go back there yet. Could we go to your place for a little bit?"

"I guess so," I said.

We crossed the street and walked up the long path to my front door.

"This was Professor Seifert's house," Moira said.

"That's right, I'm renting it. His wife is going to move in with her sister in Lexington."

"That's sad, the way he died so suddenly. He had our class over for a picnic once. His wife baked this wonderful German pastry for us. They were so nice."

"Well, I hope you won't feel weird being in the house again."

"No, I don't think I will."

"Okay, come on in, then."

I led the way to the kitchen and opened the refrigerator. "Let's see, there's Sprite, orange juice . . ."

"Mmm, Beck's—my favorite." Moira eyed the green bottles of beer.

I looked at her with a half-smile. "Well, sure, there's that too. I guess you're old enough."

She smirked. "Like that matters around here. But I am."

I pulled out two bottles and stood them on the counter. Moira was staring at my hand.

"What did you do to your finger?"

I glared at her. "Don't ask, okay?"

Moira made a face. "Sorry, didn't mean to get personal."

I shook my head. "It's all right. It's just that I have a tendency to injure myself. Boys my age shouldn't be playing with knives."

I opened the bottles and we walked into the living room.

"Oh, what a pretty cat," Moira said. Juniper was sitting in the dining room doorway staring at her.

"Isn't she, though? C'mere, kitty."

Juniper padded over to me and flopped onto her side to have her belly rubbed.

"She's sweet," Moira said. "What's her name?"

"Juniper. I gave her a little taste of gin when she was a kitten, and she liked it."

Moira looked puzzled.

"Juniper berries are what gin is flavored with, and they're dark blue, almost black, so. . . ."

"Oh, sure, that's clever. Will she let me pet her?"

"She might. She's pretty good with strangers."

Moira crouched down and took over the scratching. "Listen to her purr," she said.

"Yeah, she loves that. Do you have a cat?"

"Two, actually. I sure miss them. We're not allowed to have pets in the dorms, of course."

Juniper righted herself and headed for her water bowl in the kitchen.

"Have a seat," I said, walking toward the rocking chair next to the fireplace. Moira sat down on the sofa and placed her bottle on one of the beer coasters scattered around the coffee table.

"Are these all from Germany?"

"Pretty much. Germany and Austria."

"Let's see . . . Heidelberg . . . Berlin . . . oh, this is a real pretty one . . . 'Engelbräu Rettenberg'—I've sure never heard of that place."

"Rettenberg's a tiny little resort way in the south of Germany. I went skiing there once when I was a student."

Moira was scrutinizing the coaster. "It's got two little angels on it."

I got up to have a look.

"Oh, right. 'Engel' means 'angel,' of course. But it's probably the name of the brewer."

"Or Germans think beer is angelic, one."

"Also a distinct possibility. Which reminds me. . . ."

My phone rang. I answered it without looking at the number.

"Hello, Colin, it's Annika."

"Well, hello . . . can you hang on?" I held the phone against my chest and whispered to Moira, "I'll be back in a minute."

I mounted the stairs two at a time and went into my study, shutting the door behind me.

"Sorry," I said, "I have a student here who wanted some advice."

"Ah. Well, I hope she doesn't mind waiting."

"Annika, it's not what you think. That other girl, I was only a TA at the time."

"So that made it all right?"

"No! What I mean is, we were almost the same age."

"So *that* made it all right?"

I was feeling utterly exasperated. "Look, I know I shouldn't have let it happen. But that was before I even knew you. I never would get involved with a student again."

She was silent for a moment, then sighed audibly. "I certainly hope not. But I'm not calling now to argue with you. Actually . . . it seems to me that I treated you rather harshly when we talked a week or so ago."

I was starting to soften. "I'm not so sure. I think I got what I deserved."

"In a sense that may be true. But I could have been more . . . understanding. My reaction was due to shock, I think. It was the first time I had heard from you since we separated. I didn't know you had found a job, of course. You said it's a sabbatical replacement?"

"Yes, for both semesters."

"And after that you would have to look for something else?"

"Yes. Well, I'm not exactly sure. The man I replaced has died in the meantime."

"Ah, so they might keep you on."

"I have no idea. It'll depend on what they think of me, I suppose."

"Oh, I suspect you will do well. You were very popular at Macalester, judging from all that I heard."

"Thank you, that's nice of you to say."

"Not at all, it's simply a fact."

"I really enjoyed my time there. I'm sorry I had to leave—for more reasons than one."

There was a moment's silence.

"Well," Annika said, "I'd better let you get back to your student."

"Yes, I'd almost forgotten. Thank you very much for calling, Annika, I really appreciate it."

"All right. Good night then."

"Good night."

I stared at my phone, wondering what to make of the call. Taken at face value, it was simply as Annika had said: that she regretted having treated me harshly. She was sensitive to a fault about the feelings of others and disappointed with herself whenever she thought she had said something insulting or injurious. I had been on the verge of saying, "It was good to hear from you," or "Let's keep in touch," but had thought better of it. If there were to be any further communication, it would be best if she were the one to initiate it.

Lost in thought, I slowly descended the stairs. Moira had moved to the bookshelf next to the fireplace and was paging through a large-format volume. She glanced at me as I entered the room.

"What have you found?" I asked.

"Oh . . . Dürer woodcuts. We worked with wood blocks for a while in my printmaking class, but none of us ever got close to this kind of precision."

"You must've been reading my mind," I said. "I was going to check something in that very same book."

"Really? What's that?" She sat down on the sofa again and handed me the book.

"Well, let's see . . ."

A moment later I had found the woodcut of the *Rest on the Flight to Egypt*. There were in fact a good half-dozen little angels involved in various activities, but writing was not one of them.

"What're you looking for?" Moira asked again.

"You wouldn't believe me if I told you."

"No? I might. I can be pretty gullible sometimes." She looked away. "Like about my boyfriend. *Former* boyfriend, I should say. We broke up tonight."

"I'm sorry, Moira. . . . Had you been going with him for a long time?"

"About a year. He turned out to be such a jerk, and I used to think he was so nice. I even considered *marrying* him." She wiped one eye with the back of her hand. "Do you have a Kleenex?" she asked.

I went into the kitchen and came back with a box.

"Thanks," she said, taking one and dabbing her eyes. "Damn it, I hate to lose control like this."

"It's okay. It might do you good to let it out."

"I mean, he *knew* I'd never have an abortion, we'd talked about it, and then we were having this pregnancy scare, and he says, 'Don't worry, I'll pay for it.' So I ask him, 'Pay for what?' and he says, 'an abortion.' I couldn't believe it! He didn't know me any better than that? And then he said, 'We can't get married now—I've got a year of college left!' Thank God I *wasn't* pregnant—there's no way I would have married him after that! And he used to tell me all the time how totally committed he was. The lying son of a—"

Moira looked down. "Sorry," she said.

"That's all right, I've been known to use the expression myself."

"So anyway, when I found out today I wasn't pregnant, I went to his dorm room and told him I was through with him. And he says, 'Fine, if that's the way you want to be.' Can you believe it? That was his 'total commitment.'"

"Well, maybe it's for the best, then."

She started sniffling again. "I'm sure it is. But I really did like him in a lot of ways." She smiled wanly. "Thanks for listening, Colin. I needed to talk to somebody, but I didn't know who." She wiped a final tear away, then pointed at the Dürer volume that was lying open on the coffee table. "Were you going to tell me what you were looking for? Or is it really unbelievable?"

I looked down at the woodcut of the *Rest on the Flight to Egypt* again. Moira had read Baumgartner's diaries, she knew far more about the St. Eustace campus and its ins and outs than I did. I had a feeling, possibly irrational, that I could trust her. Maybe she would even be able to help me in my search.

"All right. You've shared something extremely personal with me, so I'm going to do the same with you. I'll keep what you told me to myself, and I'll trust you to do the same."

She cocked her head at me. "Depends on what you were looking for, I suppose."

I gave her a wry smile. "Look, here's a hint: it's connected with Luke Baumgartner, and it's pretty far out."

She thought for a moment. "Something to do with those crazy visions of his?"

"Volume III. No, I haven't made it that far yet."

"Oh, you should. They're screwy as all get-out, but they're fascinating."

"I will eventually. Here, let me give you a more specific clue: I was hoping to find a little angel."

She looked at me and then at the woodcut. "A little angel. Well, there are plenty of them here."

I nodded. "There are. But I need one with a halo."

Moira frowned. "I have a feeling there's something you're not telling me."

"There's a lot I haven't told you. I had an experience this afternoon that shook me up, too. Except it shook me up in a *good* way."

I proceeded to explain the whole story, from my initial reading of Luke Baumgartner's last words to my discovery in the chapel that afternoon.

"And just so you don't think I'm making it all up, I'll show you what I found there."

I went up to my study, came down with the yellowed pages, and placed them on the coffee table in front of her. She read through the letter and the poem, then sat there stunned for a moment.

"Hard to believe, isn't it?" I said.

"It's like out of this world. Has anything in particular occurred to you yet? Aside from trying to find the angel with the halo, I mean?"

"Not a thing."

She glanced down at the poem again. "How about the telling-time part? Makes me think of the Garden of Time. The 'stony pantomime' kind of works there, too—you know, all those tiny sculpted figures in the frieze above the columns."

"Maybe. I think I'll have to figure out what the angel, and the ladder, and the little maid are all about before that."

She heaved a deep sigh. "You know what I think? I think I'm at

94

the end of my rope. That beer about did me in, and I was already feeling pretty drained emotionally."

"I'm sure you were. How about if I walk you home?"

"You don't need to, Colin."

"I'd feel better if I did."

"All right, if you really want to."

We walked for a few minutes along the road to the side entrance of Amity House.

"Thanks for listening," Moira said, "And thanks for trusting me."

"Sure. Thanks for being my partner in crime."

"Oh? What crime are we committing?"

"We're not. We do have to keep all of this *unter vier Augen*, though, as the Germans say."

"Between the two of us, right?"

"Right. See you in class on Monday?"

"Okay, see you then."

As I watched her climb the stairs and unlock the door with her key card, I wondered: when had she started calling me by my first name?

Back at the house I continued to page through the volume of woodcuts; there was nothing even close to what I was hoping to find. Next I pulled a book of Dürer's engravings and etchings off the shelf and began flipping through the pages. But images of Jason Miller kept intruding on my consciousness. Jason was nasty enough, but was he vicious? Did he have serious neo-Nazi leanings? Those tattoos on his arms—it almost seemed as if he wished they weren't there. Would he have had the physical strength to push someone off a bridge? Impossible to say.

All these thoughts about Jason, and then Annika's phone call. I needed to do something to clear my mind. I had borrowed the second and third volumes of Luke's diaries from the library a few days before and they were lying at the back of the desk in my study. Mounting the stairs, I flopped in my chair and picked up Volume II, *The Challenge of a New World*.

Chapter 12

Cincinnati, 25 April 1854

I can scarce believe it: I am in America, which many call the land of opportunity. Will it be thus for me?

Having braved the vast ocean, I continued my voyage, first by railroad to Pittsburgh in the state of Pennsylvania, and thence by steamboat along the Ohio River to Cincinnati. Why have I come to this distant location? During the crossing I met several fellow countrymen whom I deemed to be trustworthy, and who told me that every other person in this city was of our nationality, and furthermore that jobs for experienced shipwrights were plentiful. While the first claim turned out to be slightly exaggerated (though not terribly so), the second was accurate enough – to the extent that I am now employed at Huger's Boatyards in this city called by the locals the "Queen of the West." Having escaped from queens, kings, and other such royalty – for all time, as I hope – I have endeavored not to take offense at this designation.

Cincinnati, August 4, 1854

Now that I have been working at the Huger Shipyards for three months, I will give a brief report of my experiences there. Mr. Egge-mann, my employer, was appreciative of my three years' experience at the shipyards in Le Havre, for which reason I had only to perform me-nial tasks (for the most part hauling heavy planks and such) for a short period of time, after which I was promoted to the rank of overseer. I can assert that I am quite content with this new position.

My fellow workers, who are almost all of German origin, are industrious and friendly enough, but they make occasional derisive comments about my having worked with the "Frenchies" in Le Havre. I do not understand why so many people feel the need to belittle other nationalities (whether French, Italian, or Polish), since we are all equal brothers in the flesh.

So far, so good. In future it is not likely that I will report in these diaries about my daily work experiences, but will limit myself to mat-ters of greater interest – matters which, I may hope, will be of some interest to those who come after me.

Cincinnati, 20 July 1855

I note that it has been almost a year since I have written in my diary. Now, however, I have a most unusual event to record. Since taking up residence in Cincinnati, I have enjoyed many a steamboat trip to cities and towns both near and far. On some of these excursions, I have noticed the propensity of certain paddleboat captains for challenging others of their ilk to test which of their vessels is the faster. This, then, is what transpired while I was a passenger on the "Lexington" just a few days ago. I do not know which of the captains instigated this particular race, but I do know that I found myself in the bow of our ship with several other young men, cheering for all I was worth.

Suddenly I heard a tremendous "boom," and felt myself being flung over the railing into the water. Somehow I had the presence of mind to swim away from the boat with all my strength. Once I was close to the Kentucky shore, I dared to look back at the ghastly conflagration as the vessel listed to one side. I have not yet heard how many lives were lost, but I fear it must have been hundreds. I have since been told that there are innumerable corpses lying at the bottom of the Ohio, having in many cases suffered the explosion of a boiler as was the fate of our boat.

May God rest all those who have perished. I myself will never again engage in such folly.

Cincinnati, 5 August 1857

Over the past years I have continued to enjoy steamboat excursions on our mighty river, but today I must comment on a matter I consider reprehensible, in that it concerns human dignity. I refer to the minstrel performances I have witnessed on more than one river showboat, and in particular one that I happened upon just yesterday.

There were four "performers" in blackface – if such individuals can be dignified with this term. One played on a banjo, producing terrible twanging sounds, while another sang out of tune. The remaining two performed what looked to be a parody of an African tribal dance while waving sticks about and at times "accidentally" striking one of his mates, who put up a terrible howl. The object of what I describe here seemed to be to remove any vestige of humanity, of human-ness, from the characters portrayed. I thought back to my comrade François, who had been so brutally killed by Prussian soldiers and who was undoubtedly one of the noblest men I have ever met.

I left the miniature theater as soon as I could. To what depths will mankind stoop next?

Cincinnati, 12 May 1859

I have now lived in this city for five years, and have certainly encountered more than a few attractive young women, whether through friends, at dancing parties, evening soirées and the like. But never have any compared to the young lady I am about to describe. I met her, along with her parents, a well-bred couple of English stock who reside in Louisville. The girl's name is Catharine, her hair and eyes are dark, and she is of medium height – in short, nothing I have written yet would distinguish her from many others. Yet there was a charm about her that I find difficult to describe, a naturalness, untainted by the stilted conventions of society. Even at her tender age – I would put her at about fifteen – she is already a lover of poetry, as am I. She seemed familiar with all the great British and American poets, who are, alas, only names to me. Surprisingly, she had heard of both Eichendorff and Heine, though for her as well, they are only names. Were she only a few years older, or I a few younger! The fellow who will some day make her his own will be fortunate indeed. To me, she was like an angel passing through a dream – but a dream only.

Cincinnati, 21 December 1860

What a catastrophic event! Brazen South Carolina has dared to secede from the Union. This is only the beginning, I fear. Other states will soon follow suit, and what is to happen then? Mr. Lincoln cannot and will not allow this great nation to be cleft in twain. But how is he to prevent it? War, alas, will be his only recourse. Ah, that it must come to this!

Cincinnati, 5 February 1861

Word has come of the formation of an unholy alliance which those in the South call the Confederate States of America, and it is apparent whither this will lead. Will I, too, soon have to go to war again?

Cincinnati, 13 April 1861

Fort Sumter has been attacked. War between the two powers is now inevitable. But this must be seen as a necessary evil. The disease which has raged in the South of this nation for two centuries, eating away at the moral fibre of those who dwell there, both colored and white, must be combatted with strong medicine. Slavery is the name of this disease—nay, it is worse than a disease, it is a crime against humanity which may no longer be tolerated. Mr. Lincoln is right in all that he has said concerning this subject.

I pledge my honor that I will march with my fellows when the time comes.

Cincinnati, 17 April 1861

The throngs at Turner Hall this evening uplifted my heart. It was as if every young German of the city, and many not so young, had appeared at Mr. Lincoln's call to volunteer. Many with whom I spoke had, like myself, fought against the Hessian or Prussian troops during the revolution in Germany. Fine speeches were made, upholding the cause of freedom. There will be no difficulty in finding the thousand men who will make up the Ninth Ohio Regiment. We have been told that it will be sent for training in a matter of days to a camp not far from here.

Camp Harrison, Ohio, 26 April 1861
We arrived at camp two days ago by train. There are several other regiments gathered here as well, but as long as I remain in the area in which the Ninth is quartered, it is almost as if I were once again in Germany. Almost, I say, because one does hear the occasional and unavoidable English word. Only our Colonel McCook, beloved by all, speaks but little of our language.

When I went to Baden, I was young and foolish. How could I have imagined that a handful of irregulars and a few revolutionary-minded soldiers could overthrow the combined forces of several German monarchies? In the present instance, however, the bulk of the country is on the side of right, as is the power of the established government. And Mr. Lincoln has said that we must have faith that right makes might. Victory will surely come swiftly.

Camp Harrison, Ohio, 17 May 1861
Our training here draws to a close, as tomorrow we are to depart for Camp Dennison, the main collecting point for Ohio troops. There we are to receive uniforms and rifles and will, I believe, be heading into action sometime in June. I can imagine no better commanding officer than our Colonel McCook, and spirit among the men continues to be high. From this point on, I suspect that I will have little time to add to the pages of my diary.

Mill Springs, Kentucky, 20 January 1862
Over the past months our regiment has been involved in several inconsequential skirmishes, which pale in comparison to yesterday's encounter. The Ninth had already won respect on both sides for its bravery, and this will be even more the case following our bayonet charge which routed the enemy. We mourn the loss of six of our number, and many more from the other Union regiments involved, but the Rebel losses must have been far greater.

near Athens, Alabama, 5 August 1862
I must record a terrible act of treachery. Our beloved Colonel McCook, while lying ill in an open ambulance and defenseless, has been

killed by so-called guerrillas! The vengeance taken by several of our side in burning down the houses where these men live, is of little consolation to me and my comrades. Our division commander, General Thomas, has announced that it would be better for us to seek vengeance on the battlefield, and this we will certainly strive to do.

> *Chicamauga, Tennessee, 22 September 1863*
> *Our division, already famous for its bayonet charge at Mill Springs, has succeeded in another which scattered the enemy and resulted in the recapture of an artillery battery. Thus the Ninth has once again shown its undaunted bravery. The battle was not won, however, and we were instructed to retreat to Chattanooga and work to build fortifications. The war continues and does not appear to be approaching its end.*

> *Chattanooga, 29 November 1863*
> *Once again I am part of this world; I was, so I am told, unconscious for the better part of three days. When I awoke my dear friend and fellow "Niner" Fritz Bauer was sitting by my side, his arm wrapped in bandaging. Fritz reminded me of our division's activities on the 25th inst. – our taking up of positions alongside Missionary Ridge, the enemy's fierce cannonading, and our bayonet advance on the rifle-pits at the foot of the ridge. All this I remembered as if it had happened but an hour before. As for the rest, I can only believe what Fritz has told me: that I threw myself between him and two rebel soldiers as they charged him. Suddenly I saw a blinding flash of light – a light so intense, so searing, that it seemed to set my brain on fire. A moment later I perceived myself as something akin to a rifle-ball, being propelled at enormous speed through a gun barrel; I swirled and swirled along the rifling, but did not grow dizzy.*
> *Soon my journey was over, and the most ineffable beauty I had ever experienced lay before me: a world of the greenest grass and trees, and the bluest, clearest sky – a world in which it seemed that time did not exist – a world populated by countless animals of every description, all at peace with one another, and by people of all races, frolicking hand-in-hand through the woods and meadows. Far, far away in the distance, there stood a splendid castle.*
> *I saw all these things as I roamed about this world. Then, suddenly, I was awake again. And my head, my poor head – never before have I known such pain.*
> *Fritz has kindly put these words down on paper for me, for I felt the need to preserve them. But now I can speak no more, I must rest.*

Louisville, 9 December 1863

Mr. Wilhelm Bauer, the gracious father of my comrade-in-arms Fritz Bauer, has, following our mustering out, installed me in his splendid house, where he has lived alone since the death of his wife two years ago. Here I am to stay bedridden for as long as is necessary. Fritz himself, I am happy to say, is doing quite well and stops by my bedroom every day to visit. For my part, though I notice some slight improvement, I am still subject to blinding headaches and fainting spells. A nurse is at hand to see to my needs; I cannot thank her enough, nor the Bauers, father and son, for their kindnesses.

Louisville, 18 December 1863

I can hardly express my joy at the recent visits of a guardian angel who learned of my plight through an article in the the city's Daily Journal, describing what had taken place at Missionary Ridge and the subsequent solicitations of Mr. William Bauer on my behalf. This angel is none other than the self-same Catharine Alexander whom I met on a steamboat several years ago and who, in the meantime, has grown into an utterly delightful young lady of nineteen. Miss Alexander has visited me for three days running now, and promises to continue until I am restored to health. Given her fondness for literature, she is happy to read to me for as long as I can stay awake. Our present reading is the moving account of slavery by Mrs. Stowe, titled "Uncle Tom's Cabin." Passages in this work frequently reduce both of us to tears. Miss Alexander has said that, once we are finished with the novel, we will begin reading poetry.

Louisville, 9 January 1864

The new year has brought with it a distinct improvement in my faculties. I am now able to go for short walks each day, always on Catharine's supporting arm, and have suffered only rare fainting spells. I am pleased to note as well that the pleasure I used to take in playing harmless tricks has returned after a hiatus of several years. This amounts to no more than my spiriting away Catharine's handkerchief, or shawl, or some such thing, and then playing the innocent when I suddenly find the item in the most unexpected place. Catharine inevitably realizes that the culprit was none other than myself, and dismisses the deed by declaiming, hands on hips, "Oh Lukas, not again!"

Our current reading is a lengthy poem called "The Song of Hiawatha" by the American Henry Wadsworth Longfellow. Most captivating, and one stands to learn, I believe, a great deal about the original inhabitants of this country, who have been used as unkindly as the Negro slaves of the South.

I have no new knowledge of the Ninth, but its soldiers should be mustered out in a few months' time, having served their three-year term in an exemplary manner.

Louisville, 27 January 1864
I am unspeakably happy. I have dared, and I have won: that is, I have asked Catharine for her hand in marriage, and she has agreed! She is of the opinion that the eleven years that separate us are of no great import, and I must say myself that I feel more youthful with every passing day. Catharine's parents having blessed this union, the wedding will take place in June, by which time I expect to be fully restored.

Louisville, 5 March 1864
My dear father and mother have surprised me by writing to congratulate Catharine and me on our planned nuptials. May this be the beginning of a familial reconciliation!

Louisville, 12 March 1864
Thanks to Catharine's ministrations and those of the Bauers as well, I feel that, despite an occasional bout of faintness, I am once again as healthy as I have ever been. Mr. Bauer treats me like a second son, and has shown great confidence in my abilities in appointing me a co-employee, along with his son Fritz, of the Louisville and Nashville Railroad of which he is regional superintendant. I am extremely grateful too to Mr. Alexander, the father of my bride-to-be, for assisting me in the purchase of a house, which is to become the home of the future Mr. and Mrs. Baumgartner.

Louisville, 3 May 1864
In the midst of my great good fortune comes an event that has cast a dark shadow – Fritz Bauer has contracted typhoid fever and the family doctor fears for his life. I pray for the recovery of my dear brother-in-arms, but I have been cautioned not to build up my hope. Why must God's ways be so mysterious and, in this instance, so unjust? Yes, I know this is blasphemy, but I must speak what is on my mind!

Louisville, 8 May 1864
Early this afternoon I received word of Fritz's decline and rushed to the Bauer residence. The day had begun with a sunrise of such glory that I had taken it as a good omen – the dawning of a bright new day for our ailing Fritz. But this was not to be. By three o'clock the fever had racked his poor body so, that he seemed to lose all remaining will to continue the struggle. An hour later this brave fellow soldier and devot-

ed son had breathed his last. God have mercy on him, and on his loving father, who himself has now contracted the disease.

Louisville, 10 May 1864

Alas, Fritz's death has proved too much for his father to bear. I believe it was less the disease than his loss of the will to go on living that carried him off. Not an hour before his passing, he called me and his lawyer to his bedside and stated that, having no other heirs, he wished to bequeath his entire estate to me and have me assume the position of superintendent of the Louisville and Nashville Line. I am honoured by the trust he has hereby placed in me and will make every effort to carry on the business of the railroad in a manner worthy of his name.

Louisville, 12 June 1864

A day of joy, darkened only by the memory of my recently departed friend Fritz Bauer and his father. Our wedding ceremony, simplicity itself, was held at the home of the Alexanders, with only family members in attendance, as seemed fitting to Catharine and myself. Reverend Thompson of Christ Lutheran Church was kind enough to come out and officiate. My father has written once again offering his best wishes on behalf of the family in Germany. Given developments there in recent years, in specific the growth of Prussia's domination, he now has some sympathy for the rash acts of my youth and has forgiven me. I look forward, as does Catharine, to paying a visit to my family home one day.

Louisville, 12 April 1865

Lee has surrendered at Appomatox, and the war is finally over. May all parties who were involved in it henceforth live in peace and harmony!

Louisville, 23 February 1869

My work as superintendent occupies me so fully that I have neglected my diary, and I cannot imagine that I will ever find again the resolve of my youth to write in it with any regularity. My physical health is long since restored, and I have no difficulty in conducting the business of the railroad, but certain of my mental facilities leave something to be desired. My former fainting spells have been reduced to occasional dizziness; far more worrisome are the images I see, or believe that I see, from time to time. The worst of these have been of my beloved wife, dressed in black and walking down a seemingly endless corridor. I have not told her of this, of course.

Catharine's father has noticed certain oddities in my behavior as well, and recently suggested that I might have a country retreat built, to be used as an escape from the exigencies of the city. I am giving his suggestion serious consideration.

Louisville, 9 March 1869

Our search for a suitable building site has been fruitful. Catharine and I traveled by train from Louisville to Lexington on Friday last; there we spent the night in a pleasant hostelry and set out early the next morning by hired coach toward the hills to the east. Our three-days-long excursion yielded what I believe to be an ideal location in the beautiful rolling countryside. Our residence will take the form of a castle surrounded by a moat; this is certainly a gross indulgence on my part, but I believe that the memories of my youth it will recall will help me to relax all the more. I will seek out the best building firm I can find and have the construction begun as soon as possible.

Louisville, 11 May 1869

The foundation is laid and the course of the moat has been established, though not yet dug; the overseer tells me that the entire project will be finished by late summer. I have taken quite an interest in the artistic aspects of stonemasonry, and the chief mason has expressed his willingness to instruct me in the art of carving in stone. My excitement and Catharine's anticipation grow by leaps and bounds!

Louisville, 19 August 1869

When Catharine and I first laid eyes on our new country dwelling, she exclaimed: Why, I could believe we were in Arcadia! – Which immediately became the name we decided upon. I will leave the details of the interior furnishings to her, and we should be able to spend the night there in a month's time.

Castle Arcadia, 10 September 1869

Neither my wife nor I can fully express our delight at the finished product! We have spent two nights now here, doing precisely nothing. No, that is not quite true – for reading the poetry of Wordsworth, with whom I had previously not been been familiar, can hardly be termed doing nothing! Catharine has the most melodious voice and is a joy to listen to. How wonderful it has been to discover that there is more to the world of poetry than Goethe, Schiller and Heine!

Louisville, 25 September 1869

This week we have continued to read Wordsworth, whose poems in their immediacy and sensitivity touch my soul. In return for hav-

ing introduced me to Mr. Wordsworth, I have been reciting to Catharine this or the other poem by my favorite German nature poets, followed by my feeble attempts at translation. Catharine takes great delight in hearing my native language, even though the words I speak are no more than peculiar sounds to her.

> *Louisville, 3 October 1869*
> *I have recently memorized a few lines of a favorite Longfellow poem and often recite them to my dear wife at bedtime:*

> *Come, read to me some poem,*
> *Some simple and heartfelt lay,*
> *That shall soothe this restless feeling,*
> *And banish the thoughts of day . . .*

Inevitably, Catharine finds it impossible to resist the invitation and grants me my wish. The feeling I have of communing with her at these moments is beyond description. In a few days, she has promised me, we will begin with Tennyson.

> *Castle Arcadia, 9 October 1869*
> *I have begun to compose my own little love poems and have recited them to Catharine, who seems immeasurably touched. Since, however, their sentiments are for us alone, I will not record them in these diaries.*

> *Castle Arcadia, 20 October 1869*
> *This is the beginning of our second stay at Castle Arcadia, and we have decided to spend two entire weeks; my secretary at L&N has convinced me that my absence will pose no hardship for him or his co-workers. We read poetry in the evenings, of course, while I have been doing a fair amount of stone carving during the daylight hours. My first attempts had to be consigned to the scrap heap, but since then, under the tutelage of Mr. Meier, my stonemason friend, I have had some success. Among Catharine's favorites are several small gnomes, in the guise of gardeners, who will one day "work" a strip of ground between the castle and the moat. Of these, her especial favorite is a sort of "manneken pis", inspired by the statue in Brussels (which I know only from book illustrations). These creations are far from perfect, but once they have been painted in bright colors, I believe they will do quite nicely.*

> *Castle Arcadia, 23 October 1869*
> *When I contemplate the days of my youth, my lofty ideals, my*

opposition to the powers that be – I cannot but realize that I have now become all that I then objected to so strenuously. I must, I simply must, find some means of sharing my good fortune with others. Mere charity will not suffice, I must seek out some greater purpose. My Catharine and I often speak of this, and I am confident that we will finally discover what that greater purpose might be.

Louisville, 23 November 1869
The railroad having continued to run with no difficulties in my two-weeks' absence, Catharine and I are now contemplating a much longer leave of absence, the goal of which will be Germany, and Nuremberg in particular. I long to see my family and my beautiful home city again after so many years, and Catharine, too, is anxious to experience something of the Old World. Thoughts of Nuremberg inevitably make me think of Albrecht Dürer, her most illustrious son; a stay in Germany may well provide me with the possibility of purchasing some of that fine artist's works. I will look into booking passage immediately for the spring of the coming year.

Nuremberg, 27 May 1870
Catharine and I endured the crossing quite well and have been welcomed with open arms by my parents and my brother, who is now a well-established art dealer in the city. Stefan has been able to locate a fine print of the "St. Eustace" engraving, a favorite of mine for reasons that go back to my childhood. Furthermore, he is quite sure that he will be able to find prints of the three master engravings of 1513 and 1514 in the near future. These four pieces will be a wonderful addition to my almost-German castle in the far-off hills of Kentucky.

Louisville, 11 December 1870
How fortunate that Catharine and I left Germany before the current conflagration between two emperors began. I will not take sides—indeed, how can I?—but will only express our great happiness at living in a blessed island of peace and tranquility!
My dear brother continues to outdo himself in finding superb Dürer prints, both engravings and woodcuts, to the extent that I have decided to turn a sizable room in the castle into a museum. I have also had Stefan commission a local sculptor with the carving in wood of a life-sized St. Eustace, who will stand inside the little chapel in my castle and welcome the few visitors who put in an appearance.
A humorous moment: this past September, as Catharine and I were unwrapping the engraving known as "Knight, Death and Devil" which Stefan had sent, she noted that she detected "a distinct similarity

between the features of the Knight's profile and your own." I laughed at this, saying that I was gratified she found it was the <u>Knight's</u> face, and not one of the two other figures, that bore the similarity. We have had many a good laugh at this since!

Louisville, 5 April 1871

My beloved wife has found yet another way of delighting me – by telling me this morning me that she is expecting! At each yearly examination, our Dr. Davies has pronounced Catharine to be in the best of health and sees no reason for concern at this point.

Louisville, 17 October 1871

Dr. Davies has detected some irregularities in the development of Catharine's child. Needless to say, we are worried, but hope and pray that all will go well.

Louisville, 25 November 1871

I have not been able to find the strength to write for several days now. But this, too, must be recorded. My beloved Catharine, my dark-haired beauty, lives no more. This most delightful, most pious, most cherished woman has been taken from me. The light of my life has been snuffed out, and not even the child could be saved. I ask you, God, why not the child? Could you not have granted me at least this blessing as a living memory of her mother?

But I was permitted to share in Catharine's life for seven long, tender years. What man can claim that he has known such joy as this? I pray now that one day I will be reunited with her in that place where all memories of pain are washed away.

Requiescat in pace.

Castle Arcadia, 5 June 1873

I have not written in all these months since the passing of my Catharine. But I have not lain idle during this time, neither in business matters nor in the execution of a lasting memorial to my beloved wife. This has taken the form of what I call a Garden of Time – a rotunda in the antique style. Twelve columns, most of them fragments, are arranged in a circle and represent the devastations brought about by the passage of time. One will approach the rotunda in later years by means of a maze of hedges, representing the difficulties and struggles we all encounter in making our way through life.

In the center of the garden stands a statue of Catharine in the guise of an angel bearing an inverted, and hence extinguished, torch. I have sculpted the statue myself, and for the torch I am indebted to the German writer I feel closest to, Gotthold Ephraim Lessing, who describes its symbolical use in antiquity in a treatise I read several years ago. Lessing was frequently on my mind following Catharine's death, since he had suffered the same blow as I, having lost both his wife and new-born child at one stroke.

Castle Arcadia, 19 November 1876

On this, the fifth anniversary of my dear wife's death, I contemplated my own past life and once again was forced to admit that all I have achieved – success in a commercial sense, the amassing of a collection of Dürer's works which are a rarity in these United States – has been for my benefit alone. How shall I fill the emptiness in my life? When will I undertake some project whereby I might serve the greater good of mankind, as Goethe's Faust does at the end of his life? What might this project be? Of this I have no notion. I will do my best to keep my eyes – and my mind and my heart – open, in hopes that this wish may ultimately be granted me.

Castle Arcadia, 18 May 1878

Until recently, I had not been able to bring myself to step inside Christ Lutheran Church after so many years, since it was there that Catharine and I were married and that her obsequies were held. But now I have braved its portals again and have found both pastor and parishioners to be extremely caring. I have also come to know a widow of about my own age. I find Christina both intelligent and attractive, and I believe that she considers me in the same light. And yet I have resolved that our companionship must remain purely platonic, for I knew at the moment of my marriage to Catharine that we had somehow been chosen as life's partners for each other. I will remain true to my beloved wife's memory until my dying day.

Castle Arcadia, 12 June 1885

Alas, my poor diary, how I have neglected you! I have not yet recorded my retirement from my position with the Louisville and Nashville two years ago, at which point I decided to move permanently to the peaceful setting of my castle; given my vast holdings in lumber to its north, I expect to have no financial difficulties.

Since then, however, my life has been a hodge-podge of emotions. Hallucinations, as Dr. Davies calls them, have resumed with increasing frequency. Some, for example when I see Catharine walking through the castle grounds wearing a beautiful gown, give me a measure of joy – until, that is, I return to my senses and discover that she is not there. Others take place while I am walking on the grounds myself and spot several foxes in the distance, or even an occasional deer. Do I really see these creatures? I cannot tell, but when I blink my eyes they are suddenly gone. Still other visions, as I prefer to call them, are of joyous children frolicking on a meadow. Sometimes I see myself, as a man, joining in with them, playing pranks, or running through a maze.

I do not know where my life is taking me.

Castle Arcadia, 7 August 1898

The fourteen Apocalypse woodcuts of 1498 arrived yesterday, almost four hundred years after they were printed. They will fill the remaining wall space in my little museum and thus conclude my collecting activity.

Castle Arcadia, 30 August 1898

These past weeks I have been beset with vision-like dreams, which must have as their inspiration my Apocalypse collection. Sometimes I see myself about to be trampled by galloping horsemen, or put upon by many-headed monsters; sometimes I feel my flesh burning as fiery stars fall from the sky. On other occasions, however, I have been blessed with quite positive dreams, though certainly of the same provenance. In the one I seemed to be a slain martyr, but in the absence of pain; on the contrary, I was surrounded by light and was wearing a white robe. In another I was the apostle John himself, being shown the New Jerusalem by an angel.

Young Dr. Davies, my personal physician following the death of his father a year ago, reassures me that such dreams are quite common and should cause me no concern.

Castle Arcadia, 17 September 1899

Several newspapermen have contacted me of late – from Louisville, from Frankfort, from Lexington – all of them wishing to give accounts of my Dürer collection in their papers. I am both surprised and pleased that a cultural matter of this sort has inspired so much interest.

Castle Arcadia, 25 October 1899

Recent events at my castle have saddened me. What aggrieves me most is that my manservant has been as much as accused by the police . . . But I will let the following newspaper commentary tell the tale.

The theft of an engraving valued at several hundred dollars was reported on Wednesday of this week to the Lexington police. The engraving, *Knight, Death, and Devil* by the German artist Albrecht Durer, disappeared from the country dwelling of Mr. Lukas Baumgartner, formerly of Louisville, sometime before midnight on the previous day. A servant of Mr. Baumgartner's averred that he had found an open window in his employer's display room at eleven o'clock that evening. According to his testimony, he noticed a moment later an empty space on the wall where the engraving had hung. Not wanting to disturb his master at such a late hour, he decided to despatch a rider immediately to Lexington to summon the police. To date, no clues have been found. Mr. Baumgartner himself asserted that he had no reason whatsoever to doubt the veracity of his servant's statements, adding that he had the utmost trust in his loyalty and honesty. The matter continues under investigation, but police officials stated that they consider the recovery of the work of art unlikely.

- Lexington *Morning Herald,* Saturday, October 24, 1899.

Castle Arcadia, 25 December 1899
    On this Christmas Day, twenty-seven years after the passing of my wife, I betook myself to my chapel, where the statue of St. Eustace which I commissioned many years ago greeted me at the door. Seeing him there on this day of our Lord's birth transported me back to my childhood days in Germany – in specific, to a day in December on which Stefan and I were allowed to accompany our father to the Royal Picture Galerie in Munich, where we beheld Dürer's wondrous altarpiece of the Nativity with its side panels depicting St. Michael and St. Eustace. On that occasion, and on subsequent visits to the museum in recent years, I must say that I felt no little pride in the fact that it was my ancestor Martin Paumgartner who had commissioned this remarkable painting.
    I prayed in my chapel for some time, thinking especially of my wife, and when I left I was filled with a comforting sense of peace. Whatever the new year may bring, I shall meet it with courage and composure.

Chapter 13

How could anyone have gone through all the physical and emotional pain that Luke Baumgartner had and still look ahead calmly to the coming of another year? There could be no question about it: Luke was a survivor. Now there was just one volume of his diaries left, with all its "weirdnesses," as Moira had put it. But these would have to wait; the discussion evening at Klaus Hochstraaten's house was coming up in a week and I still had a lot of homework to do.

I began spending the time I had between classes and after supper reviewing what I liked to call the Age of Dürer, which overlapped very closely with the Age of Luther and all its religious controversies. The reformer's righteous fervor had riled up the various sides to the point where the Lutherans hated the Catholics, the Anabaptists the Lutherans, the Calvinists the Anabaptists, the Zwinglians the Calvinists. And everyone hated the Jews. There was no way of telling what, if any of this, would come up in a discussion of Dürer's own religious views. But by the time Friday rolled around, I felt reasonably confident that I would not make a complete fool of myself.

At a few minutes before seven a battered old Buick pulled into my driveway. Pastor Roland had relinquished his customary monkish look in favor of a black jacket, slate-gray shirt, and clergyman's collar. I climbed in and we stopped at the Rossis to pick up Michael, then headed along the road that led down through the woods to the highway.

"We'll take the shorter route and be there in ten minutes or so," the pastor said. "Klaus insists on the longer alternative himself, to avoid gravel roads. His devotion to the well-being of his Mercedes is slightly exaggerated, to put it mildly."

"Now why doesn't that surprise me?" I said, looking over my shoulder and grinning at Michael. "You've been to Klaus's house before, I suppose?"

"Charlotte has, but I haven't. Klaus isn't exactly a social butterfly."

"Which is a shame in a way," the pastor said. "His house is old but quite beautiful. He had it completely renovated many years ago. And he keeps it spotless, of course. His housekeeper does, that is."

"A housekeeper, sure," I said. "I can hardly imagine him dusting and vacuuming."

"She's a woman from town who comes every week, I believe. But Klaus doesn't let her touch his houseplants. They're at least as important to him as his automobile."

We drove along the highway for what I judged to be about two miles.

"Ah, here's our cut-off," the pastor said, "at that 'fresh eggs'sign. It has always been my faithful landmark, though I've never taken the time to stop at the farmer's to sample his wares. I really must do that sometime."

We were now bumping along a gravel road that gradually turned and wound its way up a wooded hillside. A dilapidated old house stood far off in a clearing on the right, and another on the left several hundred yards farther along. At the crest of the hill, where the road abruptly became paved, Pastor Roland began leaning forward to look past me out the window.

"Ah, here we are," he said finally, turning in at a narrow drive between rows of pine trees. "Klaus has his place well-hidden, as you can see."

A two-story brick house stood at the end of a long driveway. Ionic columns adorned the front porch and a smaller sleeping porch on the second floor, lending the place a touch of elegance. Pastor Roland pulled up to the detached garage and parked next to it.

"We're a few minutes early," he said, "but I'm sure Klaus won't mind."

We climbed the porch steps and the pastor knocked on the door—there was no doorbell—and then a second time, more insistently. I looked through a window into what seemed to be the living room and saw no signs of life.

"I wonder where he could be," the pastor said. We followed him down from the porch toward the garage. Michael peered in through a side window.

"Don't see any car in there."

"Oh, dear," the pastor said. "I hope this is the right day." He pulled out his date book and checked it.

"Yes, this is definitely the day we agreed on . . . ah, but we weren't to be here until seven-thirty—somehow I had seven-fifteen in mind. Well, I'm sure that Klaus will be along soon, given his habitual punctuality."

While he and Michael chatted on, I walked around to the backyard, where several apple trees had been planted in rows. Overripe and rotting apples littered the ground. The rear of the house was dominated by a large screened porch that jutted out into the yard and contained a jungle of house plants. Immediately above it, a room of the same size appeared to have been added on; its brick walls didn't quite match the rest of the house and looked less weatherbeaten. Two skylights perched on top of the roof, and an almost continuous row of narrow horizontal windows ran just below the gutter. Could this be another plant room, for certain types that had special lighting needs? That seemed unlikely.

Hearing the crunch of gravel, I joined Pastor Roland and Michael as Hochstraaten's black Mercedes crawled up the driveway and parked next to the pastor's car. Hochstraaten got out laboriously, an annoyed expression on his face.

"We had said seven-thirty, had we not? You are early."

"Yes, Klaus," Pastor Roland said, "I was a bit off with the time. Well, better early than late, *nicht wahr*?"

Frowning, Hochstraaten led the way up the porch steps with no further comment. He unlocked the front door and let us pass before him, still without saying a word.

A short entryway led to the living room, which was dominated by plants of various sizes. Landscapes and still lifes filled the available wall space. Aside from plant tables, the only pieces of furniture in the room were a small sofa and coffee table across from the fireplace, and a leather easy chair and rocker to the right and left of it.

"You're a plant lover," I said, wishing that I had been able to think of something less obvious to say.

"Certainly," Hochstraaten replied. "I could almost say that my plants are my family."

I was tempted to ask which were the brothers and sisters, which the cousins, but thought better of it. There was, after all, something poignant in my solitary colleague's remark.

"Quite a collection of paintings you have," Michael said, stepping over to examine two small landscapes.

"They are all by anonymous artists," Hochstraaten said. "As an art historian, you will immediately see that they are attempts at imitating the realistic style of painters of earlier centuries, but without a great deal of success. It goes without saying that I am not in a position to own a Ruisdael landscape, or a still life by Pieter Claesz, or even a van Thielen *Blumenstück*—a flower piece, as you say in English."

"But these are . . . quite decorative," Michael said.

Hochstraaten dismissed the comment with a wave of his hand.

"This is quite an occasion, Klaus," Pastor Roland said, "as you will remember, we have had only one other evening devoted to Dürer. I was telling Colin how we invited Ronald Fleishman to join us two years ago. . . ."

Hochstraaten's eyes flashed. "I remember such a meeting, but only vaguely."

"But surely—"

"May I suggest that we get on with *this* evening's discussion? I will bring the cognac. Please be seated."

The pastor stepped past the coffee table to the easy chair, a puzzled expression on his face. I glanced at him, wondering what he was thinking. Michael and I sat down on the sofa and Hochstraaten returned a moment later with a bottle of what appeared to be very old Martell and four cognac glasses on a tray. He poured a generous amount into each and passed them around. Pastor Roland sniffed his glass, nodded appreciatively, and held it aloft.

"May I offer a toast to our dear departed friend Walter Seifert," he said.

"To Walter Seifert," Michael and I repeated. Hochstraaten was silent, but raised his glass slightly before drinking.

"Ah, remarkable!" Pastor Roland said, relishing the cognac.

Hochstraaten sat down in the rocking chair next to the fireplace. "Shall we begin? You suggested, I believe, the topic of Albrecht Dürer's religiosity."

"Yes, something on that order. It seemed to me that, given the times in which Dürer lived, this could lead to a profitable discussion."

Hochstraaten folded his hands as if he were about to pray and rested his chin on them. "And not one which might be turned, adroitly or no, toward the attempted conversion of one of the members of this group? This, I assure you, would prove to be quite as fruitless as have similar attempts on previous occasions."

Pastor Roland shook his head and frowned. "Ah, my dear Klaus, as suspicious as ever, I see. And, I suppose, with some justification. If only you would realize that I have your best interests at heart."

Raising his eyebrows, Hochstraaten sat back in his chair. "My best interests? You wish me to burn along with your illustrious coreligionists? And you call this my best interests?"

The pastor cast a frustrated glance at me. "The fellow is hopeless, I'm afraid, quite hopeless. But perhaps you do not share my opinion? I have not had occasion to talk to you about your own religious convictions."

Things were getting more personal than I had banked on. Oh well, I thought, why not plunge in head first.

"As a member of yet another of the great confessions of the world," I said, "I'm not sure I should be the one to comment on either of your positions."

Pastor Roland looked at me in mock horror. "Great heavens above, you're not a Buddhist! A Zoroastrian?"

"Or a Jew?" Hochstraaten's mouth twisted scornfully.

Michael shot him an angry glance. "Would you have a problem with that?"

Hochstraaten shook his head impatiently and looked away. "It was merely a question, nothing more."

"Well, if you have to know," I said, "I'm an agnostic."

The pastor raised both hands. "Ah, good, then there still is hope for you," he said, smiling.

"A lazy position," Hochstraaten said, "a position—how do you say it?—a position with weak knees."

"Maybe so, but it's the only position I'm able to take. At this point in my life, at least."

"Yes, you're still young," Pastor Roland said. "In any case," he added with a twinkle in his eye, "I am of the opinion that next to Lutherans agnostics have the best chance of attaining the Kingdom."

"Fine, go ahead and make your little jokes," Hochstraaten said. "Joking is a sign of insecurity."

I glanced at Michael. It was clear that he was feeling uncomfortable with the turn the conversation had taken.

"What ever became of Dürer?" he asked. "I thought that was our topic for the evening."

Pastor Roland smiled. "A very good question. And if we modify it slightly, we have yet another good question, namely: what *would* have become of Dürer? That is, had he lived a few years longer than he did. I believe, you see, that he would have left the Roman Church and declared himself even more unequivocally for Luther than he had already."

"Nonsense!" Hochstraaten exclaimed, his voice almost a shout. "Nowhere does he mention this as a possibility!"

"Not in writing, perhaps," Pastor Roland replied, "but what do we know of conversations he might have had?"

"Nothing, we know precisely nothing of them! Are you going now to speculate on what he *might* have said?"

"But my dear Klaus, please remember that Dürer lived in a city which, during the last three years of his life, had become thoroughly 'Lutheranized,' if I may use this term, and that several of his friends had gone over—"

"Precisely! And if he had by that point not left the Church, how can you speculate that he *might* have at some later point? Dürer was a faithful adherent to the Faith. Of course he saw that there was corruption, yes, even in the very highest ranks—but that would have been removed in good time, in *God's* time. What hubris, for a renegade monk to try and split apart an institution which had united Europe for a millenium and a half!"

Pastor Roland frowned. "I don't agree that that was his aim, Klaus. He was hoping for *change*, not for a split. Now it is certainly true that he said some nasty things about Pope Leo along the way, but there's good evidence that he and other officials of the Church deserved it. Not that Luther himself was without blemish, far from it. I find it quite reprehensible, for example, the way he castigated the Jews later in life."

Hochstraaten made a dismissive gesture. "That was the least of his sins. The Jews simply had no role to play in Christian Europe, they—"

Michael fired another angry look at Hochstraaten. "No role to play? Ask some of the rulers of the time who needed to borrow money from them!"

"Be that as it may," Pastor Roland said, "as Michael pointed out a moment ago, it was *Dürer* we were to discuss this evening. May I suggest that we leave questions involving Luther for another session?"

"Fine, let us do that," Hochstraaten agreed, lowering his voice. "As I was saying, Dürer was a faithful child of the Church. He had been to Italy on two occasions, and although he received certain impulses there which were damaging to his art, being in the cradle of Mother Church only strengthened his allegiance—"

"Ah, but Klaus, who, may I ask, is speculating now? We know little of his experiences there, aside from those in artistic circles. And are you forgetting that *Luther* had made a trip to Italy, too? He had been in Rome, in fact, the heart of 'Mother Church,' as you characterized it."

Hochstraaten had been silenced for the moment. I was feeling about as much a part of the conversation as the ferny-looking plant in the large pot next to me.

"I'd have to support Pastor Roland on this," I said. "Judging from what I've read, Luther and Dürer had cordial relations with each other, even though they never met—they exchanged treatises, prints, and so on. And the most telling thing, it seems to me, is the utter horror that Dürer expressed during his trip to the Netherlands when he heard rumors that Luther had been killed. And that we *do* have in writing."

Hochstraaten stood up and began pacing jerkily back and forth, cognac glass in hand, his gaze fixed on the carpet.

"I am pleased that you have cited this example, *Herr Ritter*, very pleased. To quote him exactly, he said, *'ist Luther todt, wer wird uns hinfürt das heilig evangelium so klar fürtragen?'* He saw Luther not as one who would bring a new, somehow improved, religion, but solely as one who explicated the texts clearly. And that, I will concede, Luther did in many instances, as scholarship has shown." He glanced sharply at Pastor Roland. "Although I am loathe to grant *anything* to that pompous seeker of publicity."

The pastor cast his eyes to the ceiling. "That remark, Klaus, is beneath the dignity of a response."

"And what did Dürer then write," Hochstraaten went on, ignoring him, "in that same diary entry? Whom did he call upon to come and replace the presumed dead, but unfortunately very much alive Luther?"

He looked at me penetratingly, as if he were asking an examination question. I had read through Dürer's diaries just that past summer and remembered the passage well.

"He made a plea to Erasmus—"

"Precisely!" Hochstraaten exclaimed triumphantly. "Erasmus, the defender of the Faith and enemy of Luther, who would subsequently show definitively the foolishness of the latter's views on free will . . . "

I felt out of my depth. There was still a lot I didn't know about the period, especially in the area of religious controversies. Grudgingly, I had to admire the breadth of Hochstraaten's knowledge and his ability to quote detailed passages from obscure texts.

Michael sat frowning to himself and Pastor Roland didn't appear to be up to challenging Hochstraaten yet again. He slumped in his chair, looking resigned rather than defeated. This struck me as an appropriate time to try and change the subject.

"When we were talking about Dürer's trips to Italy a minute ago, you said something about 'damaging impulses' to his art. What exactly did you mean by that?"

"This should be quite apparent," Hochstraaten said, sitting down in his chair again. "To suggest how Dürer's art might have developed had he *not* made those trips would involve further speculation, and we certainly do not want to indulge ourselves in that"—he glanced at Pastor Roland again—"but there can be no doubt that his creations would have remained more clearly Germanic in spirit. Something more in the direction of Matthias Grünewald, shall we say. —Whose works, incidentally, I find in some ways superior even to Dürer's . . . "

"More Germanic," Michael echoed. "Are you thinking of the Italianate look of his Madonnas, say, at that time?"

"That is correct, but not only this. Though these works are perhaps the most flagrant examples—such soft, sensual, simpering creatures—"

"Very nice alliteration, Klaus," Pastor Roland said, looking up from his now almost empty glass. With a smirk, he emptied it in one large gulp and placed it on the coffee table. "May I?" he said, and began to pour without waiting for an answer.

"Where was I?" Hochstraaten went on, acknowledging only that he had been interrupted. "Yes—Dürer's Madonnas. Certainly these women have never known a moment's suffering in their lives. And what was the *raison d'être* of the Mother of Christ, if not suffering?"

Though no longer a believer myself, if I ever had been, I took offense at what I perceived to be a dismal view of Mary. "Maybe motherhood?" I suggested. "Maybe tenderness? Maybe *love*?"

"Sentimental nonsense! And theologically quite untenable!"

"*Whose* theology, Klaus?" Pastor Roland countered. As before, Hochstraaten ignored him.

"Man's lot is suffering," he went on in a more subdued voice. "We are born in suffering, we die in suffering. And the death of the man Jesus symbolizes this. Suffering is a fact of our existence, one which we can rarely, if ever, overcome. I believe, however, with Schopenhauer, that some of us, if we have the requisite aesthetic sensibility, may be able to transcend suffering for brief periods of time, by listening intently to the great composers—Mozart, Beethoven, Schubert, Bruckner—or by contemplating great works of art."

Hochstraaten's fixed gaze had taken on an almost ecstatic cast. "Such moments as I myself have experienced," he continued, "I can only describe as touching the Godhead."

I glanced around the room, wondering just what aesthetic transcendence the particular works of art hanging on Klaus's walls were capable of offering.

In the meantime, Pastor Roland had apparently become more interested in the contents of his glass than in the conversation, and Michael seemed to be doing some sort of deep-breathing exercise. I decided to use the excuse of going to the bathroom to escape for a while. Hochstraaten, visibly displeased at my request, nodded toward the stairway at the opposite side of the living room.

"Turn to the right when you reach the second floor. You will find the bathroom on the left at the end of the hallway."

The staircase reversed directions halfway up at a small landing. Mounting the last few steps, I found myself at the angle of an L-shaped hallway, each section dimly lit by a single ceiling lamp. Straight ahead, a door on my left and one at the far end were closed; this second door had to lead to the added-on room at the back of the house. Following Hochstraaten's instructions, I turned to the right. When I reached the bathroom, I noticed that the door directly opposite was slightly ajar. After a moment's hesitation, I gave it a push and looked inside. In the gloom, I could make out a desk and row upon row of bookshelves. Cocking my ear toward the staircase, I heard the beginnings of another vehement argument. The study was on the opposite side of the house from the living room; any floorboard squeaks would not be heard below.

I stepped gingerly into the room and shone my penlight around. Several plants stood on tables at the two front windows. On the wall above the desk hung a glass case containing two crossed daggers and what looked to be a classic Luger pistol. A silver-framed black-and-white photograph of a handsome young man in an SS officer's uniform stood at the back of the desk. The inscription on the photo read: *Meinem geliebten Sohne Klaus zu seinem 4. Geburtstag, den 20. September 1943*—To my dear son Klaus on his fourth birthday. I was barely able to stifle a whistle.

The argument downstairs was still going full tilt. Nonetheless, I couldn't chance lingering in the study for very long—Hochstraaten would raise holy hell if he found me prowling around his inner sanctum. Turning back to the desk, I noticed a foot-long object against the wall that was rolled up and loosely secured with a rubber band. It appeared to be a piece of fabric; bits of color were visible along the edge. I leaned over and ran my fingers along the inner surface, which was slightly rough and uneven. Slipping the rubber band off, I unrolled the object.

It was a painting of flowers in a glass vase standing on a marble table. There were roses, tulips, irises, poppies, and a few others that I couldn't identify. A blue-and-white butterfly had landed on one of the roses, and two brownish beetles crawled around near the base of the vase. The artist hadn't missed the opportunity to show his skill by painting, with almost photographic precision, the reflection of a four-paned window on the rounded surface of the vase. I could barely make out a signature near the bottom: I. P. van Thielen. I mumbled the name out loud: van Thielen . . . wasn't that one of the artists Hochstraaten had mentioned earlier that evening? A *Blumenstück* by van Thielen. Or was I remembering it wrong? I was familiar with the other two painters, Ruisdael and Claesz, but the third wasn't one I had heard of. I gazed at the painting again and ran my hand over the surface. This was clearly not a reproduction—not that Klaus would have countenanced such in his house.

The voices from the living room had become louder again. Turning my head toward the door, I heard Hochstraaten and Pastor Roland trying to out-shout each other. I'd been up here too long already. As I started to roll up the canvas, I noticed a few faded words on the back, written in the old Sütterlin script on a fragment of a label: "Samml--- -- -----nstein, München 1924." The first word had to be *Sammlung*—collection, and the last six letters part of a name. In between there seemed to be an initial—something with a loop below the line in the old script, like an 'H' or a 'G,' but the first letters of the name itself were missing. Bernstein, Rosenstein, Rubinstein . . . There were many possibilities, but whatever the name was, it was certainly Jewish. How in the world had Hochstraaten come by a painting, by all appearances a valuable one, that had belonged to a German Jewish collector in the 1920s?

I glanced at the father-and-son photo again. Was it possible? His father had given him an expensive emerald ring last summer. Had he given him a painting as well? I quickly slipped the rubber band around the rolled-up canvas and put it back on the desk, then crossed the hall to the bathroom and flushed the toilet.

I reached the bottom of the stairs just in time to hear an especially harsh edge in Hochstraaten's voice: "We should have burned him while we still had the chance, just as we did Jan Hus a hundred years earlier. But no, we allowed that scapegrace elector Friedrich to spirit him away so that he could do more mischief."

"But don't forget," Pastor Roland replied, "that this 'mischief' included translating the New Testament, and then the Old. And you yourself conceded earlier this evening that Luther was an excellent explicator of the Gospel."

"I did not say 'excellent,' I said—"

Hochstraaten slowly lowered his head, closed his eyes, and began to massage his forehead with both hands. "Gentlemen, I am sorry," he began, his voice sounding weak and strained.

Pastor Roland looked concerned. "Klaus, what is it? Don't tell me—is it a migraine coming on?"

Hochstraaten nodded, continuing his massage. "I am afraid you will have to excuse me for the rest of the evening, gentlemen."

"Is there anything we can do?" Michael asked.

"No, no . . . I will be all right eventually. This pain, too, I must embrace."

Pastor Roland and Michael got up from their seats.

"Forgive me if I do not see you to the door," Hochstraaten said.

"Of course," Pastor Roland said, "don't even think of it. We'll let ourselves out." He patted him on the arm. "Good night, and get yourself to bed."

"Thank you for hosting our discussion," I said. "I'm sorry this had to happen."

Hochstraaten looked up at me with an expression that was difficult to define. Pastor Roland and Michael offered their final good wishes.

"Ah, poor fellow," the pastor said when we were outside. "He's been suffering from these attacks for as long as I've known him."

"Yes," Michael said, "Charlotte has mentioned them, too."

"That's terrible," I said. "How often does he have them?"

"I doubt that anyone knows—except his doctor, if he has one. Klaus is a solitary soul, always has been, it seems. He neither seeks nor does he attract sympathy."

We got into the car and drove off. I looked back just in time to see the last light on the main floor go out.

Chapter 14

If Pastor Roland had been tipsy before, he seemed to have sobered up in a hurry; he had no problem negotiating the gravel slope and the adjoining road that led to the highway. The three of us had been silent up to that point. Then Michael leaned forward from his seat in the back to make himself heard.

"Well," he said, "I guess that confirms my suspicions."

"How do you mean?" I asked.

"That Klaus Hochstraaten is xenophobic, and anti-Semitic to boot. He got to me on both those fronts tonight."

Pastor Roland let out a sigh as he turned onto the highway. "What you say is hard to refute, Michael. Though I don't believe he intended to attack you in particular."

Michael shrugged. "I'm not so sure about that."

"I didn't know you were Jewish," I said.

"Only one-quarter, on my father's side. You'd be surprised how many Italians named Rossi have Jewish blood. I'm not observant, as you might have guessed. But I don't suppose that makes me any less Jewish in the eyes of certain people. And as for Hochstraaten not attacking me personally—you do tend to give people the benefit of the doubt, Martin."

"I certainly endeavor to do so. I believe it's part and parcel of my profession."

We grew silent again until we reached the large granite slab bearing the inscription *St. Eustace College* and began climbing the winding road through the forest.

"You can let me off at Michael's," I said. "That will give me at least a little bit of a walk."

"Very well." The pastor pulled into the Rossis' driveway. "Thank you both for coming along tonight," he said as we got out of the car. "Klaus needs, even craves, some companionship, if only rarely. He has made his own bed, so to say, but I cannot help thinking that he is a very lonely man. Such bitterness as he harbors is one reflection of that, it seems to me."

"It's nice of you to care," I said. "To be honest, I've had a hard time warming up to him ever since I met him."

"Well, again, it's part of my being a *Seelsorger*, as the Germans so poetically put it. And I do try to care for Klaus's soul. You can perhaps see why after this evening. The fellow *believes*, I am convinced of that. Yet I am not quite sure *what* it is he believes. And that is the problem. If he believes in the word of God, then, as my faith teaches, he will be saved. But if it is something else, if he puts so much emphasis on the necessity of suffering and pain. . . ."

The pastor shook his head woefully as Michael and I stepped out of the car.

"Well, thank you both again for joining me. I hope the rest of your evening is more pleasant."

We stood in the driveway and waved as Pastor Roland backed out into the street.

"He's such a decent man," Michael said. "Which can trip him up sometimes. It's a terrible thing to say, but I think it's true." He paused. "Anyhow, I can't deny that it was an interesting evening."

"Interesting in more ways than one. What struck me at the very beginning was how Hochstraaten seemed to barely remember that earlier evening, the one Pastor Roland mentioned. Seemed to me he wanted to avoid talking about Ronald Fleishman, even though the pastor had told me they had been friends."

"Friends—that's a good one! The one time I saw them together they were arguing like crazy about something. Though I suppose friends can do that, too."

"Did you know Fleishman very well? He was a passing acquaintance of mine when I was an undergraduate. Didn't strike me as a particularly argumentative type."

"I can't really say. I only knew him as Charlotte's colleague. I don't think either of us felt the need to get to know each other. His views were pretty orthodox, and mine are anything but."

"Which makes it seem all the less likely that he and Hochstraaten would have become friends."

"Seems so to me, too."

"About tonight, though . . . remember when I went upstairs to go to the bathroom—"

"Of course I do, you missed out on several choice skirmishes—from both parties, I'd have to say."

"Sorry to leave you in the lurch like that. But let me tell you what I discovered. I peeked into Hochstraaten's study and there was a signed photograph of his father from 1943 on his desk; he was wearing an SS-officer's uniform. And there was a Luger and two daggers in a case on the wall."

"I'll be damned! But why should I be surprised, that would explain a lot. Including why his family moved to Argentina. Or fled, maybe, if it was before the war was over."

"That was the first thing that crossed my mind when I saw the photo. Not that we should automatically jump to conclusions about

Klaus—like the apple not falling far from the tree, I mean."

"Maybe not, although . . . " Michael shrugged. "You know, I'm not going to say anything about this to Charlotte. She always wants to think the best of people, no matter what. She's kind of like Pastor Roland that way. All these years she's treated Klaus the same as she does anybody else. Sometimes it's like she doesn't even see his nastier qualities, so knowing what you just told me would at the very least make her feel awkward around him. She's a true innocent, and that's one of her most endearing qualities."

"All right, I'll keep my mouth zipped too. What will you tell her when she asks how the evening went?"

"Oh, I won't sugarcoat things too much, but I'll definitely leave out the vicious comments."

"Good. Maybe you could tell her about all the great art Klaus has hanging in his living room."

Michael laughed. "You know, that really surprised me. Surely he could afford something a *little* better than what he has there. Been a bachelor all his life, with no particular expenses, I don't suppose, beyond the occasional trip to Argentina."

"I wondered about that too. Not that any of us could afford paintings by the artists he mentioned—Ruisdael, Claesz, and . . . who was the third one again?"

"Jan van Thielen—he did mostly floral paintings. I know of a couple, one in the museum at Oxford and another one in Cambridge."

"Oh. All I knew was that it was someone I hadn't heard of. So paintings by any of those three would be out of sight, I suppose."

"Well, Ruisdael would be *way* out of sight. I remember a couple of auctioned pieces in the '90s that brought in over a million dollars each. Claesz isn't as well known, but I would think some of his paintings would be up in the mid-six-figures range. It would depend on the individual still life. And there's so many other variables at auctions, too."

"How about this van Thielen guy?"

Michael thought for a moment. "Seems to me there was an auction in Amsterdam a few years ago where one of his pieces went for over two hundred thousand euros."

I nodded, trying to look nonchalant. "It kind of blows the mind, doesn't it, how much art can be worth."

"It does. And no depreciation, like with cars or almost anything else you could name. With top-rung art it's exactly the opposite."

"Yeah. Too bad the artists themselves aren't around to reap the benefits. Well, look, I'll head on home now and listen to some nice soothing music—à la Schopenhauer, the way Klaus suggested."

"You noticed the composers he named? Only Germans and Austrians. Funny he didn't mention Mendelssohn."

"Right. Or Mahler, maybe?

He gave me a grim smile. "Not a chance. So what will you listen to tonight?"

"Oh, a Carly Simon tune, I suppose."

Michael grinned. "Don't think that's exactly what he had in mind."

"No, probably not."

"But go for it."

"I might. Give Charlotte my best."

"Thanks, I'll do that."

Truth to tell, I had no intention of listening to music. I ran up to the study, turned on the computer, and began making a list of all the names ending with 'nstein' that I could think of: Bernstein, Bronstein, Ehrenstein, Weinstein, Ohrenstein, Rubinstein, Wittgenstein, Eisenstein, Blumenstein, Feinstein, Einstein, Lichtenstein . . . There were certainly others, but these were the ones that occurred to me at the moment. My plan was to first try googling *Kunstsammlung*—art collection—followed by each of the names, one after the other. If that led to nothing, I could try adding the initial 'H,' and possibly 'G.'

I went to Google and typed in several of the names, with discouraging results; all that turned up were a museum curator, several contemporary American artists, a late-nineteenth-century German couple who had collected Impressionist paintings, and a private collection of twentieth-century Russian artists. Finally, when I entered the name Blumenstein, I found what I was looking for on the third Google page.

Heinrich Blumenstein had owned an art gallery in Munich from 1910 until the infamous *Kristallnacht* of November 1938, when countless Jewish shops and synagogues had been attacked; he had specialized in Dutch and Flemish art of the sixteenth and seventeenth centuries. Nothing more had been heard of him following the war, but it was believed that he had ended up in Auschwitz. Blumenstein's heirs claimed that twenty-seven paintings had been taken from his Munich gallery.

I pounded the palm of my hand with my fist. This had to be it. But what now? Who did you go to if you had information concerning a painting with the presumed provenance of the one on Hochstraaten's desk? The CIA? The Israeli secret police? And what would I tell them? 'I have reason to believe that someone I know has a painting that was stolen from a Jewish art dealer . . .' The very idea was preposterous; surely some form of hard evidence would be required. Could there be a list of paintings appropriated from Heinrich Blumenstein's collection somewhere?

Suddenly an image flashed through my mind, of the room that had been added on at the back of Hochstraaten's house, with its skylights and windows placed high in the wall. An extra plant room, for more of his 'family'? Not bloody likely.

There were no two ways about it, I had more snooping to do. When or how that would happen, I had no idea.

Chapter 15

Following Con and Comp on Monday I sat in my office, pissed off that Jason Miller had not been in class. Was this going to become a pattern? It looked like I would have to play the scolding teacher again, something I hated to do. I would wait and see if he showed up on Wednesday and take it from there.

There was a knock on my door. It was Moira, who had been lacking in her usual enthusiasm on the previous Friday and today had seemed even sullen. Had there been repercussions from the breakup with her boyfriend?

"Sorry," she said, "I know I haven't been up to snuff in class lately."

"Well . . . your energy has certainly seemed lower than usual."

She frowned. "It's because of my photography show. The opening is this Friday, so I have to mount it on Thursday. I've been working pretty much night and day on it. I never thought it would take this long to winnow four-hundred-odd photos down to forty."

I shook my head. "Sounds like a monumental task to me. I'm really looking forward to the final product."

She smiled. "Thanks, we'll see how it turns out. Better get back to it now."

"Okay. See you Wednesday?"

"Right, see you then."

Once Moira had left, I closed my door and pulled Luke's pages with the poem out of the drawer where I had stashed them. Of the several interconnected problems I had to solve, the most immediate was to find the elusive 'little angel.' That had been one of the definitions in the *Times* puzzle I had been working on over breakfast, and I had laughed out loud as I filled in the presumed answer, 'cherub.' Had to be an omen, right? Or more likely the crossword demon laughing up his sleeve at me.

The hitch, of course, was still that damned halo. If I could find a Dürer angel that had one, it would presumably lead to the ladder, and that in turn to the 'little maid.' I wished I could check the Dürers in the museum, but I wouldn't have time until after my Beginning German class. For now, I would type out a copy of the poem on my computer—there was no way in hell I was going to take the original out to the scanner in the anteroom; if Klaus was in his office, he could appear at any moment. Feeling more than a little paranoid, I typed the poem out and hit the Print button.

Suddenly my office phone rang. Shit, what great timing.

The caller was one of my overly conscientious students. She'd been having stomach cramps all morning and had tried to reach me several times to tell me she wouldn't be in class today, blah blah blah.

"Sorry I missed your call, Heather," I interrupted.

I heard a floorboard creak out in the anteroom.

"Look, stuff happens," I said, staring at my office door. "There's nothing for you to worry about—you're doing fine in the course. If you like, you can come by tomorrow and we can go over what we cover this afternoon. Take it easy and get well soon, okay?"

I hung up, walked quickly to the door, and opened it as quietly as I could. Composing myself, I stepped out into the anteroom. Hochstraaten turned abruptly away from the printer with a sheet of paper in his hand; apparently we had been running things off almost simultaneously. He nodded curtly, then limped back to his office and closed the door behind him.

Swearing under my breath, I slowly walked over to the printer. The poem lay there in the tray, printed out in fourteen-point Times New Roman—a font style and size anyone could read a mile away. Damn, why hadn't I used my usual twelve-point? But that could be read easily enough at a distance, too. Whose sheet of paper had come out first, Hochstraaten's or mine? Not that it mattered that much—he had to have seen the poem either way. Had he read it? Or had he treated it with the customary disdain he accorded other people's work and simply ignored it? I picked the sheet out of the tray and went back into my office. After brooding for a few moments, I left the building to have lunch at home.

Turning onto Faculty Row, I caught sight of someone dressed in black trotting up my driveway four houses away. Whoever it was rang the doorbell, waited for a moment, then tried the front door handle. What the hell was going on? As I broke into a trot, whoever it was looked over his shoulder and rushed around the far side of the house. Was it Jason? Had he decided to stop by to offer some sort of excuse? No way, that would have been completely out of character.

I ran all the way around the house, but the apparent intruder had to have escaped into the woods. Inside, I double-checked the lock on the kitchen door. I would talk to Jason for sure if he showed up for class next time. But it might not have been Jason at all. It probably would be best to let this sleeping dog lie.

"How do, Professor Ritter," Bobby said as I stepped into the museum that afternoon after my Beginning German class.

"Hello, I'm back for more." I noticed with dismay that there were several other visitors, mostly students, in the room.

"Well, it's allus a pleasure to see you here," Bobby said.

"Thanks. It's always a treat to be here."

Crossing over to the fireplace, I stood in front of the *St. Eustace* and pretended to study the foreground details. A moment later I walked on to my right, past several saints and Madonnas, none of which, predictably, had halos. At the corner where the *Knight, Death, and Devil* had once hung I came to the *St. Jerome* and the *Melencolia*.

The *St. Jerome* was one of my favorite Dürers, possibly my very favorite. I could think of no other black-and-white piece, by this or any other artist, in which the quality of light was used so effectively. The wall recesses next to the windows reflected the brilliant rays of the sun as they passed through the individual panes, while the objects in the room cast shadows of varying intensity. Could a little angel possibly be crouching in the relative darkness near Jerome's feet, offering him encouragement for his Bible translation? I scoured this area and every other section of the print and found nothing. It had been a silly idea to begin with; surely the small crucifix standing in front of the saint's writing desk would have supplied him with all the inspiration he needed.

I barely glanced at the *Melencolia* as I walked past, since it was not a manifestly religious piece. Wait a sec, I said to myself—the engraving did contain two angel-like figures . . .

My gaze was drawn almost magnetically to the small winged boy who sat on a millstone writing on his tablet. A ladder leaned against a wall behind this little angel, and directly above his head the basin of an apothecary's scale seen at an angle looked for all the world like a halo.

"That devil of a trickster," I whispered.

Glancing over my shoulder, I saw that the other museum visitors were all at the far end of the room. I slipped my copy of Baumgartner's poem out of my jacket pocket and read through the first four stanzas.

> Sitting in a night of light,
> a little angel, halo gleaming;
> he seems to be about to write
> or is mayhap he only dreaming?
>
> Were he to do as I advise
> and look about, his eyes new-seeing
> would spy a ladder, and he'd rise
> to reach a state of higher being.
>
> Anon he'd see a little maid,
> who points quite clearly toward the goal;
> but how she does this, I'm afraid,
> is not, perhaps, so clear at all!

The angel's eyes are falling shut,
'tis <u>you</u> must climb, then, in his stead;
seek one and two to crack the nut,
then look afar from head to head.

All the images in the first two stanzas fit: the little angel who appeared to be writing, the 'night of light' resulting from the comet in the background, and the ladder behind the angel. The reference at the beginning of the fourth stanza to the angel's eyes falling shut seemed reasonable, too, whether or not it had been Dürer's intention.

The rest of the poem, though, was still a puzzle. Could the numbers one and two refer to the magic square, or to the tiny numbers on the sundial just above the hourglass? Neither of these possibilities seemed to lead anywhere. There was also the Roman numeral I in the engraving's title on the wings of a bat-like creature. But of what help to me was the 'I' without a 'II'?

Most aggravating of all was the reference in the third stanza to the 'little maid who points quite clearly.' The only thing that *was* clear was that she wasn't anywhere in the engraving.

The first item of business, then, would be to figure out that reference. If the angel climbed the ladder—the one in the engraving—he would find her, so the poem said. But the ladder's topmost section wasn't visible. Where would it lead, if it were possible to extend it upwards? To a 'state of higher being,' according to the poem. Was that phrase really a reference to heaven, as I had initially surmised? If so, the 'climbing' obviously could only be meant figuratively and had no value as a clue. This didn't seem likely, since up to that point everything in the first two stanzas had been firmly rooted in the physical world. But what—or where—could this 'state of higher being' be?

Making a show of massaging my neck muscles and stretching my arms, I stepped back from the *Melencolia* and looked up to where the ladder might reach if it continued beyond the picture frame. All I could see was the cream-colored wall, the off-white ceiling, and the narrow oak cornice that ran around the entire room. This ladder seemed to lead . . . absolutely nowhere.

Concerned that someone might have noticed me lingering too long in front of the *Melencolia*, I began walking to the opposite side of the room, where the *Apocalypse* woodcuts were hung. As I glanced toward the door, I caught sight of Jason Miller quickly turning his head away before hurrying out into the corridor. Had he been there the whole time? Snooping around my house earlier that afternoon, if in fact it had been him, and now here. What was he up to? Disquieted, I headed for the exit, barely noticing Bobby as I walked past his chair.

"'Bye, Professor Ritter, come back now."

I looked around with a start.

"Oh—sorry. My mind was a million miles away."

"No problem a tall, I know you professors is allus off somewhere else, thinkin' great thoughts." He smiled at me.

I shook my head and smiled back. Great thoughts, I said to myself. When did I last have a great thought? I certainly had none as I crossed over the moat and headed for home, nor later that afternoon and evening as I sat at my desk poring over the *Melencolia* in one of my Dürer volumes in the hope of noticing something I hadn't before.

There was no question about it: I needed a change of pace. Luke Baumgartner's third volume, *Visions*, lay within easy reach at the back of the desk; since I couldn't come up with a vision of my own, I would check his out.

Soon I was immersed in an aspect of Luke's world that was, quite literally, out of this world.

Chapter 16

Castle Arcadia, New Year's Day 1900
My hand trembles as I write. God has granted me a great boon,
though I do not yet know its import: he has appeared to me in a vision.
The transition from the old year to the new was devoid of signif-
icance for me, as it has been for the last several years. Indeed, what can
yet another new year mean to a man of almost sixty-six who has lost his
beloved wife and the greater part of his family and friends?
Such were my self-pitying thoughts during most of this day.
Following supper, I went as usual to my little chapel for my evening
prayers. Yet I was little comforted by them.
Darkness having long since fallen, I stepped outside and
breathed in deep draughts of the crisp, invigorating air. Despite the
coldness of the evening I determined to take a turn around the moat.
When I had reached the half-way point, I paused for a moment's rest.
Looking up into the clear sky above, I had begun to marvel at the beauty
of God's starry canopy, when all at once I was engulfed by the blackest
blackness I have ever experienced. The stars, the castle, the surrounding
woods – all had vanished. I sank to my knees and cried out, "Hilf mir,
lieber Gott!" No sooner had my prayer been spoken than a new light
shone all around me, a light brighter than the brightest daylight. My
castle now stood on a distant rocky peak. Off to one side I saw several
trees, and at first only these. As I looked more intently, however, I de-
tected something moving; to my astonishment, a majestic stag stepped
forth, himself bathed in light. As he approached me I saw that, like St.
Eustace's stag, he bore a crucifix between his antlers, and there the light
was at its most brilliant. He stopped a short distance away and gazed
at me. I was dumbstruck. He had the kindest, gentlest face I think I have
ever seen. Slowly the image began to fade and then disappeared entire-
ly.
I found myself lying on the gravel path looking up at the stars,
which shone as brightly as before; one star in particular seemed to beam
forth miraculously with nine points of light. I felt drained of energy, and
it was only with great effort that I collected myself and made my way
back to the castle. I climbed the many stairs to my rooms with the help
of my servant and, once there, fell into bed and slept for an hour, after
which I felt refreshed enough to rise again and put pen to paper.
My only fear is that my experience of this evening was nothing

more than *"ein eitel teuflisch Blendwerk"* – a vain work of the Devil, who seeks to ensnare us in the most devious ways possible. I only pray that this may not be so.

Castle Arcadia, 2 January 1900

Today was spent in reading Holy Scripture and in contemplation, which gave me a great feeling of peace. In the evening I undertook the same walk as I had yesterday, and stood again looking up at the sky from the same vantage-point. The heavens, however, were overcast and revealed not the least pinpoint of light. A few drops of rain began to fall, and I walked briskly back to the shelter of my castle. I must wait now, and see what the morrow brings.

Castle Arcadia, 3 January 1900

The Lord be praised! He, or his emissary, appeared to me again this evening. The clouds and light rain of this morning had begun to dissipate by early afternoon, and the evening sky was resplendent with stars again. Repeating my practice of the two previous days, I set out around the moat after having said my prayers. At the same point along the path I looked up at the starry heavens as before, and once again I was transported to the land of my first vision. It was as if the same play were being reenacted: the stag stepped forth, surrounded by his aura of brilliant light. All at once he began to move his mouth as if he wanted to speak but could not. I looked at him imploringly for some time until his image grew dim, as it had on the previous occasion, and I was again left staring up at the stars.

What, I asked myself, did the stag want to tell me? But I could find no answer.

Castle Arcadia, 4 January 1900

Upon rising this morning, I immediately experienced a sense of incompleteness, which continued throughout the morning. Would I be granted yet another vision? If so, when? I felt impatient – how was I to know what to do without some instruction from God's messenger?

As I thought these discontented thoughts, I became aware that the sky was beginning to darken. Soon it began to rain. It rained as I have never seen it rain before, until two hours later the moat had climbed over its banks and reached the path, rendering it impassable. I began to pray fervently, and soon thereafter the deluge began to subside. The sky has remained overcast throughout the evening, however, and I have not ventured out. I will go to bed now, and take my Bible along to comfort me.

Castle Arcadia, 5 January 1900
I glow with the radiance of God's spirit. My beloved stag has made yet another appearance before me and left me with a message which I can only describe as divinely irrational. Yet, on the chance that I have fathomed its meaning, I will do all that is in my power to heed it.

This evening I beheld once again the same miraculous scene in all its splendor. Again my castle stood on a far-off rocky slope, and again the stag appeared and gazed at me in silence. Then, a moment later, his warm, brown eyes took on an admonishing glow, as if he were telling me: it is you who must speak. I understood this well enough, but what does one say to a deer, especially one sent from God?

I stood there at a loss, watching the beast's gaze become more insistent and impatient, when suddenly a poem from my distant childhood, an incantation of sorts, proceeded to issue from my mouth:

> *Edler Hirsch,*
> *Sei nicht unwirsch;*
> *Liebes Tier,*
> *O sprich zu mir!*

At this, the radiance around the animal's head grew more and more intense. He seemed to nod to me, and then looked toward the castle. Suddenly the mountainside supporting it came crashing down, leaving it standing, as it does today, surrounded by the moat. Beams of light, nine in number, began to emanate from the castle in all directions, each creating a beautiful building out of the remaining formless rock. It was as if the New Jerusalem were coming into being before my very eyes. And out of nowhere throngs of people came streaming toward these resplendent buildings.

As I stood awe-struck, not knowing what all this could mean, a bat-like creature came soaring across the sky, on whose outspread wings were emblazoned the words: LUX HOMINIBUS. The stag gazed at me again and nodded his head as if in approval, and the scene vanished.

I went back to my rooms and pondered at length what I had seen. "Light to mankind." How was I to make sense of this proclamation? Of what significance was it that my castle had stood amidst so many other splendid buildings? Then it came to me in a flash: I was to bring this light! Luke was to bring Lux – of course! And the buildings that had sprung up – they were not the New Jerusalem, they were the buildings in which this light was to be radiated, in which learning was to take place: they were the buildings of the college I was to found.

This, then, was the great project which I had so longed for. I have an enormous task before me. I will begin immediately.

Castle Arcadia, 15 January 1900
Today I met with three respected business associates whom I know well from my years with the railroad in Louisville and from my church attendance in that city. They are Mr. Simmel, Mr. Hoffmann and Mr. Renner, all upright citizens and willing to assist in this grand undertaking. I will prepare a letter, to be sent to the General Assembly of the Commonwealth of Kentucky, in which we will state our desire to establish a college in what is quite a remote part of the state. My colleagues and I are agreed that applicants of any and all religious affiliations will be welcome, and that our college will turn away no potential student because of financial distress. I daresay that these principles, as well as the signatures of four businessmen of considerable stature, will make a favorable impression on our esteemed legislators.

Castle Arcadia, 3 March 1900
My activities of the past several weeks have occupied me to such an extent that I have neglected my diary-writing. I will try to fill in this hiatus now.

In my letter to the General Assembly, I did not, of course, mention the visions that I had had, for fear of being taken for a raving madman, though I did use the word 'vision' a time or two in an effort to convey my hopes and wishes for our future institution. In this same context, I was also concerned lest my castle be regarded as a mere folly, such as those built by many of my English contemporaries on their estates. My explanation, however, as to how the castle would become part of the very fabric of the college, was apparently enough to reassure the Assembly members.

Be that as it may, my letter occasioned a flurry of questions, concerning the precise nature of the education we hoped to impart, our method of seeking teachers and students, the size and membership of our proposed governing body, and many others too numerous to mention. I trust that my three colleagues and I have in the meantime responded satisfactorily to these queries. In the end, it may be that money will have spoken with the loudest voice, as we have made it clear that we have more than sufficient means to endow the planned institution and, further, that I myself will provide the necessary land. I am most hopeful now that the Assembly as a whole will approve our project. I wait with bated breath for word from the capitol.

Castle Arcadia, 19 March 1900
I need but few words to express my pleasure. A message arrived

yesterday, informing me that the General Assembly has granted our charter as requested. I will leave for town as soon as possible to have our constitution recorded at the office of the County Clerk.

Now the physical labour must begin. For want of adequate space, we will enroll no more than a dozen students for the coming academic year, all of whom will pursue the same curriculum. The construction of our first building will begin this spring, and will serve to house everyone and everything during our first year: quarters for the students and faculty, classrooms, record-keeping and dining facilities, and whatever we are able to put together by way of a library. At the same time, the Great Hall of my castle will be transformed, through the addition of pews and the replacement of the plain-glass clerestory windows with stained glass, into a place of worship for the student body and faculty.

Thereafter, we plan to erect one additional building per year for the following eight years, and dormitories as needed. With the exception of the planned library, which will be named after my revered Lessing, each building will bear the name of a town or city in, or near, my beloved Frankenland. The result will be a circle of structures, a miniature realm of sorts, free of partisan strife and in a bucolic setting conducive to learning.

I foresee that I will most likely neglect my diary over the next several years, due to my occupation with the planning and execution of the buildings, interviewing appropriate teaching candidates, etc. I will, however, at the very least, commemorate every milestone along the way with a few words.

Castle Arcadia, 7 August 1900

Upon the present completion of Eichstätt Hall, with its slightly rounded façade reminiscent of the Cobenzl Schlößchen there, I look forward with confidence to the ultimate completion of our great project. We must rush now to make sure that all will be ready come September to welcome our very first academic class, minuscule though it may be, as the new century begins!

Castle Arcadia, 30 August 1901

Another new building for our budding century: Oettingen Hall, in the southwestern quadrant of our future campus, stands complete, and a handsome edifice it is – in Tennessee pink marble, which will be the construction material for all of our buildings. The planned conversion of my Great Hall into a place of worship, however, will not be completed until the following summer, yet in time for our few students, many of whom will begin their third year of study.

Castle Arcadia, 15 August 1902

The double dedication of Rothenburg Hall and of the recently finished student chapel in the castle's center took place on a wondrously beautiful day. Clement weather beginning in early spring has helped to secure these two monumental achievements.

Castle Arcadia, 24 August 1903

I have welcomed many friends from Louisville to come on the morrow to witness the laying of the capstone of Kitzingen Hall, fashioned after a modest side wing of the otherwise lavishly decorated Luitpoldbad in that city. I expect a great crowd of enthusiasts!

Castle Arcadia, 2 September 1904

Bamberg Hall now stands ready for occupancy – a building which is meant to emulate the fortitude, and to some small degree the form, of that city's Altes Rathaus.

Castle Arcadia, 18 September 1905

I find it necessary to make clear on this the founding day of Bayreuth Hall that the building is not meant to reflect on the pompous Richard Wagner, but on the Markgraf Friedrich – a peaceable man and one tolerant of all religions..

Castle Arcadia, 23 November 1906

The completion of Weiden Hall has taken longer than initially planned, since it was ultimately deemed necessary to modify the original plan in order to accommodate the various studios of painting, sculpture, etc. which it will eventually house. It is thus, and will likely remain, the sole L-shaped structure on our campus.

Castle Arcadia, 19 December 1907

This newly completed building, the pièce de résistance of our campus with its pleasant courtyard and fountain, will be, as I have previously indicated, the only one named for an individual rather than a city. The individual in question is Gotthold Ephraim Lessing, the brilliant writer and champion of religious tolerance. As the future library of our college, the building will also be the largest and hence has taken longer than envisioned to construct.

Castle Arcadia, 9 September 1908

Riedenburg Hall now stands, as the last building of our new campus. As we now set about to establish fixed scholarly determinations for each building, it has been decided that it will house foreign languages – Greek and Latin, for those of a classical or ecclesiastical bent, German and French for those whose penchant is toward a language of more "practical" use. Two years' study of one of these languages will be required of every student.

We express our boundless gratitude to the architects and laborers who have achieved the completion of the campus of our St. Eustace College! With the official dedication on Sunday next, the circle, in the words of Miss Habershon's moving Gospel song, will indeed be unbroken.

Castle Arcadia, 24 September 1908

I will travel to Cincinnati in the coming week, accompanied by my good friend and personal physician Dr. J. Earl Davies, for the purpose of visiting a foundry there which will see to the manufacture of a certain item – one considerably smaller than anything built on our campus these past several years, but which will one day serve well, it is to be hoped, in its intended function. When this item is in place, my one remaining task, about which I have not written in these pages, will soon be nearing completion. When that day arrives, I will be ready to depart this earth; surely three-quarters of a century is a sufficient span of life for any man. I look forward to joining my beloved Catharine in the hereafter. That circle, too, will then be unbroken.

Castle Arcadia, 26 October 1908

This afternoon I received the sad news of the passing of my brother Stefan, who soon would have attained his seventy-second birthday. He died peacefully in his sleep; for that at least I can be grateful. Stefan never married, and so left this world childless, and me without a living relative. May you have gone to a better place, my dear brother; indeed, I trust that you have. Now, more than ever, I sense that my own will to live is gradually slipping away.

Castle Arcadia, 18 November 1908

Twilight has come, and with it the conclusion of my diaries. I offer the fervent wish that those who read these volumes may discover something about themselves; certainly we can all learn from the study of other men's lives.

I wish also that one fine day there may happen along an uncommonly clever reader who, by discerning the true significance of my last words, seven in number, and by following the number three, may ultimately be led to a certain objet d'art of inestimable value.

One small hint (or two): the appropriate turn of mind and literary interests of the seeker may well prove helpful in the search.

What mystery may our great God
hold hidden where his books are stored,
reveal to one who finds that place
where pen is mightier than sword?

Such person, if I might advise,
may speed the pathway to success
by altering one certain word
to smooth my grammar's awkwardness.

So now, o sleuth, use well your time,
and fashion reason out of rhyme.

Chapter 17

Bobby was settled in at his usual post as I stepped into the museum late Tuesday afternoon. I had finished the final volume of Luke's diaries the previous evening and was still wondering about the mysterious apparatus that a foundry in Cincinnati had apparently made for him shortly before his death. From what he had said, this was connected to the "one remaining task" that he had mentioned equally vaguely. But all that was irrelevant at the moment. What I had to do now was figure out where that damn ladder went.

"How do, Professor Ritter," Bobby said, looking up from his paperback. "Kinda humid today, init."

"Yes, it is. I think there's some rain on the way." I glanced around, pleased to see that no one else was in the room today.

"Seems you cain't get enough of this place, now can you."

"I guess not, Bobby. These prints have a freshness for me every time."

"Well, I have to agree with y' there. I allus say, great art may *be* old, but it never *gits* old. Even for me, who don't have any book-learnin' to speak of. Why, I walk around here lookin' at these pitchers ever' day, and ever' time I see somethin' new in 'em."

I nodded. "I know exactly what you mean, that happens to me quite often too." And I hope to God it happens today, I said to myself.

Deciding not to put on any needless show this time, I walked straight to the *Melencolia* in the far right-hand corner of the room and took the poem out of my pocket. Oh, little angel, I said to myself, if only you'd climb up that ladder and tell me where the hell it leads! But you're not going to, are you, because that would mean I was having a vision and going loony. I continued to stare at the engraving without seeing anything new.

"Now that un's the biggest puzzler of 'em all, init," Bobby called over from his seat at the door.

"That's for sure," I said, alternately looking at the engraving and the poem. Bobby was a veritable font of wisdom today, though for the moment I wished that he would keep his comments to himself so that I could concentrate. But he had nothing further to add in any case.

In the ensuing silence, it suddenly seemed to me as if a distant voice were telling me: look at the fourth stanza, it's right there. *The angel's eyes are falling shut, / 'tis you must climb, then, in his stead.* If I, as the seeker, was supposed to take the place of the angel, the earlier admonition had to apply to me as well: *Were he to . . . look about, his eyes . . . would spy a ladder . . .* Slowly I glanced around the room. Ladder? There was no lad—

I stared past Bobby, who was still gazing absently in my direction. Beyond the open door, directly in my line of vision, a metal ladder ran up the wall on the far side of the corridor.

"You all right, Professor Ritter? Look like you seed a ghost."

I was speechless for a few seconds. "No—no, I'm fine, Bobby. I just . . . thought of something I have to do. I'll be back another time." I hurried toward the exit.

"All righty. Have a nice afternoon." Bobby went back to his detective novel.

Outside in the corridor, I lingered next to the ladder. I had walked by there dozens of times without ever noticing it. But why would I have? Nothing but an unobtrusive, functional ladder, painted the same color as the wall and leading to a trap door in the ceiling. And beyond that, the roof of the castle, and . . . of course! I grabbed hold of the ladder's side rails just as two students came in through the Rapunzel tower. One of them gave me a funny look, then walked on by with his companion. A moment later Bobby stepped out into the corridor, stretching and yawning. When he saw me he did a double take.

"You sure you're okay, now?" he said. "Looks like you're hangin' onto that ladder for dear life."

"Oh, no," I stammered, looking up at the ceiling. "I just happened to notice it, and I was kind of wondering . . . well, there's that little statue of a dwarf up on the roof, and I've always wanted to have a closer look at it."

"Oh, yeah, she's a little cutie, all right. Not that I've ever seed her up close or anythin'. This here ladder won't take you there, though. That trap door been sealed up for Lord knows how many years. There's a stairway leads up to the roof over in the bell tower on t'other side, though. You'd need to get Ned to let you up there, 'cause it's kept locked. Don't want any students prowlin' around up there or nothin'."

Bobby looked at his watch. "Ned should still be here," he added, "he doesn't gen'rally leave till after four, so's he can git all the blackboards warshed after the last class lets out. And then he's back in the mornin', bright and early, to make sure the floors is all lookin' good. Conscientious feller, that Ned."

"That he is. Thanks, Bobby, I'll see if I can track him down."

I found Ned in the main chapel, wiping the marble altar table with a rag. This was the first time I had seen him since the jazz evening in

Bamberg Hall.

"Hello, Ned," I called out.

Ned looked up and smiled slightly.

"More drawin'?"

"Probably," I laughed, "if I can get up on the roof. But first I wanted to thank you for your part in the jazz concert last week. I thought you were great. You've got a wonderful tone."

Ned leaned against the altar table, three steps above me. He looked skeptical.

"It still needs workin' on."

"I don't know—if I could play like that, I'd be doing it professionally."

"Well, I did have a gig or two back in St. Louis."

"Is that where you're from, St. Louis?"

"Yeah, grew up there. Played in clubs whenever I could."

"So what brought you here?"

"A woman." He shrugged and looked off into the distance. I wasn't sure if the message was that this was a trivial matter, or that it was none of my business. Either way, Ned didn't seem to want to elaborate.

"You must've played with those students before," I said. "You worked so well together."

"Yeah, once last spring. They're good kids—I like playin' with 'em." Ned climbed down the altar steps. "What'd you say about goin' up on the roof?"

"Well . . . it seems ridiculously frivolous . . . you know that statue of the little dwarf-girl up there? The one who's waving her arms—"

Ned looked amused. "I know her, all right. I know her real good. I was up there for a week last summer helpin' to tar the roof. What about her?"

"Well . . . I'd like to examine her up close. Maybe make a drawing. I've done some of the other dwarfs already. I hear there's a stairway to the roof on the other side of the building."

Ned started to grin. "You want to have a look at a little stone girl. Sure, why not? Just gotta unlock the door."

He dried his hands on his shirt and we walked through the front tower to the corridor on the opposite side.

"I know it sounds crazy," I said. "It's just that I've gotten kind of hooked on the guy who founded the college. Which is why I've been investigating his various creations on campus, including all these little statues he carved."

Ned looked over his shoulder and smiled. "Oh yeah, uh-huh." I wasn't sure if he believed me or not.

A moment later we were standing in the bell tower at the rear of the building. A single bell hung high above us, and a metal staircase led to a small landing and a door next to it. Ned took the stairs two at a time and unlocked the door, then leaned on it with his shoulder till it opened.

"Just pull it shut when you leave, it locks automatically," he said as he came down. "But only from this side. Don't worry, you won't get trapped up there."

"Okay. Thanks for helping me out again."

I climbed the staircase and stepped out onto the roof. Directly ahead, the Rapunzel tower soared up for another twenty feet or so. Standing at its base, I looked up toward Luke Baumgartner's apartment. What a lonely life the man must have led. And for how many years had it been? Something like twenty-five. Enough to drive anyone to distraction.

Continuing across the roof, I avoided puddles of water here and there; apparently it had rained briefly while I was in the museum. The sun beat down on me from time to time as it moved in and out of dark clouds. Just past the tower, the private chapel's slate roof covered its clerestory windows at the height of my shoulders. A few steps farther on I noticed the tarred-over outline of a trap door, and suddenly there was the dwarf girl's rear end protruding from between the battlements.

Baumgartner had placed his "little maid" in such a way as to make it look as though she had just stepped up into one of the embrasures in the crenelated wall. Even from close up she appeared to be looking directly at the dwarf-culprit who was doing his business among the rose bushes; Luke had carried out his tomfoolery with characteristic precision. The girl's arms were raised, the right one higher than the left, in an expression of seeming outrage.

I reached into my jacket pocket and pulled out Luke's poem. Leaning against the wall next to the statue, I studied the third and fourth stanzas again:

> Anon he'd see a little maid,
> who points quite clearly toward the goal;
> but <u>how</u> she does this, I'm afraid,
> is not, perhaps, so clear at all!
>
> The angel's eyes are falling shut,
> 'tis <u>you</u> must climb, then, in his stead;
> seek one and two to crack the nut,
> then look afar from head to head.

This much was clear: since the angel was too tired, I, as the seeker, was to climb up to the roof—the "state of higher being" in stanza two (rotten joke, Luke, really rotten!), and there I would find the little maid. Fine, I had done that. But the phrase about the girl pointing toward the goal was, as the poem itself indicated, anything but clear. Stepping back,

I looked at the statue again. Damn, she wasn't pointing at all, except maybe up at the sky! Was that where the next clue was, somewhere in the clouds? That, of course, made no sense. What I apparently had to do was figure out the *manner* in which she was pointing. This, then, seemed to be the nut I had to crack. And to do this, I had to find "one and two," whatever that meant.

I studied the girl's gestures more carefully. She was holding her right hand slightly above her head, with only the index finger raised . . . *one*. The palm of the left hand, at about chest height, was turned inward, and the last three fingers were curled inside, leaving only the thumb and index finger extended, much as little boys do when forming their hand into a pistol . . . *two*.

I was getting excited. Was it in fact a pistol, or did the girl seem to be pulling back on an imaginary slingshot with her other hand? What would happen if I sighted along a straight line from the tip of the index finger of her right hand to the "V" formed by the two raised fingers of her left. . . . I climbed up into the next gap in the parapet to get a better angle, then lined up the fingers as if they were gun sights.

Good God in heaven, I said in a whisper, then checked again to make sure I wasn't fooling myself.

I wasn't. Sighting along the make-believe gun barrel, my line of vision led across the moat, past the bushes beyond the Promenade—to the Garden of Time, where it struck the life-size statue square in the face. *Look afar from head to head,* the poem instructed me, and the following stanza began: *And next, sir, you must tell the time!* The Garden of Time, I said to myself, is where the next step will be.

As I stood staring out over the parapet, my eyes focused on a figure sitting on a bench just beyond the moat. Partially obscured by a large black umbrella, he (or she?) seemed to be looking up in my direction. But maybe I was imagining it. If anyone happened to ask later what I'd been doing on the castle roof, I'd repeat the story I had told Ned.

The wind had picked up and it had started to rain again; the contours of the Garden of Time were already beginning to grow unclear. A visit there would have to wait until the weather took a turn for the better. I had done all I needed to with the 'little maid' and felt satisfied. As I began to walk back toward the bell tower, I glanced across the moat again. The figure with the black umbrella had vanished.

Chapter 18

The weather wasn't much better on the following morning, but, impatient to find out what my discovery on the castle roof might lead to, I walked to the Garden of Time in the steady spitting rain. On the plus side, there were few students out and about. I ducked in under the dripping latticework entrance and went through the rigmarole of opening the gate at the end of the arbor. Faced with the maze, I found the right path after one false start and a moment later I was standing inside the circle of broken columns.

The angel looked even sadder on this gloomy day. Water dripped from her veil as if it were saturated with tears. Standing on her pedestal, I looked toward the castle as I had done the first time I was there. But today I saw something I hadn't noticed before, simply because I hadn't been looking for it: the gesticulating dwarf on the castle roof, tiny in the distance.

Climbing back down from the pedestal, I pulled out my copy of the poem. By now I had it virtually memorized, but I still found it easier to refer to the printed text. Only the final two stanzas remained to be solved.

> And next, sir, you must tell the time!
> Is't one, is't two, or three, or four?
> Be led by stony pantomime
> and there will be but one step more.
>
> Time stands not still, as well we know;
> the hour at hand must therefore turn,
> advancing in its clockwise flow;
> this hour, my friend, is your concern.

It was clear enough: the twelve columns represented the hours of a clock, and just now I noticed that small stones embedded in the ground before each one bore Roman numerals from I to XII. It was up to me to determine which one held the key to the next step. Was Luke trying to be helpful in his poem by limiting the choice to four? Or was that just his shorthand for saying that it could have been any of the twelve? Was his earlier suggestion to 'follow the three' still in effect? That possibility made most sense to me, but it was little more than an educated guess.

Apparently 'stony pantomime' would give me the answer. I walked around the circle and examined the few fragments of the frieze to see if there might be any indication there. But I could find no half-hidden arrows, or pointing fingers or whatever. It seemed that the only source of anything like a pantomime was the angel-figure herself.

I climbed up on the pedestal and stood behind her. Her left arm, the one that held the inverted torch, hung by her side, and her veiled face looked down as well. Her slightly bent right arm projected outward and appeared to point in the general direction of the third column, a fragment about two feet tall. What choice did I have but to go with that?

The poem's last stanza started out as what looked to be a simple homily on the transitoriness of existence, but it had to have another dimension for me as the seeker. I stood next to the broken column, trying to get my thoughts straight. *Time stands not still . . . the hour at hand must therefore turn . . .* yes, figuratively—and also literally? Was I supposed to twist the column to loosen it? And in which direction? *Advancing in its clockwise flow*—could it be that simple?

Suddenly there was a loud crack of thunder and the skies opened up. I grabbed my umbrella out of my briefcase and opened it. A message from the gods, maybe, saying: this is not your day yet, be patient.

I trotted toward the maze and was halfway through it when I heard the dull thud of the wooden gate ahead of me falling shut. Who could be coming here now? I would greet whoever it was as casually as possible and make some comment or other about the weather. Anyone interested in visiting the garden on a day like this wasn't likely to wonder what anyone else was doing there.

As I turned the last corner of the maze it occurred to me: the sound I had heard could just as well have been made by someone *leaving* the garden! Rushing up to the gate, I pulled it open and caught sight of a pair of black-clad legs rounding the corner at the far end of the arbor. I struggled with the umbrella as I hurried along under the vines, swearing the whole time. Out on the path, I almost crashed into two women students as they ran past. No one else was in sight.

On Friday morning the rain was coming down steadily again as I sprinted to Riedenburg Hall for my Con and Comp class. Moira seemed relaxed and enthusiastic. After class she gave me the thumbs-up once the other students had filed out of the room.

"I assume that means things have been going well?"

"They really have. Mounting the show took a while, but I feel confident about it."

"Good. I have lots of news to tell you, too, but it might as well wait till the weather improves."

She gave me a puzzled look. "Hmm. Can't wait to hear what the weather has to do with it."

"All we need is a little bit of sun. Or a lot would be even better. So the opening's at four?"

"That's right. There's two other guys and me exhibiting, and we each have to give a brief talk first. There'll be lots of snacks and stuff, so come with an appetite."

By late afternoon the sky was showing some signs of clearing. The college's brief fall break would begin on the weekend and run through the following Tuesday; some of the students would be leaving campus, but I doubted that the ones who stayed would be likely to spend their few days of freedom hanging out in the Garden of Time. If only the weather would cooperate. . . .

As I walked up the front steps to Weiden Hall, I saw Pastor Roland approaching on the path from the castle. I waited for him and shook his hand.

"I fancy we have the same goal in mind?" the pastor said.

"I wouldn't be surprised. One of my students has her Senior opening today."

"Ah. Since the other two in the show are male students, this can only be Moira MacGregor."

"That's right. So you know her?"

"Not personally, but I've seen her work in previous years and found it very impressive."

We walked down the hallway toward the student exhibition gallery. The pastor pointed to an orange and black poster outside the door announcing an upcoming Halloween party on Friday, October 31.

"This is always great fun," he said. "The students organize it, and they do all they can to make the gymnasium look as frightening as possible. Some of the costumes are quite wonderful. My wife and I never miss it—we're very fond of dancing, though that seems to surprise many people. Quite a few faculty attend."

I looked at the poster again. "So three weeks from now. Are costumes required?"

"Well, a mask at the very least."

"I have a costume I wore at a Fasching party once. It's stored away in my apartment in Minneapolis, but I can have my subrenters send it to me."

"I think you would enjoy the occasion," Pastor Roland said. "I can almost guarantee that the Rossis will be there, I've never known them to miss." He paused, then added with a twinkle in his eye, "You would get to see Charlotte in a strikingly different role."

I smiled. "That clinches it, then. I'll be there."

We stepped inside the gallery, where several visitors were milling about looking at the three exhibits. Dressed in a black sheath that emphasized her slender figure, Moira stood next to four horizontal sequences of photographs and appeared to be in an animated conversation with Michael and Charlotte Rossi. Somewhat closer to us I spotted renderings of Dürer engravings, but with colors added. The third exhibition consisted of a fifteen-foot plank of wood painted stark white and narrowing from about two feet at one end to a couple of inches at the other. Its surface was covered with row upon row of small markers bearing Stars of David and crescent moons. At the widest point of the board, miniature Palestinian and Israeli flags were displayed. A title placard between the flags read: "No End in Sight."

"How sad," Pastor Roland said. "But terribly brave of the student to tackle such a controversial topic."

"Yes," I said. "I'm sure whoever it was will take a fair amount of flak from people on both sides of the issue."

A bearded man I recognized as the Chair of the Art Department announced that the three presenters would now make brief introductory statements. Moira was the first to speak, followed by a swarthy student with Middle Eastern features and a third with hair dyed bright red. They talked about their main interests in the field of art and added that they hoped their exhibits would speak for themselves.

Pastor Roland and I crossed the room to Moira's exhibit, which she had called 'Communication.' Each of the four sequences contained nine or ten paired portraits showing the heads and torsos only. The quality of the photos changed gradually in their progression from left to right, from blurry at first to perfectly in focus. As the subjects slowly turned toward each other, their expressions changed, too, from dead-pan to tentatively smiling and back again to dead-pan. At the same time identifying objects began to become clear—a bookcase behind a middle-aged woman, a pizza oven next to a young man.

"It's like they're getting to know each other," I said. "But in the end they're still separated, stuck in their own individual lives."

"Yes," said Pastor Roland, "and the final sequence is especially poignant. In the last few photographs one of the two figures has simply vanished. A situation that happens all too often."

"Yes, I'm afraid that's—" I stopped in mid-sentence. "Look's like we're about to have company."

Pastor Roland turned to look. "Ah, your colleague, yes. Klaus is, as you know, quite a connoisseur of art."

"An unusual exhibition," Hochstraaten said as he came up to

us, "those colored representations of Dürer's engravings, including the *Knight, Death, and Devil* that is missing from the museum. How strange. Does the student fancy himself another Andy Warhol?" The corners of his mouth turned down at the mention of the name. "Be that as it may— has either of you formed an opinion about this . . . study in white?" He gestured toward the cemetery display.

"Oh, I'm quite impressed," Pastor Roland said. "I must say, it presents a most dramatic statement."

"Structurally, at least, it is quite well done," Hochstraaten began. "The message which the student is trying to convey, however, is much too obvious. Yes, there will be continuing wars in the future, between various parties. Does this need to be pointed out?"

Pastor Roland smiled wryly. "As is frequently the case, Klaus and I do not entirely agree in our assessment of works of art. I believe, however, that we do share a similar view concerning the paintings in his own collection. As you yourself conceded at our *Tafelrunde* meeting, Klaus, they are not quite of the first rank—"

"Nor of the second or third, to be quite frank. But I do stand to inherit my father's small collection of early Germanic paintings."

I nodded my head slowly. How about that painting by a certain Jan van Thielen, I wanted to ask, or haven't you even unrolled it yet?

"That reminds me," I said, "I have a Jewish friend in New York who collects old German paintings. I've gone through his gallery with him a time or two, but I don't think he really enjoys them for what they are, only for what they're worth. Sometimes I wonder if he even deserves to own them."

Pastor Roland pursed his lips. "I suppose it is difficult to determine exactly what one individual or the other gets out of a work of art. Perhaps your friend merely likes to talk about the value of his pieces, but really does treasure them?" He touched the arm of Hochstraaten's jacket. "In Klaus's case, of course, there is no question but that he finds only the intrinsic value of a painting important."

"I daresay this is true," Hochstraaten said. He studied my face for a moment. "Concerning your Jewish collector, of course, I have no opinion. But I believe indeed that there have been and are certain individuals who do not deserve, as you put it, to own fine works of art. The reasons for this can be many, but the most egregious are instances in which the works in question were acquired simply by being passed down from generation to generation within a family—a family which in many instances had made its fortune by underhanded means. What right does such a beneficiary have to an art collection about which he himself knows nothing and cares nothing?"

Hochstraaten's gaze darted between Pastor Roland and me, as if he was searching for confirmation.

"I'm sure you're right about that," I said. "Were you thinking of any cases in particular?"

Hochstraaten gestured dismissively. "They are too many to enumerate. Their name is Legion."

"Aha," Pastor Roland said. "And you would have them exorcised?"

"Aptly put, my dear pastor." Hochstraaten glanced around the room. "But if you will excuse me, I must examine Moira MacGregor's exhibition now."

He bowed slightly and began to walk stiffly across the room.

"He sure doesn't mince words," I said when he was out of earshot.

"Oh, no, not our Klaus. By the way, I don't believe I've heard you speak of your New York collector friend before."

"Probably not, seeing he's my imaginary friend."

"I see," the pastor said with a glimmer of a smile.

"Going back to what Klaus just said, could you refresh my memory about the 'Legion' bit? I know it's from the Bible, but I have no idea where or what the exact significance is."

"Certainly. It's from a passage in Mark, in which Jesus has just cast out demons from a possessed man. The demons tell him that their number is 'Legion.' Then they enter into a herd of swine, who rush into the sea and drown. One of the many puzzling texts in the New Testament."

"What were pigs doing there in the first place?" I asked. "I'm not exactly an authority on the New Testament, but we're still talking about the land of the Jews, aren't we?"

"A very good question. I would have to check the passage, but I believe the area where Jesus was preaching at the time was not necessarily populated by Jews. That, I think, would be the only way of accounting for the presence of pigs."

"Klaus must know that story pretty well. He picked up on your exorcism reference without missing a beat."

"Indeed he did. He is quite a scholar, you know, in diverse areas, including the Bible. I've heard him quote chapter and verse on many an occasion."

"Well, he is a confirmed Catholic, after all."

"Truer words were never spoken." A frown briefly furrowed Pastor Roland's brow, then his expression brightened again. "Well, shall we have a look at the Dürer display?"

The student artist had begun with enlarged copies of the *St. Je-*

rome, the *Melencolia*, and, as Hochstraaten had pointed out, the missing *Knight, Death, and Devil*. To each he had added touches of color: shades of yellow for the saint, brightest around his head, less intense on the heads of the lion and dog in the foreground; blue for the angel-architect in the *Melencolia* and pale green for the little writing angel; crimson for the knight and dull brown for the death and devil figures.

Pastor Roland stood scratching his chin. "I don't feel competent to comment on what the student had in mind, but I am pleased that he drew his inspiration from works in our museum—plus another that unfortunately is no longer there. Imagine, one hundred years ago the museum was still a private collection. And now it is a resource of learning for all who care to stop by. And this is how it should be, a truly public treasure. A treasure, of course, in the sense of enriching our mind and spirit."

I smiled. Slightly overblown, maybe, the way he put it, but he was absolutely right. What were museums if not public treasures?

Out of the corner of my eye I caught sight of Moira, who was standing at a respectful distance behind us.

"Hi, Moira," I said, motioning to her. She came up to us and shook Pastor Roland's hand.

"I'm Moira MacGregor—we met way back when I was a First Year, I think."

"Did we now? My memory is not what it used to be. Well, as I was telling Professor Ritter, I've been admiring your work over the years. Your last show was of watercolors, I believe, some abstract and some representational?"

Moira smiled. "That's right, in my Junior year. Nothing wrong with your memory there."

"I find your current photographic display most effective. It's difficult to combine art with a message, without being maudlin. You have succeeded admirably in that."

"Well, thank you, Pastor Roland, it's nice of you to say so."

"I wish you great success in your further studies. You'll be going to graduate school, no doubt?"

"Yes, I just got my acceptance yesterday afternoon from the Savannah College of Art and Design."

"That's wonderful, Moira," I said. "Congratulations!"

"And from me as well," Pastor Roland said. "I will have one more look at your display, and then I must be going. So much to do, even though the arrival of our fall break means that I have no sermon to prepare for this Sunday. It was a pleasure meeting you."

"Thank you, very nice to meet you too."

We watched the pastor head off toward the other side of the gallery.

"What a nice man," Moira said.

"Yes, he is. And very knowledgeable when it comes to art. He was spot-on about your show, Moira."

"Thanks, Colin," she said, blushing slightly. "You didn't think it was too negative?"

"Realistic, is what I would say. A lot of students would have shied away from portraying life the way it often is." I hesitated for a moment, then gave her a quick hug.

"You didn't tell me you were applying to graduate schools."

"No, I decided not to in case I wasn't accepted. I only applied to the one. I thought about New York or Chicago, but I was pretty sure I wanted to stay in the South."

"Well, that's great. So you'll start next fall?"

"No, this winter quarter, at the very beginning of January."

"Wow! That's what, just three months from now."

"I know, it's kind of scary. Moving away from here and all that."

"It's bound to be at first. But I'm sure you'll do fine."

I pointed over toward Pastor Roland, who was engrossed again in Moira's display. "We were talking to Klaus Hochstraaten before. How did he respond to your show?"

"Mixed. He thought the photography was good, he liked the fade-ins and fade-outs. He said I got one of the sequences right, at least. Didn't say which one, but I can guess."

I nodded. "Yeah, so can I."

Moira frowned. "What is it about Professor Hochstraaten? He gave a chapel talk a couple of years ago about art being one of the pinnacles of human achievement. But I've never seen him show anything like human warmth."

As I glanced around the gallery, Pastor Roland was just leaving and gave a cheerful wave. "What makes anyone the way they are?" I said. "What makes the pastor such an upbeat kind of guy? Is it in the genes? Or is it the way people were raised, the circumstances they grew up in? We'd have to know much more about Klaus Hochstraaten than we do to figure him out, and even then a lot would still be a mystery."

Moira nodded. "I wonder if there's anything at all in his life that he views positively—aside from art, I mean."

"Right. Art . . . and his plants. His house is full of them."

"Yes, I know. I water them for him whenever he's gone for any length of time."

"Do you really? That must take forever."

"A good hour, anyway. There's the back porch and the living room, and then there's a whole 'nother bunch in the sleeping porch upstairs and a few in his study."

"And more still in that second-story room at the back of the house?"

Moira looked puzzled. "Well, there's a spare bedroom up there that's pretty much empty, and there's a door at the end of the hallway toward the back that's always been locked when I've been there. No idea what's inside, but it can't be plants."

"No, I don't suppose so," I said, scratching my chin.

Someone called out to Moira from across the room. She turned and saw three women students approaching with big smiles on their faces.

"Looks like your fan club is about to arrive," I said.

Moira chuckled. "Yeah, they're my buds. They'd say nice things about the show even if they didn't mean it."

"I don't think you'll have to be concerned on that count. Well, I'll be heading off now. What do you have planned for the break? More photography?"

"No, I need to do somethng different for a change. Maybe some drawing."

"Sounds relaxing. By the way, as I intimated before, if the weather's nice one of these days, I'd like to do a little . . . exploring with you. In the Garden of Time."

"Exploring? So you think . . ." She glanced over her shoulder and saw that her friends were only a few feet away. "I'll be at my folks' house till Monday morning," she whispered. "Could you send me a text?"

"Sure, what's your cell? Just say it, I've got a good head for numbers."

"Mine's sort of easy anyway: 531-642-0987."

"Cool. It's like a Sudoku row plus zero."

I nodded to the students, one of whom was already giving Moira a hug. "I'll leave you to your next group of admirers."

"Okay, talk to you soon. Thanks for coming to the show!"

"My pleasure."

I looked around the gallery. Hochstraaten seemed to have left already. Too bad, Klaus, I said to myself, I had a question or two for you: would you mind telling me what's in that room at the back of your house? . . . and how about that "friend" of yours, Ronald Fleishman . . .?

Chapter 19

The rain returned during the night and continued on and off for most of Saturday and until noon on Sunday. By contrast, Monday had the look and feel of Indian summer. The local weather predicted temperatures in the 80s and light winds; after the previous day's partial sun, the ground would soon dry out. Before going downstairs I sent Moira a text: Meet at 10 by Rapunzel tower? Then to G of T.

Her reply came as my coffee was brewing: OK, will you be on time? :) —Damn, she'd noticed my tendency to be late too.

Over breakfast I worked on one of my downloaded Times crossword puzzles and was amazed at how many of the solutions I knew at first crack. Maybe the puzzle angel was hovering around in the vicinity that morning. I left the house at 9:55 on the dot according to my cell phone.

Moira was sitting on a bench immediately across from the Rapunzel tower, seemingly engrossed in a book. As I rounded the lower end of the moat carrying my briefcase, she gave me a minimal wave, but didn't look up again until I was a few feet away.

"I'm on time," I said. "In case you didn't notice."

"I noticed. Have you turned over a new leaf?"

"I'm doing my best. Am I really late all that often?"

"Pretty much. Look, if you just set your watch ahead—"

I glared at her. "The few times I ever owned a watch, I broke the crystal within a couple of days. Didn't see any future in it. I do hate being late, though. It annoys people. It annoys *me*."

"Hey, don't worry about it, there are worse character flaws." She smiled up at me. "I like your name for this tower," she said. "My momma used to read me the fairy tale when I was a little girl."

"Wish I'd thought of it myself. I heard it from Charlotte Rossi."

I sat down on the bench next to her and related my steps and missteps of the past week, from figuring out who the "little angel" and the "little maid" were, to my supposition as to which column in the Garden of Time was the right one. Next I handed her my copy of the puzzle-poem to refresh her memory.

"Crazy," she said, shaking her head. "How could he have written such a complicated poem?"

"Not much like the romantic poems he and his wife liked to read, is it. So should we get going? It'll all make more sense when you're there."

We had the campus almost to ourselves as we walked to the Garden of Time. Once we had gone through the maze, I pointed out the small numbers at the base of each column, which Moira vaguely remembered having noticed on some earlier visit. I positioned her on the pedestal behind the statue and handed her the poem again. Bending over, she ran a hand along the angel's right arm.

"Amazing, it really does look like she's pointing to the three. To say nothing of Mr. Baumgartner's fetish for the number three."

"Right, we agree on that, then. So what do you think about the last stanza, the bit about the hour turning?"

She looked down at the page and read the text aloud.

> Time stands not still, as well we know;
> the hour at hand must therefore turn,
> advancing in its clockwise flow;
> this hour, my friend, is your concern.

"'The hour at hand' must refer to the column, and it sounds like you have to turn it clockwise . . ." She stared at me intently. "Do you really think that's what you're supposed to do? It sounds so crazy."

"I know. But he did have me digging out a block of stone in the chapel to find the first clue, and if *that* didn't seem crazy at the time! Besides, what else could it mean? I was about to try moving the thing when I was here the other day, but then it started to pour. So I figured I'd leave it for a better day."

"Okay, what are we waiting for?"

"Well . . ." I glanced around the circle. "Hang on a minute, I'm just going to check out the area."

I found my way back through the maze and peered along the arbor. Seeing no one, I hurried back to the rotunda.

"Coast is clear," I said, and dropped to my knees in front of the three-o'clock column.

"You sure you can do that all right? I mean . . . your hand . . ."

"Look, Moira, my hand is fine. That was a good two weeks ago." I held it up for her to see.

"Okay," she said, shrugging.

Grasping the column as tightly as I could, I tried to twist it as if it were a giant screw with the threads reversed.

"Nothing doing. It feels like it's set in concrete."

I took a deep breath, then let it out as I tried again.

"Almost felt like it moved a tiny bit that time. Could you see anything?"

"It might have. But it might have been wishful thinking."

I took a moment's breather, then made a third attempt. A barely audible noise rose from the ground, something between a groan and a gasp, as if a corpse below had been disturbed.

"No doubt about it that time," I said.

Moira knelt down next to me. "So you're thinking it's attached to some kind of huge screw under the ground, sort of like a light bulb?"

"Yes, except you'd turn a light bulb in the opposite direction to loosen it. But that wouldn't have fit the poem—the clockwise flow of time and so on. Anyway, if that's what it is, it stands to reason it's going to be harder than hell to move a hundred years later. All I can do is keep trying."

"Maybe I can help. How about if I grab the column near the top, and you grab it lower down."

"Okay. Let's try turning it back and forth first, clockwise then counterclockwise, instead of always going in the same direction. That might help to loosen it up. On the count of three each time, clockwise first. We'll take a breath between each turn."

We positioned ourselves on either side of the stump and grabbed hold of it as tightly as we could.

"One—two—*three* . . . reverse . . . one—two—*three* . . ."

With each clockwise turn the column moved slightly farther on its axis, grating and rasping as before. After six or seven tries, there seemed to be a sudden blockage. Two more attempts proved futile; the column wouldn't budge beyond a certain point.

"How far do you think we've moved it by now, Moira?"

"A couple of inches, maybe?"

I sat back on my haunches, panting. "We might've hit a rusty spot in the threading."

"But it moved relatively easily in both directions up to that point, almost like it was oiled. Why would it suddenly stop, unless we'd hit some kind of barrier?"

I thought for a moment. "Our light bulb analogy could be wrong . . . or we might have been visualizing the wrong kind of light bulb. There's another type I've seen on my wanderings in Europe—instead of threads it has little protruding pins that fit into grooves in the socket. To get it out, you just give the bulb a partial turn and pull. Maybe what we have to do now is *lift*."

"Oh, sure, like with little automotive bulbs, for turn signals, back-up lights and so on."

"Really? I guess I've never noticed. How do you know about stuff like that?"

"Easy. My daddy's a mechanic, he has a garage in town. My momma works there, too, she keeps the books. When I was little I loved to prowl around the workshop and look at the replacement parts and all."

"No kidding? So your momma and your daddy both work there?"

"That's right, both of the two of them."

I had to smile to myself. Before moving to Kentucky I'd never heard anyone over the age of twelve refer to their parents like that. Mr. Locke did too, now that I thought of it, though I couldn't remember him ever mentioning his 'momma.'

"So what do you think, Moira—should we give it a try?"

"Like, turn and then lift?"

"Exactly. This hunk of marble is going to weigh a ton, of course."

"I'm ready when you are."

"All right. Let's turn it counterclockwise a little, then clockwise again to make sure we've gotten it as far as it'll go. . . . Good, now let's try lifting it. Same as before, on the count of three."

With a slight scraping noise, the column slowly rose out of the earth. As it reached the edge of the hole I felt a twinge in the small of my back.

"Okay," I said, wincing, "let's stand it up right here . . . okay . . ." My hands automatically went around to my back.

Moira looked worried. "Maybe I shouldn't say anything, but if you ask me—"

"Look, it's nothing. I have a history of back pain." I massaged my lower back, taking deep breaths. "I'll take a couple of ibuprofen and ice it when I get home."

It looked as if Moira wanted to say more, but she apparently thought better of it. She looked at the column, gave it a rap, and tipped it on its side.

"The darn thing is hollow. No wonder it wasn't as heavy as it looked."

I nodded and began to examine the way the mechanism had been put together. My assessment had been right: a cylindrical brass sleeve, several inches from top to bottom, had been attached to the base of the column, and three thick metal pins protruded at equidistant points around its circumference. These corresponded to L-shaped slots in the bucket-like housing that had been anchored in the hole in the ground. A thin film of some slippery substance coated both sleeve and housing.

"Luke Baumgartner never ceases to amaze me," I said. "What precision!"

"Do you suppose he made it all himself?"

"You know what? I just read the third volume of his diaries. Near the end he says something about going to a foundry in Cincinnati. That had to be—"

"Whatever. Are you forgetting why we went to all this trouble? Look what's in the bottom of the hole."

I reached in and lifted out a package wrapped in oilcloth that felt firmer than the one I had dug out in the chapel. The object inside the wrapping turned out to be a metal box with a hinged top and a simple clasp.

"As a reward for your efforts, you get to open it," I said, handing the box to Moira.

She smiled, opened the clasp, and flipped the lid back on its rusty, squeaky hinges. What was inside was no surprise to me: another small parcel wrapped in oilcloth, held together this time by two red ribbons tied in bows.

"Such style," I said. "The first package had a single white ribbon. Guess what the third one will have?" I stowed the package in my briefcase. "Let's wait and open it at my place. Have to clean up the mess here first, though."

I dropped the empty box into the hole and, with Moira's help, slid the column back into its casing and twisted it counterclockwise. Everything looked as it had before, except for the matted-down grass on one side of the column, which I scuffed up with the edge of my shoe.

"Try to look natural," I said with a smirk as we left the Garden of Time. I made sure to walk behind Moira so that she wouldn't see I was limping.

Back at the house, I sat down on the sofa and began to loosen the bows.

"Aren't you . . . forgetting something you were going to do first?" Moira asked.

I looked up at her, puzzled for a moment, then shook my head. "No, no, I'll do that later. It's feeling better already. Look, I know you're trying to be helpful, but I can take care of myself. Most of the time."

With a sigh, Moira sat down next to me as I continued to unwrap the package. In the process, a small brass key fell onto the coffee table. I examined it from all sides and nodded slowly. It was beautifully wrought and had a bit shaped like the number two.

"Hmm. I have an idea about this . . ."

I passed the key to Moira without further comment, then smoothed out the yellowed pages I had just unwrapped.

"Here, we can read this together if you want."

"Well . . . how about if you read it out loud, Colin. I haven't been read to since I was six—Rapunzel and all that."

I raised an eyebrow. "Okay. Let's just hope this whole business doesn't turn out to be another fairy tale."

The letter began with the most unusual dateline I had ever seen. Leaning back in the sofa, I began reading.

My dear friend,

You will permit me, I trust, to use this intimate form of address? We have, after all, known each other for some time now – that is to say, you have known me for some time, while I have known you for a certain period of eternity, as viewed from my perspective. But alas, I fear that the term "period of eternity" is a contradiction in terms – such are the difficulties of communication from our side to yours. Be that as it may, I wish to inform you that I have been watching your every move of late – and when I say "I", I mean I, Lukas Baumgartner, not that other "I" who inserted himself into my previous communication, apparently in some vain attempt at usurping my authority. That "I" has since taken leave and will not, let us hope, be seen again.

As I was saying, then, I have been watching over you, as a guardian angel of sorts, and I have been quite pleased with your most recent achievement and hope that you have been equally pleased with mine, to wit: the device which you were recently able to unearth. The concealment of the pages which you now hold in your hands, you see, required no inconsiderable amount of effort and ingenuity on my part, if I may be so immodest to say so. For the labor of construction we are both in the debt of Mr George Morrison, a fine craftsman employed by Schilling Metalworks at Cincinnati, though the emplacement itself was accomplished by my dear physician-friend and myself alone. Well, I am delighted that our little invention has functioned adequately and that I am as a result able to visit you once again.

Let me now offer a few quite transparent verses, and then proceed to others which I suspect will be somewhat more challenging.

O earnest, stalwart knight,
with armor shining bright,
upon a mighty steed,
most noble of his breed.
Strong faith in him abides:
past gruesome death he rides,
nor can the devil's stare
reduce him to despair.
He and his loyal hound
the fearsome ones confound,
e'er keeping them at bay
along life's arduous way.

But now, alas, alack,
they've left their wonted track
and vanished from our sight –
o awful, awful plight!
Yet still they may return
if you can but discern
the sense of what I say
and not be led astray.

Old Boreas the Greek
can help you as you seek;
or will you think it best
to choose south, east, or west?
Three lindens are your goal
upon a grassy knoll;
the one between the two
will give the answer true.
Then, once you've found the spot,
will you, as like as not,
decide to climb on high
toward the azure sky,
since climbing once before
was not mere metaphor?
Or might you scorn the heights
and, lowering your sights,
discover some small sign
which further will define
what you are next to do?
– This, friend, I leave to you.

I glanced at Moira. "You know what he's referring to in the first part of the poem, right?"

"Of course. I wrote a paper about it for an art history course. But how can that be? It was stolen from the museum."

I shrugged. "Beats me. It must've been recovered somehow."

"Or never really was stolen?"

"Your guess is as good as mine. Anyway, let's look at the clues and consider the possibilities. Three lindens on a grassy knoll . . ."

"Sounds like the ones in the library courtyard. Remember when I showed them to you a few weeks ago?"

"Sure. *Tilia europaea.* The problem is, they're planted in a perfect triangle. How could any of them be 'the one between the two'?"

"Good question. Maybe if you look at them from a certain angle . . ."

"Doesn't seem likely."

"I know, I'm grasping at straws. So who is this Boreas in the line just before that?"

"Boreas is the north wind."

"Really? I wouldn't have known that. It sounds kind of like the poem is emphasizing that direction, seeing the others don't have names."

"Interesting logic, I tend to agree."

"You know what, though? The more I think about it, the library courtyard doesn't seem like a likely location. Would Mr. Baumgartner expect you to go grubbing around in such a public place?"

"So it's a red herring? Could be. Actually, another possibility occurred to me while I was reading through the poem—the painting of Dürer's *Three Lindens* in the museum."

"Interesting." Moira glanced through the poem again.

"Are Dürer's trees on a grassy knoll?"

"I don't know. Seems to me he didn't do much with what's under them. But maybe Luke just needed 'knoll' as a rhyme word."

"That doesn't sound like him, as precise as he was. Well, if it is the painting, at least you wouldn't have to clamber up any trees."

"Right. Which is much more appealing. And here's something else: the painting is on the north wall of the museum."

"Is it really?"

"Yes. And what's on the other side of that wall? The private chapel. Maybe the middle tree in the painting marks the spot where the engraving is hidden, but you get at it from the chapel side. Does that make any sense?"

"Kind of. But it would take some pretty precise measuring, both in the museum and in the chapel."

"Which, by the way, would be the perfect place for the third clue—inside the chapel, where he'd hidden the first one. Luke was big on balance and symmetry, after all."

"Hmm. I don't know, Colin, it seems a little far-fetched to me. I'm trying to think like him, and he loved trees so much . . ."

"But he loved Dürer too. And since it looks like what he's hidden is a Dürer piece that was once in the museum . . ."

Moira made a face. "Darn, this whole thing is getting so convoluted."

"It is. I may well be seeing things that aren't there."

"On the other hand, it really would be easier to check out the museum option, wouldn't it."

"Yes. I'll do that as soon as I can. The museum won't be open until after the break, of course."

We got up from the sofa.

"Thanks for including me in this, Colin."

"Not at all, you had some good ideas. And it's nice to have a co-conspirator."

Moira smiled. "Co-conspirator. I like that *much* better than 'partner in crime.' Well, see you soon . . . and don't forget about your . . . you know."

"All right, all right, I'll deal with it." As I opened the front door for her, I said, "Are you sure you don't want to become a nurse?"

Chapter 20

I sat down at the coffee table again and admired the key's beautifully wrought design. With both the museum and the chapel out of reach for the moment, I called Clay Locke's number to see about making an appointment.

"Locke, Locke & Gates, how may I help you?"

"Oh, hello. My name is Colin Ritter. I stopped by a couple of months ago to talk with Mr. Locke—"

"Why, yes, sir, that would have been at the beginning of August, I believe."

"Yes, that sounds right, I'm surprised you remembered. I was wondering if Mr. Locke might be able to squeeze me in again sometime today or tomorrow, just for a few minutes."

"I'm afraid not, sir. He and his son left for Louisville early this morning, due to a death in the family. He won't be back in the office until Thursday."

"Oh, I'm sorry to hear that. Hmm, let me think for a minute . . . would he have any time on Thursday morning, say?"

"I believe so, I'll just have a look here . . . yes, he'd be free at ten-thirty if that would suit you."

"Ten-thirty on Thursday would be perfect, I'll stop by then."

Not a bad plan. I'd have to wait until after my Beginning German class on Wednesday to scope out the *Three Lindens* situation, then I'd invent some story and have Ned let me into the chapel. I picked up the key again. It *had* to fit the metal box down at the law office, didn't it? I could hardly wait to find out.

On Monday night my dreams were filled with innumerable Dürer pieces, each flashing by and then disappearing like parts of a sped-up slide show. The ones I could recall most distinctly when I woke up had some peculiar twist to them: the *Paumgartner Altarpiece* with the infant Jesus missing; the *Four Riders*, each holding a giant key aloft; St. Eustace kneeling before a horned creature that appeared to be right out of the *Knight, Death, and Devil* engraving.

The next day was the last of our brief fall break, so I spent almost the entire time working on class preparations for the rest of the week. Whenever anything related to the three lindens threatened to invade my mind, I opted for a quick walk around campus or fifteen minutes' worth of calisthenics on the living room floor. Despite several interruptions, I was able to finish my preparations by evening.

As I considered my planned museum visit over breakfast on Wednesday, a potential problem occurred to me: what would I say to Bobby to justify the measurements I would have to make? Shit, maybe the plan wouldn't work after all. Just in case, though, I stashed a tape measure in my inside jacket pocket as I left the house.

After Con and Comp, Moira waited until everyone had left before coming up to the front of the classroom. I had noticed her giving me an occasional knowing look during the hour.

"Planning on doing some measuring today?" she said.

"Thought I might. If I can figure a way to get around the guard."

"Well, good luck. Let me know how it turns out."

At two-fifteen I hurried over to the Dürer museum. Aside from Bobby, not a soul was in sight.

"How do, Professor. Hope you had yerself a nice long weekend."

"I did, Bobby, thanks. Mostly catching up on school work and stuff like that. How about you? Did you have a chance to do anything special?"

He scratched his head. "Well, no, I wouldn't say that. Just a tad more relaxin' than usual, with the missus on the front porch. 'Course, I get to do quite a lot of that right here, now don't I."

"Yes, but you've got to keep your eyes open, too. Wouldn't want anyone to go walking off with another one of these prints."

"Lordy, no, that would cost me my job! Anyway, I'm glad to see you're here again for another visit."

I smiled and took a few steps into the room. "Thanks. It's always nice to have you as my welcoming committee. I just need to check out a few things today. For one of my classes."

"All right, then, I'll leave you to it."

With a nod to Bobby, I walked over to the north wall and stood staring at the *Three Lindens*. Moira's point had been well-taken—the surface beneath the trees could in no way be construed as a "knoll." But there was another, possibly more significant, problem that I hadn't considered: the piece was small to begin with, only about fifteen by ten inches, so that the distance between the trunk of the middle tree and those flanking it amounted to three-quarters of an inch at the most. How in the world was I supposed to make a measurement that precise and transfer it to the other side of the wall? I stood there stroking my chin. Well, maybe it wouldn't be necessary after all—maybe the chapel wall would be marked in some subtle way that would indicate where to chip away at the mortar.

I stepped back and tried to consider the whole situation more clearly. It was probably a mistake to get hung up on the notion that the chapel was necessarily involved. Maybe the answer was somehow concealed in the painting itself, rather than on the other side of the wall. Where, though? I scrutinized every inch of the tree in the middle to see if there might be some hidden writing or markings. But beyond an occasional irregularity here and there—a blemish on the trunk, an oddly-shaped space in the foliage—there was nothing that might even be remotely construed as a clue.

"Excuse me, Professor," Bobby called out, sounding slightly hoarse, "I got this awful tickle in my throat all of a sudden—if you're goin' to be here a couple minutes longer, I'll just step on down the hall to the fountain and have me a drink. If you don't mind, that is."

"No, no, Bobby, not at all. Go ahead, take your time."

"Thank you, sir, 'preciate it."

Bobby got up and walked out into the corridor. What a stroke of luck! As the sound of his footsteps died away, I whipped out my tape measure and knelt on the floor, letting out enough tape to reach from the corner of the room to a point directly below the center of the painting. Just a hair under seven feet; I stood up again and wrote the exact figure on a pad of paper: eighty-three and a half inches. The next measurement would be from the floor up. But what part of the tree should I measure to? At this point, it was all a guess, so I decided to take the distance from the floor to the very bottom of the trunk and then measure the height of the entire tree. This gave me two more figures: fifty-three inches and ten and one-quarter inches.

I heard footsteps approaching and stuck the tape measure back in my pocket just as Bobby came through the doorway.

"That do the trick?"

"Yessir, I reckon it did. Normally, I'd have a bottle of water in here with me. Clean forgot it today."

I nodded and turned back to the painting. There was nothing left to do in the museum as far as I could see. Was I on the right track? I was less than convinced. But I'd come this far, so there would be no point in giving up now. I'd get Ned to let me into the private chapel on the pretext of making more drawings. In fact, maybe I should actually make some this time, in case he happened to ask to see them. Not likely, but you never knew.

By this point the *Three Lindens* had become a greenish blur. I turned and walked toward the museum entrance.

"So long, Bobby, see you next time. Keep that throat of yours well lubricated."

"Yessir, I'll certainly do my best. You come back now."

Lost in thought, I strode through the castle looking for Ned. He was nowhere to be seen, so I had no choice but to wait till the following morning. What to do now? Maybe check out the library courtyard? It couldn't hurt.

As I approached the library I looked through the archway that led into the inner courtyard. From there I could see only one of the tall linden trees, from the trunk up to the lower branches, and the Neptune fountain spurting behind it. Once inside the courtyard, I could see the other two trees on the far side of the fountain as well. Because of my viewing angle at the moment, the three formed a straight line, with those on the left and right seeming to be standing extremely close to the one in the middle. Their proximity made the whole scene look surprisingly like Dürer's painting! What was it that Moira had said about looking from a certain angle? Could it be that at this very moment I was doing exactly that? Or was I just . . . grasping at straws.

I sat down on a bench close to the archway and let the last lines of the puzzle poem—by this point, I had it memorized—run through my mind. *Will you as like as not, / decide to climb on high / toward the azure sky* . . . I glanced at the middle tree again and said to myself: the stairs inside the library are all I'm gonna climb for now.

It was cool, almost cold, inside the building. I dragged myself up to the third floor and walked over to the windows that overlooked the courtyard. The tops of the trees rose still higher and their dense foliage, just beginning to turn its autumn yellow, made it hard to distinguish anything. What had I imagined I would be able to see anyway? A disguised bag, maybe, attached somehow to a branch? Ridiculous. I climbed down the stairs to the floor below to check out my nonsensical idea again. This was utterly pointless. The only way to see if some object was attached to the tree would be to climb it.

Besides—why hadn't this occurred to me right off the bat? How large would these three lindens have been in Baumgartner's day? They hadn't been planted until near the end of his life, after all. How in the hell could he possibly have hidden a package or whatever it was in a little sapling? Well, he couldn't have, obviously! So what choice was I left with now? *Might you scorn the heights / and, lowering your sights, / discover some small sign* . . .

Hurrying down the stairs, I went into the courtyard again and sat down on the same bench as before, then slowly looked around to see if there was anyone I knew. Fortunately there were only two students in the entire area, sitting on a bench just past the fountain and chatting with an older professorial-looking man. Anyway, who would notice if or for how long I examined one of the trees? And since I certainly wasn't in any mood to be cautious, I got up from my bench and climbed up the gentle slope to the tree that I had identified as *the one between the two*.

Falling to my knees, I hopped rather than walked around the

entire circumference, feeling the bark whenever I thought I had spotted some sort of irregularity. Next I poked around every smaller or larger hole between the roots. Nowhere was there anything that even remotely resembled a hiding place. Maybe Moira was right again: would Luke really have expected anyone to go poking around in such a public space? The only possibility left was Dürer's painting.

Damned lindens anyway, I thought, as I looked up at the magnificent trees again. *Unter den Linden* . . . I had strolled along that wide boulevard in Berlin with Annika one summer. How long had it been since she phoned me? Coming on for three weeks. It didn't seem likely that she would be upset if I called just to ask how her dissertation was progressing. I took my phone out and scrolled down to her name.

"Hello, Colin, I recognized your number this time." Annika's voice sounded calm and relaxed.

"Did you? Well, both of us were always good with numbers. Look, I hope you don't mind my calling—"

"No, it's fine. I was just about to take a break from my diss."

"That's exactly what I was calling about. How is it coming along?"

"I've actually finished. I'm just proofreading now for anything I might have missed. And I've scheduled a date for my defense, in mid-November."

"Wow, that's terrific! Do you anticipate any problems?"

"No, none at all. Everyone on my committee has been very supportive. And after the defense I will begin the job search, of course."

"Well, I hope you'll have more choices than I did."

"I'm not very hopeful. There may be something at a large university, but beyond that positions for medievalists are bound to be scarce. And what have you been doing? Do you have any time for scholarly work?"

"Not much, other things keep coming up. But the deadline for the Lessing paper I've been working on is the last day of October, so I'll have to get cracking."

"Lessing again, good. What it is you're writing about?"

"It's a relatively obscure essay, about Van Eyck and the origins of oil painting. Whether he really did invent the process and so on. Actually, I'm more interested in exploring Lessing's thought processes than the subject itself."

"That will be an interesting approach, I'm sure."

"I think so too."

There was a pause of several seconds.

"Annika, you still there?"

"Yes."

"Look, can I just say again how terrible I feel about that business with Nina—"

"Yes, of course you can say it. But this is not something that is easy to talk about on the telephone. And I must run across the street now to Bordertown and get myself a coffee. Then it will be back to the dissertation."

"Of course. Well, I wish you all the best again."

"Thank you. And thank you for calling."

Good move, Colin, I said to myself as I put the phone away. Talk about an inopportune moment to mention Nina.

Glancing up at the trees one last time, I walked through the archway and headed for home.

Chapter 21

Ned stood at the door of his utility room with an amused look on his face.

"Howdy, Professor. Doin' more explorin' today?"

I laughed and pulled out my sketch pad. "No, no. I thought I'd try making a few more drawings in the private chapel, if you don't mind opening it up for me again. The sun's so nice and bright this morning."

Ned nodded. "No problem." He took the key out of his desk drawer and we set off along the corridor toward the Rapunzel tower.

"Been playing any jazz with the students lately?" I asked.

"Yeah, we been jammin' every so often."

"Are you going to be putting on another concert soon?"

"Probably. Don't know when, though."

"Okay. I'll keep an eye out for announcements."

We had arrived at the chapel door. Ned turned the key and the lock clicked open as easily as it had the last time.

"Works great now," I said. "You must be keeping the lock well oiled."

Ned pulled the door open and shrugged. "Just that one time. Seems to be all it needed."

"Thanks a lot," I said and stepped inside.

"Sure. Same as last time, just let me know when you're through."

"Right, I will."

I shut the door and turned around, almost bumping into the statue of St. Eustace. Would he turn out to be my patron saint today? Smiling what felt like a crooked smile, I deposited my briefcase in the last row of pews and took out my tape measure. I walked to the right-hand corner at the rear and began measuring. Eighty-three and a half inches took me to a point about a third of the way along the side wall and even with the third row of pews. There were lots of threes here. The next number, too, measured fifty-three inches up from the floor to about chest height. I made a small 'x' with my pencil at the spot, then another one ten inches higher.

There were no unusual marks on the stones at that point, in fact no marks at all aside from the ones I had just made myself. Pounding on the wall with my knuckles yielded no evidence of a hollow spot anywhere. Was I supposed to be looking lower down, but on the same vertical axis? *. . . should you scorn the heights / and, lowering your sights, / discover* *some small sign . . .* I ran my hand down the wall all the way to the floor, rapping every few inches. Nothing doing. The morning light was less direct at the rear of the chapel, but bright enough for me to detect even a slight difference in the color of the mortar. There was none.

Edging back, I sat down in the nearest pew and rested my chin on the backrest. So much for *that* theory—I had really pulled a fast one on myself. I stood up, erased the pencil marks I'd made, and blew the crumbs away. Luke would definitely have been pleased with me for doing that, once he'd stopped laughing.

The whole process had taken only fifteen minutes, leaving me with plenty of time to make some drawings. I considered the various motifs the chapel presented. If Dürer had been here, he would no doubt have found some brilliant way of treating the bright sunlight flooding the space, as he had done in his masterful *St. Jerome* engraving. But I was under no illusions of being another Dürer.

When I left the chapel forty-five minutes later, I'd completed three sketches and was fairly satisfied with how they had turned out. Ned was nowhere to be found, so I slipped a note under his door letting him know that I had finished in the chapel for the day. I'd have to get a move on now, if I was going to make it to my appointment at the law office on time.

I pulled up in front of Locke, Locke and Gates just before ten-thirty; I had allowed myself plenty of time to get there for a change. The secretary greeted me and gestured in the direction of Clay Locke's office. I rapped on the door and stepped inside.

"Well, Professor Ritter, nice to see you again, please have a seat. And to what do I owe the honor of your visit?" Mr. Locke leaned over his desk. "Just between you and me, I have a feeling it might have something to do with a certain Luke Baumgartner."

I smiled. "As a matter of fact, it does. I've made a fair amount of progress since I last saw you."

"Well, that doesn't surprise me a tall. After our talk last time, I thought to myself: now there's an enterprisin' young man if ever I saw one." He leaned over his desk again and lowered his voice. "And when I said 'just between you and me' a second ago, I meant it quite literally. Anything you want me to hold confidential, I will. Guaranteed."

"Thank you, Mr. Locke. I wasn't even going to raise the point."

"So what is it you've come up with?"

I reached into my shirt pocket and pulled out the key. "This, for starters," I said, handing it across the desk.

"My, my, my. Now what in the world do you suppose this could be for?" He examined the key carefully before passing it back to me. "Very unusual, that numeral two on the end. Just hang on for a sec while I make a little trip to the vault." Giving me a conspiritorial wink, he got up out of his chair and stepped into the hallway.

A few minutes later he returned holding something concealed inside his jacket. "Our principles of confidentiality extend to the secretary, of course, and Elaine's a good gal. But she doesn't need to know about this just yet."

He produced a sturdy metal box and handed it to me. "Judging by the shape of your key, I have a sneakin' suspicion it will fit this lock perfectly."

I let out a deep breath. "Here goes."

The key slipped into the keyhole and turned as if it were a precision-made tool—which in effect it was. A handwritten inscription on the envelope inside read: 'To whomsoever it may concern, with congratulations. – L.B.'

"Shall I open it?" Mr. Locke asked.

"Please do."

The envelope contained a sheet of letter paper and another small brass key.

"Look at that," I said, "it's the number three this time."

Mr. Locke nodded. "But how about key number one? That seems to be missing."

"No, not really. The key to the private chapel has a one on its end, and that was where I made the first discovery."

"Well, if that doesn't beat all! The number three often has a certain finality to it, so . . ."

"I sure hope you're right. So what does the letter say?"

He adjusted his glasses. "Here, lemme read it to you."

"Codicil to the last will and testament of Lukas Baumgartner:

I, Lukas Baumgartner, residing at Castle Arcadia, Commonwealth of Kentucky, do hereby append to my last will and testament this codicil, concerning the engraving of Albrecht Dürer's "Knight, Death, and Devil", missing since 20 October 1896 and presumed stolen from what is now the Dürer Museum of St. Eustace College. To wit: any person able to find said engraving (verifiable by my monogrammed family crest in the lower left-hand corner) shall be declared its rightful owner and free to dispose of it as he may see fit.

P.S. The small brass key contained in the envelope in which this note was found will prove to be necessary as the search continues.

(Signed) Lukas Baumgartner, 9 November 1908. Witnessed by J. Earl Davies and Clay Locke."

Mr. Locke and I stared across the desk at each other.

"The missing Dürer engraving," I said. "So it looks like it wasn't stolen in the first place."

"Apparently not."

I took the codicil from Mr. Locke and glanced through it. "This might help to explain one thing, at least—that phrase of Baumgartner's, 'in perpetuum, or until further notice. . .'"

Mr. Locke thought for a moment. "I reckon it does. In any case, I'm guessing that you know a little more about the whole business by now than I do and that you're able to do as the stipulation requires?"

I took a deep breath. "Not yet. Hard to say how much longer it'll take. But I do have the second clue in hand and there's only one more after that."

Mr. Locke gave me a quizzical look.

"I'm sorry, I was forgetting that you don't know the whole story yet. I can fill you in if you have another twenty minutes or so."

He smiled. "We lawyers pride ourselves on bein' cool as cucumbers, you know—but I have to admit, I'm on pins and needles. I have a client due in soon, but it won't hurt him to wait a little." He pushed the intercom button. "Elaine, when Mr. Lewis arrives, would you tell him I might be delayed a few minutes? Thanks, darlin'."

I outlined the story of my various discoveries as briefly as possible. When I was finished, Mr. Locke leaned back in his chair and nodded his head.

"Well done, young man, well done! I'm sure I'll see you here again shortly once you've solved the rest of the puzzle. And at that point, you will be entitled to take possession of the 'missing' engraving."

"Entitled, so no longer untitled?"

"Beg pardon?"

"I'm sorry, it's just a silly little private joke."

"Well, in any case, we'll keep the codicil safe in its box in the vault for now. And you hang onto that key, of course."

I got up to go. "Mr. Locke, you're a true Southern gentleman. Thank you for all your help."

"You're most welcome, it's been a pleasure. I'll take the box right back to the vault now so's my next client won't ask any awkward questions."

I walked along the hallway to the receptionist's area, stunned at the prospect of owning one of Dürer's greatest engravings. There was a bare wall in my bedroom where it would fit perfectly. I could picture it already—getting out of bed every morning, looking up . . . and there it would be.

I said goodbye to Elaine and nodded to the man sitting there, presumably Mr. Lewis. Pausing on the steps outside, I glanced around the square and came close to pinching myself to make sure I wasn't dreaming. Not until I had climbed into my car and closed the door with a resounding slam was I sure: this was no dream.

As soon as I got home I sent Moira a text: "New development. Confer tomorrow after class?" Her reply was a simple "Yes!"

"I have amazing news," I said as we walked to the library courtyard. "Remember the box I mentioned, the one Luke left with his lawyer? The little key fit it, and a note inside said that the *Knight* engraving was what was missing, and whoever finds it becomes its owner."

"No way!"

"And there was another key in the box, too, whatever it turns out to be for. Got to figure out that damn poem now. And then there'll be another one after that, Luke said."

"But how can that engraving be the missing one? Would have to be a different print, wouldn't it?"

"Not from what the note said. Another mystery."

"That's pretty exciting, Colin! So where are you going to hang it?"

"Hold your horses, Moira, there's still the small matter of solving the clues."

"Well, we'd better get going. We have to figure all this out before I leave at the end of the semester!"

"Good, I like that attitude. So now I'll tell you about what happened—or didn't—in the courtyard. Don't expect much."

We paused at the archway, where I explained my sighting device.

"Sounds pretty cool, the way the trees lined up like that."

"Yeah, I thought so too, but I finally decided that you were right—the area is just too public, with people coming and going all the time. Plus, the trees would have been tiny in 1908. Not exactly suitable for hiding anything."

"No, I suppose not. So it has to be the Dürer painting by default."

I sighed. "After mucking around in the museum yesterday and the chapel this morning, I more or less decided that couldn't be it either. In other words, neither of our two possibilities is working out."

"Which means we'll have to think of another one."

"Exactly. You mentioned a while back that Baumgartner had planted a lot of trees in groups of three. Can you think where any of them are? Has to be lindens, obviously. And it might be helpful if there's some connection with north, just in case the Boreas reference isn't totally bogus. Is there anything on the north side of campus that occurs to you?"

"How about the North Woods?"

"The North Woods? I thought it was completely wild."

"Actually, there's a clearing a ways in with three trees out in the middle. No idea what kind they are, though."

"I thought everything around here was pine forest."

"Oh, no, there's lots of hardwoods too. The three I'm thinking of are deciduous for sure. My boyfriend—*former* boyfriend—carved our initials in one of them."

"Hmm. Do you know what the leaf looks like?"

"Kind of big, more round than oval. But that's all I remember."

"Moira, I think we'd better go on an expedition."

"Great, when do you want to go?"

"Maybe this afternoon, right after my class?"

"Okay. How about we meet at the museum? It'll be a good place to hang out if you keep me waiting." She snickered.

"No way will I keep you waiting. I'll be there by two-thirty."

She gave me a doubtful look.

"Look, I'll text you if I'm going to be delayed. Think about Boreas in the meantime. Let's hope he'll have some answers for us."

Chapter 22

Bobby had dozed off in his chair inside the doorway. I had to motion to Moira several times before catching her eye. We left the castle via the Rapunzel tower and followed the Promenade around the curve of the moat.

"Let's cut across the lawn here," Moira said as we passed the path to Bamberg Hall. Soon we were at the road that circled the campus, an extension of Faculty Row, where two large red-brick buildings stood directly across from us.

"Those are the other dorms," Moira said, "Concord House and Fellowship House. Some people think the names are hokey, but I like them."

"And you live in Amity House. Not the usual donor names you find on campus buildings. That's a nice change."

We crossed the road and walked along a path between the dorms. A few students were out and about, but no one paid any attention to us. Straight ahead, just beyond a chain-link fence with a padlocked gate, the huge trees of the North Woods rose up. I gave Moira a skeptical look.

"What's with the lock?" I asked.

"Oh, nobody's supposed to go out there. People have gotten lost, and it can get pretty cold at night. One girl apparently got hypothermia and almost died."

"Good God. You sure you know where we're going?"

Moira smiled. "Like the palm of my hand."

We squeezed through a narrow gap between the gate and the fence. What appeared to be a disused logging trail led off into the distance ahead of us. Sunlight filtered through the green canopy overhead, creating irregular shapes on the ground. It was absolutely silent, with not even a bird calling.

The trail curved to the right, then straightened out again for as far as the eye could see. I wished that I had worn hiking boots—but then, I had had no idea earlier in the day that I would end up trudging through the wilderness. The farther we walked, the more impenetrable the woods on either side seemed to become. Soon I caught sight of a silvery glint across the trail a short distance away.

"See that branch up ahead?" Moira said, pointing. "We'll cut off from the trail there and follow it a ways."

"Branch? Looks like water to me."

Moira laughed. "It is. 'Branch' is what we say in these parts."

The creek was several feet across. We walked gingerly over five or six large stones to the other side, where the underbrush was less dense, and began to follow its meanderings. The flowing water alternately widened and narrowed, gurgling gently as it passed over stones and around debris that had fallen from the trees.

Ten minutes later I could make out something through the branches that looked at first like an outcropping of rock. It turned out to be a small building—a stepped-roof stone hut standing at the edge of a large, grassy clearing. A breeze was picking up, making the grass look almost like waves. Not far from the hut, the creek formed an arc around three tall, partially defoliated trees standing close to each other. Another logging trail emerged from the forest at the far side of the clearing.

"Here we are," Moira said.

"And there are your trees," I said.

"My trees? I don't have any claim to them."

"One of them has your initials carved in it."

Her smile changed to a frown. "Yes, I'm sorry to say. And it seemed so romantic at the time."

"At any rate, they're a lot taller than the ones in the library courtyard. Maybe they were there already, and Luke just happened to come upon them. A lot better candidates for hiding something, if you ask me."

We walked over to the hut and I looked in through the doorless opening.

"Looks like a tool shed," I said.

The walls were close to two feet thick, the room itself five feet across and about twice as long. The only other opening was a large window that looked out onto the clearing. In the beams of light that came pouring in, I could make out two ancient tree saws hanging from wooden pegs, one a two-man and the other a smaller trimming saw. A weatherbeaten wooden ladder lay against the wall under the window, and a long-handled shovel hung from a peg in the far corner. Several recesses had been built into the two longer walls, presumably for storing smaller tools or other equipment. Next to the doorway, set on two stumps, stood a bench fashioned out of split logs; an axe protruded from beneath it, its blade covered with rust. None of the equipment here could have been used for years, possibly decades.

"Pretty cool, isn't it?" Moira said.

"Very, if you're into rustic."

"There's an inscription in German carved into the window sill. I remember not being able to figure much of it out."

I walked over to the window and brushed away the layer of dried leaves that had accumulated there. The well-formed letters were relatively easy to make out:

Dem Dichter Eduard Mörike zum Angedenken:
Dazumal, als du deine Buche im Walde gefunden,
Standest du völlig erstaunt unter des Baumes Laub.
So wird derjenige auch, der meine Linden entdecket,
Staunen, sie schön eingerahmt vor sich im Fenster zu sehn.

I did a double take, then stepped back from the window and looked out at the three trees in the distance.

"I'll be damned!" I turned to Moira. "For once Luke has given us a straightforward clue. Those are the lindens we've been hunting for, no doubt about it."

"So what exactly does it say?"

"It's dedicated to a nineteenth-century poet who wrote a poem describing the sense of wonder he felt when he came upon a beautiful beech tree in a clearing in the woods. What Luke says is that whoever discovers his lindens and sees how beautifully framed they are in the window will experience a similar sense of wonder."

Moira looked out the window again. "Especially if that person knows their special significance . . ."

"You're exactly right. Come on, let's go!"

Without thinking, I grabbed Moira by the hand and pulled her out the door. We ran through the long grass to the trees, which stood on somewhat higher ground.

"Does this count as a 'grassy knoll'?" she asked.

"Looks to me like it does."

Yellow leaves formed a mat beneath the trees. I reached up and plucked a still green one from a low-hanging branch.

"Look at that, Moira. It's sort of heart-shaped and it's serrated all the way around. Not quite the same leaf as on the trees in the library courtyard, but it's pretty close. And if Luke says they're lindens . . . then they're lindens."

"So what now? Are you going to have to climb the one in the middle?"

"Sounds like that would be a good starting point. How thoughtful of Luke to have left a ladder back there in the hut."

"Do you think he did? Could it be that old?"

"It looked pretty old to me. I'll run back and get it."

"Need any help?"

"No, I don't think so."

I trotted across the clearing and returned a minute later carrying the ladder.

"It's heavy enough," I said, leaning it against the tree trunk. "I guess they didn't know about aluminum a hundred years ago."

I took a few steps back from the tree and looked up into its branches.

"You see that kind of roundish protrusion, maybe twenty, twenty-five feet up?"

"Yes. Looks like there was a branch there once. Must've come off in a storm."

"I'm not so sure about that. It might be some kind of patch over a hole. I'm going to have a look." I steadied the ladder against the tree.

"Be careful. Those branches up there don't look any too strong."

"What, you don't think they'll hold my mere hundred and ninety pounds?"

"I guess we'll find out."

Moira placed a foot on the bottom rung and held onto the ladder with both hands. I climbed as far as the lowest branch and stepped onto it; the ones above it projected from the tree at convenient intervals, making it easy to continue the climb. Soon I had reached the bulge in the wood that I had identified from the ground.

"What does it look like?" Moira called out.

"You were right. There was a branch here at one time, and it's all gnarly where it came off. Sort of like a scab over a wound. Looks like an act of God, as they say, not of Luke Baumgartner."

I climbed up to the next branch and examined the trunk from all sides.

"There's another one of these gnarls around the back here. Looks pretty much the same as the one below."

"Colin, you've got to be close to thirty feet off the ground. Aren't those branches getting kind of small?"

At that moment there was a sharp crack. The branch I had been standing on hung vertically, held onto the trunk by a narrow strip of bark.

"Don't worry, I'm okay."

Grasping at branches, I eased my way down.

"Nice going, Spiderman," Moira said.

"Guess it was a dumb idea to begin with. Let's go to Plan B."

"Looking lower down, you mean? Did you bring the poem along?"

"Sure, for your sake. I have it memorized by now."

I handed it to her and looked on as she ran a finger down the margin and read a few of the lines out loud:

> will you, as like as not,
> decide to climb on high
> toward the azure sky,
>   . . .

Or might you scorn the heights
and, lowering your sights,
discover some small sign
which further will define
what you are next to do?
– This, friend, I leave to you.

"Doesn't seem to be a lot of choice left," I said. "We have to look for whatever small sign he means, somewhere lower down. On the tree trunk, I suppose."

"Or around the roots. There could be a hole filled in with stones, or mortar, maybe."

"Okay. Let's scrutinize the trunk first, starting from the lowest branch. Obviously the tree has grown a lot since Baumgartner's day."

"Any idea what we're looking for?"

"Not really. 'Some small sign,' I guess."

"Thanks, Colin, that's terrifically helpful."

A few minutes later we were close to the bottom of the tree.

"Here's the remains of our initials," Moira said. "More or less grown over, fortunately."

"Nothing else?" I asked.

"Nothing," she confirmed, coming around to my side.

"So much for that. I'll try the roots now."

She looked on as I circled the tree on my knees, prodding at every point that seemed a possible hiding place.

"Damn." I had reached my starting point. "We've covered the whole blasted tree." I squinted up toward the crown again. "Unless there's something way up at the top that I missed before—a little bag, maybe, attached to a branch."

"You'd be crazy to climb that tree again, Colin. Look at how many leaves have fallen. You can see there's nothing up there."

As I stood up, I stumbled over something in the long grass. I got down on my hands and knees again and pushed the grass away from a small metal marker that protruded from the ground.

"'American linden—*Tilia americana*,'" I looked up at Moira. "Don't tell me—"

"You've found the small sign!" She dropped to her knees. "Does it move? Could it be some kind of lever?"

I tried wiggling the marker, but it was stuck fast in the ground.

"It won't budge."

Moira was examining the nameplate. "No other writing, just the name of the tree."

The marker had been inserted into the ground at a sharp angle.

She leaned over until her head was almost touching the grass and examined the back.

"There's something written there. It's tiny, though. See if you can pull it up some."

"I'll pull it out all the way if I can."

I dug around the marker with my blunt-bladed knife, then wiggled it back and forth until it started to move. One last effort, and it slid up out of the earth. The post was eight or nine inches long and made of brass, like the nameplate itself. I wiped it on the grass to remove the dirt that was still clinging to it, then tried to make out the minuscule letters. "It looks like it's been engraved—but it's so tiny!"

"Here, let me give it a try," Moira said. "I can just make it out . . . '*Grab hier – anderthalb Fuß*' . . . '*Grab*' means 'grave,' doesn't it?"

"Yes, but it can also be the verb meaning 'dig'! 'Dig here, a foot and a half'! My God, Moira, can you believe it?"

We threw our arms around each other, laughing and whooping.

"You know what?" I said. "There's a shovel in the hut. Luke left us a shovel, bless his heart!"

"I guess you were right about the tools. He set the whole thing up for whoever figured out his clues."

"Looks that way." I trotted over to the hut again and came back with the shovel.

"Pretty old and battered, but it looks like it'll do the job. The soil should still be fairly moist from that rain we had a few days ago."

I cut through the long grass in a two-foot circle with my knife, using the hole left by the marker post as the center. Lifting out the piece of sod with the shovel, I placed it to one side and started digging the hole.

"Incredibly dull, this blade. Hasn't been used forever." I dug out a few shovelfuls. "It works, though."

"Let's hope it really is only a foot and a half down."

"Oh, it will be. Luke has spoken."

"Couldn't things have shifted in the last, what, hundred-odd years?"

"I don't know, we'll soon find out."

A few minutes later there was a clang as the point of the shovel struck something solid.

"Was that metal or a stone you just hit?"

"Sounded like metal to me. I think I've dug to about to the right depth by now."

A few more shovelfuls, and I could see a dull shine through the dirt. I manipulated the shovel carefully, then reached into the hole and pulled out a flat object wrapped in the inevitable oilcloth.

"Colin, this is unbelievable!"

"Sure is. Man, the trouble that guy went to!"

I wiped the dirt off with my hand and unwrapped the oilcloth.

"It's a duplicate of the box we found in the Garden of Time. Same little clasp, even. Here, you want to open it?"

"Sure."

There was a metallic squeak as Moira undid the clasp and raised the lid. She lifted out the package inside and handed it to me.

"Isn't that sweet," she said. "Three blue ribbons."

"That's exactly the way it had to be. From white to red to blue." I stared at the package in my hands and thought back to the day I had found the first one in the chapel. This, too, seemed to me almost like an object of veneration.

"Aren't you going to open it?" Moira asked.

"Let me fill in the hole first," I said, putting it down on the grass. "The box has to go in, too, otherwise there won't be enough dirt."

"Do you think we really have to worry about that, Colin?"

"Probably not, but I'm a perfectionist. Remember how you were talking about character flaws the other day? This is one I have to live with."

I filled in the hole with as much of the dirt as I could scoop out from the grass and replaced the sod, then pounded the marker back into the ground with the blade of the shovel. As I picked up the package again, Moira knelt down next to me and touched my arm.

"Don't turn around," she whispered.

I stared at her. "Why not? What's going on?"

"There's a stand of evergreens on the other side of the branch, and I'm sure I saw a dark shape moving under them."

Turning my head inadvertently, I caught sight of a hunched-over figure stealthily making his way through the brush in the opposite direction. I ran over to the creek, which was a good ten feet wide at that point, then stood at the water's edge looking off into the distance before turning back.

"Did you see who it was?" Moira asked.

"No . . . I'm not sure. It's pretty shadowy over there, and the light's fading. You know, the first time I was in the Garden of Time checking things out I thought there was someone spying on me. And the day before that, when I was up on the castle roof figuring out that little maid business, there was a kind of suspicious character sitting under an umbrella just across the moat from me."

"Man or woman?"

"I couldn't tell. All I could see was the person's pants. And when I left a couple of minutes later, whoever it was was gone. Anyhow, there's no point in undoing the package here. Let's take it back to the house and open it there."

Moira looked across the creek to where the figure had been hiding.

"Colin, this is kind of creepy. Do you suppose it was the same person you saw before?"

I paused for a moment. "Don't know. I have a vague suspicion, but I won't say until I'm sure. Let's haul this stuff back to the hut."

I put the shovel over my shoulder and tucked the package under my arm. Moira helped me carry the ladder.

It had to have been Jason, I said to myself. Shit. How do I deal with this?

Chapter 23

It was almost dusk as we walked up the driveway to the house. Juniper came creeping into the living room just after we stepped inside.

"Poor cat," I said, "you must be starving."

I gave her some fresh water and poured cat food into her bowl in the kitchen. She began munching away contentedly.

"Come to think of it," I said, "I'm kind of hungry myself. How about you?"

"I could eat something."

"Our unveiling will just have to wait a little. How about hot dogs and beans? That would be the fastest thing."

"Great. I love eating healthy."

We made quick work of our minimal supper and moved to the living room.

"Just so you know, Moira, I usually eat better than this."

"Oh, I'm sure you do," she said with a snicker.

As soon as we sat down on the sofa Juniper leapt up between us. Moira began to scratch her belly while I untied the three blue ribbons and smoothed out the pages.

"What does that heading say?" she asked. "'*The same . . .* '"

"'*The same u-topia, the same u-chronia.*'"

"What the heck is that supposed to mean?"

"Remember the heading on his last letter? '*A place without time, a time without place.*' It's a play on that."

"Oh, sure—'u-topia' meaning 'no place.' I remember that from More's *Utopia*. So 'u-chronia' has to mean 'no time.'"

"Right. Trust Baumgartner to invent a word if he needed it. Why don't I read the letter out loud while you see to Juniper's needs."

"Okay."

My dear friend,

I am so very pleased to have yet another opportunity to address you! (I was on the point of writing: "to converse with you," but, alas . . . Well, we need not dwell on the obvious.) Once more you have carried out your search exceedingly well, for which I congratulate you most heartily! I would like to apologize, however, for having caused you to dirty your hands during this and your previous expedition – assuming, that is, that a person of your obvious mental capabilities is unaccustomed to manual labor. But perhaps I am wrong on this account, since I for one, who have some modest intellectual ability myself, if I may say so, have in addition made abundant and productive use of my hands throughout my life.

But why do I go on so? You will certainly be quite anxious to turn your attention to the third and final clue. Here it is then, without further ado.

I put the first page on the coffee table and turned to the second. "Looks like another long one. Are you ready?"

"I can hardly wait."

I began to read again.

Greetings once more, I welcome you
and grant you the credit which you are due:
You've dug not too shallow, nor too deep
into the realm where I do sleep
(as like it or no, at present I must,
ashes with ashes, dust with dust).
Thus once more you have found your way
and brought what you sought to the light of day.

But why do I dwell on that which you know –
your deeds, that is, of a short while ago.
Let me not waste your time with such things,
you, who to me such good will brings,
knowing by now that my words are not lies,
though at times, indeed, they may disguise
the truth of what I impart to you
and becloud the sense of the message true.

In and out, then out and in,
provide a helpful place to begin;
four is thus part of the recipe,
instead of my usual number three.
Strike this balance, and soon you will be
where once you were on bended knee.
From first to last, from left to right –
the end will presently be in sight.

But let me offer a hint less obscure:
what you must seek is my signature;

you've seen it before, as I can attest,
and now it will help you in your quest.
View it once more, then a saint you must find
with the tool of his violent trade so declined
that it points, fulfilling its second role,
to the place which is your ultimate goal.

I stopped reading and studied what was written farther down the page.

"Is that it?" Moira asked. "It all seems pretty obscure. About the only things that make any sense—"

"Hang on, there's more. But it's in German."

"German? Why would he switch languages all of a sudden?"

"No idea. And it's not only in German, it's an antiquated form. It reminds me of some little poems that Dürer wrote. Hard to tell if this one's by him, or if Luke is imitating his style."

"So what does it say?"

"Here, I'll read it to you first. See how much you can catch. He calls it an 'Epilog.'"

Der narr denckt allbeg an dise welt,
Der irrdisch pesicz jm nur gefelt,
Was inniglich gut ist, daz wais er ja nit;
Sey anders dann der, jch dich pitt.

"Something about this world and earthly possessions," Moira ventured. "And about being different?"

"Not bad. Here's exactly what it says: 'The fool always thinks of this world, only earthly possessions please him, he does not know what inner values are; be different from him, I beg you.'"

"Strange," Moira said. "Doesn't seem to be a clue at all."

"No, it doesn't."

I read through the four lines again and counted out the meter on my fingers.

"Ah, now I get the irregular rhythm—it's the way German poets almost always wrote in the sixteenth century. Four-beat lines, with a random number of unstressed syllables. And always in rhymed couplets." I looked back at the clue section and glanced through a few of the lines again. "Which is exactly how Luke wrote the English verses, too."

Moira thought for a moment. "Hmm, I wonder . . . you're close to finding the hidden work of art now, so Luke takes you back to Dürer's day, maybe?"

"Very clever, Moira, you may well be right."

"None of which helps us solve any of the clues. Where do we start?"

"Maybe with the concrete things?"

"Such as . . . his signature . . . and a saint with some kind of weapon."

"Yes. He claims I've seen his signature, and I'm sure I have. On his will, probably, though I don't really remember that. But I know it was on the note he left at the lawyer's office."

"Hmm . . . remind me."

"The one in the metal box—where he says that whoever finds the missing engraving becomes its owner."

Moira glanced around the room. "By the way, where exactly would you hang it? There's not much free wall space."

"Look, how about if we try to figure out the clues first?"

"Sorry. Is there any way the engraving could be hidden somewhere down at the lawyer's?"

"Seems highly unlikely."

"So where else have you seen Luke Baumgartner's signature?"

I scratched my chin. "I don't recall having seen it anywhere else, actually."

Moira thought for a moment. "It's not on his grave marker, that's for sure."

"No, definitely not."

"How about his diaries? I remember seeing signatures embossed on the covers of books from back then."

"It's possible. I had two of the volumes here for a while, but they're back in the library now. I'm pretty sure there was nothing like that on the covers, though. And no signatures inside either, as far as I remember. Besides, where would that take us?"

"U-topia?"

"Exactly. Maybe we should be working on the saint first."

"Namely . . . St. Eustace."

"Hard to imagine a more likely candidate, given Luke's proclivities."

"But he didn't have a violent trade, did he? He was a saint, after all."

"Yes, but he was a Roman officer before his conversion. Second century, I think."

I went over to the bookcase, picked one of my Dürer volumes off the shelf, and flipped through a few pages.

"Here he is. And guess what, he has not one, but *two* weapons. Except I suppose the sword is the 'tool of his trade,' not the dagger. And Luke's poem says . . . let's see . . . it's *declined* . . . . That fits too, of course. So the question now is, which version of St. Eustace could it be? There's the engraving in the museum and that huge reproduction in the castle tower, and there's also a statue of him in the private chapel."

"Is there really? All those choices. He has to be our guy, don't you think?"

"Seems likely. Unfortunately, there's lots of other stuff in the poem we haven't even begun to figure out."

Moira took the last page out of my hand and studied it for a few moments. "Like the reference to 'in and out' . . . and the number four, which he seems to be making quite a big deal of . . . and then the 'first to last' and 'left to right' business. To say nothing of the signature again. Do you see how any of that relates to St. Eustace?"

I leaned back on the sofa and let my breath out slowly.

"Not offhand. Plus the fact that making St. Eustace the answer might have been slightly too obvious for Luke."

"Could be. Although I don't think that's a reason to rule him out entirely. Maybe it's so obvious that he thought the person doing the searching wouldn't even consider it. And for that reason Eustace might just be the one after all."

I looked at Moira and smiled. "There's a certain logic to that. An illogical logic, sort of. You're starting to think like Luke."

"I don't know about that. At the moment I feel more like I'm just thinking confused thoughts."

"Yeah, me too. Maybe we should give it a rest for now. In fact, I'm going to be completely snowed for the next couple of weeks—putting my midterms together, then three days' worth of oral exams, then grading the midterms and setting up student conferences. And the week after that I absolutely have to finish a paper I've been working on. The due date is the last day of October."

"Oh? Halloween, in other words. Have you heard about the campus party?"

"Yes, Pastor Roland mentioned it a while ago. In fact I've already called the guys who're renting my place in Minneapolis to ask them to send me a costume I'd stored away. You're going, I assume?"

"Definitely."

"What as?"

Moira paused for a moment before speaking.

"That's a secret. My initial will be . . . J."

"'J.' Only one initial?"

"Only one."

"Interesting. I'll have two myself—T. E."

Moira put a hand to her chin. "Sure you don't mean E. T.?"

"No way. I'm too tall for that. I'll be wearing a kind of goofy color combination, that's all I'll tell you."

"Maybe that'll help me recognize you. And it shouldn't be very hard for you to spot me, since I'll be one of four."

"One of four what?"

"If I told you that, I'd be giving it away. We'll all look similar, but different."

I shook my head. "Sounds like you're still in your Luke Baumgartner mode."

"Oh, this will be a lot easier mystery for you to solve."

"Well, it's bound to be a good time one way or another. I really like costume parties."

"So do I. People can get away with all sorts of things they wouldn't even dream of doing otherwise."

She got up to go and I walked her to the door.

"You okay walking home alone? It's pretty dark out there."

"I'll be fine. Besides, I have to start getting practiced up for Halloween."

"Another cryptic statement. I'm not even going to ask what that might mean."

"Wouldn't do you any good if you did. You'll find out soon enough at the party."

"Okay, guess I'll have to wait till then. Good night, J."

"Good night, T. E."

Chapter 24

In the week before the Halloween party I made excellent progress on my Lessing paper. But despite my fondness for the author and my fascination with following his thought patterns, I wished that I could have used the time to try and puzzle out the third clue. On the few occasions when a section of the poem flashed through my mind—while preparing a meal, or taking a shower—I realized what an impasse I had reached. Was St. Eustace involved, or was he not? If so, *which* St. Eustace? And Luke's signature—where on earth could it be? As I read through my paper one last time, I wondered if the orderliness of Lessing's thought processes might help me to sharpen my own. By the time I had completed the final editing and sent the manuscript off in the mail, the answer was an all-too resounding "no."

The air was muggy and the wind came in gusts the following evening as I walked down the long flight of stairs across from Weiden Hall to the gymnasium. My Till Eulenspiegel outfit had arrived in the mail with time to spare. Over a year ago Annika had helped me find the material and had done all the sewing. We had then put on a Fasching party at my apartment for faculty and students that turned out to be a rollicking success. Annika had dressed as a fairy princess, and I remembered thinking at the time how well it suited her. Now I wondered, as I often had since the break-up, if I had created a romantic image of her that she couldn't possibly have lived up to.

I followed several costumed students along the gymnasium hallway to the basketball courts, where an eerie yellowish light emanated from the open doorway. As I stepped in under a paper skeleton with arms and legs spread wide, a fiendish cackle came from somewhere in the vicinity of its grinning mouth.

The twin basketball courts had been converted into a ballroom, with round cabaret tables set up along the periphery and the center area left free for dancing. A rock band was playing at a bearable decibel level on the stage at the opposite side; the dance floor was about half-filled with gyrating, costumed bodies. Black and orange balloons festooned with matching crepe paper hung from the ceiling. Jack-o'-lanterns served as table lamps, providing most of the diffused light; the rest filtered down from orange bulbs in the ceiling fixtures. Almost all of the available wall space was taken up by Halloween trappings: skeletons, witches, goblins, sheets draped to look like ghosts.

I pressed through the crowd, heading for a refreshment booth where soft drinks were being sold. An occasional student greeted me and one even addressed me by name. Some disguise, I thought—I should have had a mask that covered more than just my eyes. So far I hadn't been able to recognize anyone myself.

Sipping on a can of root beer, I began ambling through the crowd again, wondering if Moira or any of my faculty colleagues were there yet. Finally I recognized a student from my Cultural History class and stopped to say hello. She was wearing a witch's hat and was heavily made-up with black lipstick and eyeshadow.

"*Grüß dich*, Brinna."

The student stared at me for a few seconds.

"Professor Ritter! Drat, how'd you know it was me?"

"I'm not sure—it's something about . . . you know, I'm really not sure."

I didn't want to point out that Brinna came to class wearing almost as much makeup as she had on at the moment. We exchanged a few pleasantries and I moved on.

At one of the next tables I noticed a pudgy devil, complete with horned mask and tail, sitting across from a gray-haired woman with angel wings who was dressed in white. The devil stared at me as I passed by.

"*Guten Abend, mein Herr.*"

I stopped and looked back at the odd couple.

"*Guten Abend. Mit wem habe ich die Ehre? Mephistopheles höchstpersönlich?*"

"*Nicht ganz.*" The man raised his mask and I saw it was Pastor Roland.

"Hey, great idea!" I exclaimed, sitting down in the chair next to him.

"Though not terribly original, I'm afraid. I've been wearing this same costume for the devil knows how many years now."

He threw his head back and chortled at his own joke. His wife smiled and wagged a finger at him. "Sometimes I wonder about this man," she said, shaking her head.

"As do I, my dear, as do I—ah, Colin, forgive me, I don't believe you two have met. Colin Ritter—my wife Nancy."

"Pleased to meet you, Mrs. Roland."

"The pleasure's all mine, I'm sure." She looked at me with a twinkle in her eye.

The band struck up a slow tune, and, smiling broadly, the pastor looked across the table at his wife.

"Would you care to dance, my dear?"

"Why yes, my dear, I would love to!"

"You will excuse us, Colin?"

"Of course. I'm going to move on around the circle and see who else I run into—or would you like me to stay and keep your table for you?"

"Oh, no, no, thank you. Nancy and I will dance for a while, and then we will have to be going. Neither of us is what you would call a night owl. Far from it."

He put his devil's mask back on and led his wife out onto the dance floor.

"Don't trip over your tail," I called out.

I tossed my empty pop can across the aisle into a large receptacle and was about to get up when a slender woman in a tight-fitting black cat outfit sat down in the chair across from me.

"Meow," she said, stretching out the final vowel. "My name's Juniper."

"Ahh, of course—J is for Juniper. You probably don't know my name, though—it's Till Eulenspiegel. I've been dead for four hundred years now."

"Oh, I'm sorry to hear that. Glad you could make it back for the party."

"So am I. It seemed to be an appropriate occasion for a moldering corpse."

"Hmm. It looks to me like you're in pretty good shape."

I considered returning the compliment, but decided against it.

"Juniper," I said. "Quite a coincidence. I have a cat by that name."

"Oh, do you? I *thought* you looked like a cat lover."

"Definitely—cats of all sorts. Mine has green eyes, though—and her whiskers aren't just painted on."

"Oh! Now you're getting mean!"

"Just kidding. And hazel eyes are *very* acceptable, actually."

"Well, thank you. Painted-on whiskers are really better, too, if you think about it."

"Oh?"

"They don't tickle."

Moira tilted her head slowly from side to side, the way a cat might, as she looked across the table at me.

"I like your color combination," she said. "You look good in yellow and blue."

"Thank you. You look good in black."

"I like your cap, too." She reached over and tugged on one of the drooping peaks, making the little bell jingle. "What's the mirror around your neck for?"

I held it up toward a ghost who was passing by. The ghost stepped back and raised his hands, then continued on his way. Out of the corner of my eye I noticed a gaunt figure in a skeleton outfit who seemed to be watching me—or Moira, more likely. His short-cropped blond hair was visible above his mask. Was it Jason, or was I letting my imagination get the better of me? The skeleton moved on and I turned back to Moira.

"The mirror's so that other people can see their foibles reflected in it. I have the *Narrenfreiheit* to do that."

She looked puzzled. "*What* kind of freedom?"

"Fool's freedom. We fools can get away with a lot of things that other people wouldn't even dream of doing."

"Oh, can you now? Even dancing with cats?"

I considered this for a moment. "It's not something I've done before, as far as I can recall. But why not?"

Moira smiled. "Good. Can I reserve the midnight waltz with you?"

"Well . . . sure." I looked uncertainly toward the dance floor.

"Or don't you waltz?"

"Oh, no, I do. My parents made me take dancing lessons. It's just that I can't quite imagine this kind of band playing a waltz. What do they do, put a CD on?"

"No, no, the band plays it. It's gotten to be kind of a tradition at the Halloween party. They played one last year, same band, and everybody just ate it up. The lead guitarist is a terrific musician."

Another student in a slightly different cat costume came by and put her hand on Moira's arm.

"We found a table. Right across from the refreshment stand."

"Okay, I'll see you in a little bit."

As Moira turned back to me, I thought she looked disappointed.

"There are four of us cats here tonight—guess whose idea that was. We said we'd stick together, at least for a while." She got up to go. "See you just before midnight?"

"Okay. But how will we ever find each other in this madhouse?"

"Don't worry, I'll track you down. We cats are good at that."

I watched her as she moved lithely into the crowd and disappeared. I sat for a moment, turning the mirror around and around in my hand as my masked face went flitting by. I got up from the table and noticed that a figure dressed in a black monk's robe and cowl was staring over at me from a few feet away.

"Are you who I think you are?" the monk said, coming over to the table. I recognized Michael Rossi's voice.

"Don't tell me," I said, "you're a . . . Benedictine?"

"No, an Augustinian. Like Martin Luther."

I smiled. "Of course, I should have guessed it. Well, it's a good disguise. It took hearing your voice for me to recognize you."

"Do you want to come over to our table?" Michael asked. "We're way around on the other side."

"Sure."

"I'm going to get some sodas, be there in a minute." He began walking off in the opposite direction. "Look for a fortune teller," he called out as an afterthought.

The smell of alcohol wafted by every so often as I squeezed through the growing crowd, past skeletons, Draculas, witches, and a variety of other gruesome creatures. There seemed to be more ghosts than anything else, many of them looking ominously like Ku Klux Klansmen.

I spotted Charlotte at one of the last tables. Her face was covered with gobs of makeup and she was wearing a gypsy outfit. She sat flipping through a deck of cards and studying each one in turn.

"If I didn't know better," I said, "I'd think that was Charlotte Rossi."

"Oh, darn!" she called out. "How'd you know it was me?"

"I got a heads up from some Augustinian near the entrance."

"I tell you, you just can't trust these monks anymore," she said with a laugh. "I've been wondering if you were going to make it tonight. Thought you might just stay home and work on your paper."

"Oh, no, I finished it yesterday. I've been so busy lately, I definitely needed a change of pace."

"Well, you're looking the part. You're Till Eulenspiegel, I assume?" She reached over and tapped my mirror.

"That's right. Appropriate enough for Halloween, I suppose. It's last year's Fasching costume."

"Why, I think it's splendid. Pull up a chair. I, as you can see, am Madame Medium. You may remember I suggested some time ago that I might read your cards?"

"Ah, yes. Well, as someone who did his share of trickery several centuries ago, I suppose I could subject myself to it for a change."

"Now, now—how about a little respect for the Higher Powers!"

Michael arrived at the table and held out a can of Sprite to me.

"Thanks," I said, "it's pretty warm in here."

"And I'm about to make it warmer for you," Charlotte said with a leer.

Michael smiled and nodded. "Madame M. is on a roll. She's already done two readings this evening."

As Charlotte began to shuffle her oversize deck of cards, Pastor Roland and his wife came walking over from the dance floor.

"We noticed the three of you sitting here and wondered if we could entice you to dance," the pastor said.

Charlotte put the deck of cards down on the table with a thump.

"You know, I could use a little break before the next reading," she said. "Colin, might you be interested?"

"Sure," I said. Michael indicated that he would be glad to stay behind and hold the table.

"Not a favorite activity of his," Charlotte said as we walked out onto the dance floor. The four of us danced several numbers, sometimes as couples, sometimes as a more or less connected group. As I was dancing across from Charlotte at one point, I noticed Moira and the other three cats going through a series of slinky, feline movements. Moira smiled and waved, her gesture just another element of her sensual dance.

"Now who might that be?" Charlotte asked.

"Someone who likes cats, I guess."

"Why, it's Moira MacGregor. Hi, Moira!"

I saw Moira mouth a 'hello,' and then she and the other cats were swallowed up in the crowd.

"She makes a great cat, doesn't she?" Charlotte said.

"Sure does." I quickly turned my head in the opposite direction. "Where have the pastor and his wife gotten to?"

"Looks like they're leaving." Charlotte waved to the couple as they left the dance floor and they waved back. "Think I've had about enough dancing myself."

The music ground to a sudden halt and we made our way back to the table.

"All right," Charlotte said as we sat down. "Now we find out what Fate has in store for Colin."

"Make it good, all right?" I said smiling.

Charlotte took a few sips of her Sprite.

"How much do you know about the Tarot, Colin?"

"Next to nothing."

"Okay, here's the deal. The deck consists of seventy-eight cards in all, twenty-two in the Greater Arcana and the rest in the Lesser. The cards in the Greater Arcana represent universal manifestations or qualities, you might say, and each card has its symbolic meaning, which can vary considerably, depending on a lot of things—including who happens to be doing the reading. The Lesser Arcana is similar to a regular deck of playing cards, but the suits have different names—Wands, Cups, Swords, and Pentacles—and there's one extra face card in each suit. All these cards have symbolic meanings, too. Follow me so far?"

"I think so."

"Doesn't matter that much if you do or don't. Now here's the procedure. And I have to tell you, there are dozens, probably hundreds, of different ways of going about this. Some readers use only four cards, some seven, some eight or nine, all laid out in different patterns, obviously. Some ask the person whose cards are being read to pose questions about things of special concern to them. I don't do that. And, believe it or not, there are some readers who would find my interpretations too fanciful. They're wrong, of course."

"Of course," I repeated.

"Now the way I'm going to start is by selecting one card that I, as the all-knowing medium, declare to be characteristic of you in some way. Let's see here . . ."

She flipped through the deck until she found the card she wanted.

"Knight of Cups," she said, placing it in the center of the table. "I picked this card for a number of reasons. Your name, of course—you're Colin Ritter, after all. And notice how calmly the knight is riding along on his horse—not that he's always like that, he's certainly capable of expressing his feelings. He's a very sensitive guy and he's open to others. He's a romantic in many ways, and a lover of beauty—and I know, of course, Colin, that you're very interested in art."

"That I am."

"All right, if everything is clear, we're ready to begin."

"Clear enough."

"Okay. What I'll do is lay out three cards in a vertical line to the right of the Knight of Cups, and then three more to the left. The first three will have to do with your inner life, the second three with how you relate to the rest of the world. Not that the two can always be easily distinguished from each other, so it's kind of a stretch sometimes. First I'll shuffle the deck three times and then you'll do the same."

Once I had taken my turn shuffling, Charlotte had me cut the deck. She began to lay out the first three cards.

"First card: Queen of Cups, in reversed position. Upside-down, in other words."

"Does that make a difference?" I asked.

"Most interpreters would say that it does, though it might depend on the juxtaposition we end up with. Now the second card: Two of Swords. And the third: Queen of Wands." Charlotte bent low over the table for a moment. "Very interesting, *very* interesting. Not something you see every day, those two queens there like that. They represent two women who are significant in your life, Colin. Note first of all that the Queen of Cups is of the same suit as the Knight card I chose to represent you, so there's a connection there. Now for the card itself: This queen is a contemplative sort who is interested in religious or philosophical questions; she may well be a scholar. The flow of ideas is important to her, symbolized by the flowing water that surrounds her. It's even reflected in the pattern of the cloak she's wearing. She is not one to make quick decisions, but once she's decided, she remains true to whatever or whoever is involved. But given that the card is in the reversed position, she may well be in some kind of quandary, reflecting on something that's bothering her."

"Sounds quite a bit like someone I know back in Minnesota," I said. "She's been working on her dissertation. The quandary part . . ." I motioned with my hand, as if it wasn't anything important.

"Well, we all know how difficult it is to write a dissertation."

"Right. She's blond, too, like the queen on the card."

Charlotte smiled. "The hair color on the face cards may or may not be significant. Sometimes it is, sometimes it isn't. Any more comments or questions about this card?"

"No, I guess not."

"All right, let's look at the other queen. We'll go back to the intervening card in a minute. Can you both see her okay?"

She held the Queen of Wands up for a few seconds for Michael, who was sitting on the opposite side of the table.

"Note the difference. This queen is looking out into the world. She's holding a sunflower in one hand, which indicates her sunny disposition."

"Isn't that a bit far-fetched?" Michael interjected.

"Never you mind, Michael. Let me continue. This queen is open and gregarious, she's a person everybody likes. She's positive-thinking and able to deal with any situation, no matter how difficult. The expression on her face indicates a creative mind. She could be an artist."

I noticed that this queen's hair color had a distinctly reddish cast to it. I looked at Charlotte out of the corner of my eye; she could hardly have overlooked the black cat sitting at the feet of the queen, but had made no comment about it. I hoped that she wouldn't.

"What about the card between the queens?" I asked quickly.

"Let's have a look," Charlotte said. "I would say the figure is probably a young man, though the gender isn't likely to matter in this instance. He's blindfolded, of course, not unlike the usual symbolic representation of justice, except that he's holding two swords rather than one. In almost every way the scene is perfectly balanced, including the sea without a ripple behind him. It's like the figure is trying to decide between two options—something to do with the two queens, since his card is between theirs. But he's blindfolded—in other words, unseeing—so he can't make the decision himself, he only symbolizes the necessity of making one."

"In other words, I'm the one who has to make the decision."

"Well, these are your cards I'm reading, Colin." She paused for a moment, looking pensive. "All right, if there are no further comments or questions concerning the first three cards, we'll go on to the next three."

Michael and I shook our heads.

"Remember now, Colin, these next cards will have more to do with your relationship to the external world, rather than with intimately personal matters. Here goes. Fourth card: Ace of Pentacles. Fifth card—"

"Oh, my God!" I said. "It's the devil!"

Charlotte nodded her head slowly. "The devil it is, card Fifteen from the Greater Arcana. We'll consider it later. Here's your last card now."

She placed the card on the table and gasped.

"The Death card, number Thirteen from the Greater Arcana, reversed." She shook her head slowly. "In all my years of laying cards, I've never . . . But let's start with the first of these three."

The Ace of Pentacles showed a pentagram inscribed in a yellow disk held by a huge hand projecting from a cloud. A pleasant garden scene lay below with distant mountains visible through an opening in a flowering hedge.

"Pentacles represent coins," Charlotte began, "or wealth in general. The question is, should a person accept what the hand seems to be offering, or would it be better to go on living the simple life in the garden below? Given that the Devil card follows immediately after, the meaning could be that some trickery is involved. Or there might be an enemy out there, lurking. As for the Death card—"

"Can I turn it right-side up for a second?" Michael asked. "Yes, that's what I thought—look at how similar the figure of Death and the Knight of Cups are . . . they're both in profile, they're both facing in the same direction and they're sitting absolutely straight in the saddle. Even the horses have the same stance, holding their right leg up. Doesn't that have to mean something?"

Charlotte nodded. "There's definitely a connection. Depends on how you interpret the Death card. Does it stand for danger, or is it simply an indication of an impending transition, which is often the case when it's reversed. Some transitions are painful, some aren't. All we can say for sure is that the future will tell all. Just think about it: the present doesn't really exist, except as a moment that goes flashing by. And the past exists only in memory. So what's left? The future."

Charlotte folded her arms and looked straight ahead. "I have spoken."

"You certainly have," I said, feeling befuddled.

Michael stared across at his wife, who was massaging her forehead. "That reading really seemed to take it out of you. Or is it because it was the third one?"

"Hard to say. I am feeling tired all of a sudden. Maybe it's time we were heading for home, Michael. We've been here since eight o'clock, and it's already after eleven." She started to gather up her cards.

"That's fine with me," Michael said.

"I think I'll make the rounds and see if there's anyone else I know," I said. "Thanks for the reading, Charlotte."

"Don't mention it. See you in the office on Monday."

"I hope so. What if those two queens should show up, or the devil, or even . . ."

"Not to worry, Colin. It could all just be symbolic."

Could be symbolic, I said to myself. And what if it's not?

Chapter 25

I sat for a while thinking about the astonishing sequence of cards Charlotte had laid out. It was as if she knew more about me than I did myself. The only possible explanation was that the Tarot could be interpreted in such a variety of ways that the results sometimes came close to the life circumstances of the person whose cards were being read. Of course, that had to be it. Or did it?

Despite the noise level, I was no more than vaguely aware of what was going on around me. The jumble of voices and music rose and fell as if a party were going on in a distant room. Only occasionally did a visual image register on me—an indeterminate monster with grotesque green eyes, two black students wearing brightly-colored African robes, the checkered pattern of a clown outfit. . . .

I stepped out into the hallway, found a restroom, and splashed cold water in my face. Back inside, I noticed how much the basketball courts had warmed up in the course of the evening. Putting my mask on again, I slowly walked around the perimeter. The smell of alcohol on people's breath was becoming more and more noticeable. I finished off my can of Sprite, wishing that I had something to spike it with. The clock on the wall above my head said ten to twelve; Moira would be trying to find me any minute now.

"Well, hello. Having a little drink, are we?"

I turned around, and there she was, smiling a silly smile.

"Looks like someone else has been having a little drink too."

"Mmm," she murmured, "but *only* a little one. Or maybe two. One of my feline friends has a flask of vodka in her purse."

"Where are they now?" I asked, looking around.

"Oh, here somewhere. They all found boys to dance with."

I nodded slowly.

"Don't worry, I didn't tell them who my partner was going to be." She was standing so close to me now that I could smell the vodka on her breath. I looked away again.

"Or are you having second thoughts?" she asked.

"No, why would I?"

She put a finger to her chin. "If I remember correctly, the college manual doesn't prohibit waltzing between faculty and students."

I laughed and felt a twinge in the pit of my stomach. The band abruptly broke off the rock number it was playing, and a moment later the drummer began a sustained roll on the snare drum.

"Ladies and gentlemen," a voice announced over the microphone, "in celebration of Halloween—the famous *Danse Macabre* waltz!" There were a few isolated cheers. An orange spotlight focused on the lead guitarist. "Which we will perform in the slightly unusual arrangement for guitar, bass, clarinet, and vibraphone!" The announcement of the instrumentation brought the house down.

"That's our cue, Colin," Moira said above the din, leading the way to the dance floor. The guitar slowly sounded the twelve strokes of midnight, and I felt a prickle of excitement as I enclosed Moira's small, soft hand in mine and we started our first turn. The floor was growing more and more crowded—it seemed that everyone wanted to dance the midnight waltz. Every now and then Moira and I were jostled closer together by other dancing couples.

"Pretty tight quarters," I said, noticing that I was short of breath.

"Yeah," Moira said, smiling up at me, "I like it that way."

As we swirled around, I tried my best to concentrate on the music. The quivering guitar tones insinuated themselves into my consciousness, while the eerie clarinet and vibraphone added notes of danger. Who was this dancer in my arms, this cat lady, this sorceress? Gradually, my right hand slipped down her back to her firm, supple waist. The music grew faster and faster and we spun our tight circles at increasingly dizzying speeds, to the point where it seemed that the room was turning. The music rushed on headlong, until suddenly the clarinet sounded the rooster's call announcing the dawn; there remained only a few languid notes on the guitar, and the piece was over. The dancers burst into cheers and applause. Moira and I stood for a moment catching our breath.

"We'd better not dance anymore," I said.

Moira looked at me, disappointed, then glanced around at the crowd. "Oh, I see."

"I'm not sure you do. I mean—did you maybe want to hook up with your friends again? You said before that—"

"No, no, they're well taken care of." Her look changed to one of puzzlement. "You're not quite making sense, Colin."

I forced a smile. "Maybe not. I—"

"Actually, I wouldn't mind leaving now. I can get the escort service to take me back to the dorm if you want to stay."

"Oh, no, I'll walk you home. I'm ready to go too."

"Okay. I just have to pick up my shoulder bag. I left it with the girl at the concessions stand. Be back in a minute."

"How about if I meet you outside? I could stand some fresh air."

"Sure. By that door over there?"

"Okay."

As Moira disappeared into the crowd, I turned and walked toward the exit past other overheated dancers, some of whom were fanning themselves with their hands.

Outside, it seemed even more humid than before. The air was perfectly still. I thought I heard a distant rumble of thunder—or was it just the heavy door slamming shut? I removed my fool's cap and mask, wiped my forehead, and leaned back against the brick wall. I could feel my head spinning slightly. An image of dozens and dozens of dancers in tuxedos and evening gowns flashed through my mind; Annika and I were at the center, smiling at each other as we swirled gracefully around a lavishly-appointed ballroom.

The door squeaked open and fell shut again, and Moira was standing next to me.

"You okay?" she asked.

"I'm fine. Didn't think it would still be this warm outside."

"Hey, this is the South, remember?"

The exit we had taken was at the side of the building, around the corner from the stairway up to campus.

"There's bound to be lots of people up on the road tonight," Moira said. "We can take the trail through the woods instead. It starts just past that lamppost."

"Hmm. How will we be able to see?"

"Not to worry, cats can see in the dark, you know. And we might get a little help from the moon."

Looking up, I saw the faint glow of the rising full moon behind a haze of cloud cover. Off to one side, part of the Big Dipper was visible along with several other stars. We set out along the path and stopped at the lamppost. Two wooden signs were attached to it: "Yellow Trail: Catharine's Pond .2 mi.," and: "Orange Trail: Stone Bridge .4 mi."

"I suppose that's the bridge where Fleishman was killed?"

"Has to be. There's only one stone bridge in the whole South Woods. Why do you ask? Have you been playing Peter Wimsey?"

"Well . . . not exactly."

"So how about that other mystery, Lukas Baumgartner's poem?"

"I've hardly had a minute's time to think about it. How about you?"

She shook her head. "I sort of decided I should be following your lead, I guess."

"Really? No need to. It's not like it's a dance, you know."

"Okay. I'll try to put some more thought into it, then. Maybe we should get together and look at the poem again."

"Sure. I can make you a copy."

"Speaking of leading, you were great back there in the gym."

"Thanks. I just kind of went with the flow." I looked up at the signs again. "What's Catharine's Pond like?"

"We can go there now. It's not but a tiny detour off the trail."

"Well . . ."

"Only for a minute," she said. "It's just about my favorite place anywhere."

"Okay, in that case . . . "

She removed her cat-eared cap and let her hair fall down over her shoulders. She was wearing it loose tonight; its reddish highlights glinted in the light from the lamppost.

"Want me to put your fool's cap in my bag?" she asked.

"Yeah, thanks." I handed her the cap along with my mask and the mirror and she crammed everything into her shoulder bag.

We started out along the trail through alternating patches of darkness and suffused light as the moon continually disappeared behind clouds and reappeared again. Moira's night vision did indeed seem to be cat-like and I was surprised at how well I could see myself.

"You never come out here alone at night, I hope," I said.

"No way. Nobody does. None of the women students, at least."

The trail we had taken was relatively straight, and wide enough most of the way for us to walk side by side. We went on in silence, the only sounds the soft padding of our feet, the snap of an occasional twig, and the muffled jingle of little bells from inside Moira's shoulder bag. From time to time our arms brushed against each other in the dark. Soon we crossed a trail that led up the hill to campus. A short distance farther on a simple wooden arrow carved with the inscription 'Catharine's Pond' pointed to the left.

"Not much longer now," Moira said, leading the way down a path so narrow that we had to walk single file. The moon continued to play its game of hide-and-seek, creating flickering patterns of light that ebbed and flowed in the foliage on either side of the path. From somewhere far off came the mournful hooting of an owl. I felt a strange combination of creepiness and delight as I followed closely behind Moira's indistinct form.

As the path continued to wind its way down the hillside, the moon disappeared completely. Even Moira had trouble seeing now and slowed down to a crawl.

"We're almost there," she said over her shoulder, her voice a whisper.

The path turned once more and ended at a bench a few feet above the dark surface of the pond. Moira came to a sudden stop and I bumped into her; instinctively I put my hands on her shoulders to steady myself, then quickly removed them. The moon was just beginning to emerge from behind a bank of clouds again.

"Sorry," I whispered.

Moira turned her head slightly and placed a finger against her lips, then pointed toward the opposite shore of the pond, where, not twenty yards away, a majestic stag stood drinking. We watched silently as the moon came out, highlighting the ripples on the surface of the water. Seeming to notice the change, the deer raised its head and looked across the pond toward where we were standing. Is he looking at us, I wondered? The three of us remained perfectly motionless. Suddenly there was a flash of lightning followed by the rumbling of thunder, and the deer bounded off down the hill into the woods. Masses of dark clouds began moving across the face of the moon. Another lightning flash and a loud clap of thunder, and the skies opened up.

"C'mon, Colin!" Moira called out.

She trotted along the edge of the pond with me right behind her. We ducked inside a small wooden shelter partially hidden under the trees and sat down on the bench, both slightly out of breath.

"Man, look at it rain!" Moira said. "Another minute, and we would've been drenched!" The rain was coming down so hard now that the pond was almost completely obscured.

"Luke Baumgartner would be happy to know his shelter's being put to good use," she went on. "I heard a story once that he had it built after his wife got soaked to the skin when she was out here."

"Well, this must have been one of her favorite places, if the pond was named after her."

"I'm sure it was. She's supposed to have seen a deer here too, while she was sitting at the edge of the pond reading a book of Romantic poetry. Just imagine how long ago it all happened."

"Yes. Way back in the 1860s, it must've been."

Moira looked up at me. "Who knows, maybe we're the first ones to have seen a deer here since then."

I smiled. "Only the second time in a century-and-a-half? Well, could be."

We were silent for a few moments. The rain had let up somewhat and the thunderclaps were rumbling off in the distance. Every now and then moonlight reflected on the surface of the pond.

"I can barely make out your face," I said. "You're sure it's you, and not some devil?"

She gave a throaty laugh. "It's Halloween, Colin, better watch out!" She reached into her purse, pulled out a flask, and held it up to me.

"Care for a snort?"

"Didn't you say it was your girlfriend who had the booze?"

"Oops. Guess it was me."

"Uh-huh. Guess it was." She handed me the flask and I took a swig. The lukewarm liquid burned as it went down my throat.

"Straight," I said, catching my breath.

"Sure. There was plenty to mix it with at the party." She took a sizable swallow herself.

"Dry campus," I said. "In a dry county, too. What a joke."

"Yeah. Everybody looks the other way, including the administration."

The rain was just about off now. I held my hand out and looked up at the sky. "This might be our chance," I said.

"I think it is too," Moira answered. Suddenly her arms were around my shoulders and she was kissing me. I ran one hand over the fluffy hairs on the nape of her neck, then let it slide down to the small of her back and along the curve of her hip to her thigh. The material of her costume was smooth and velvety; an incongruous recollection of the droplets of mercury I had once held in the palm of my hand during a high school science class flashed through my mind. From somewhere far away, I imagined I could hear the frenzied strains of the *Danse Macabre*.

"See?" Moira said breathlessly a moment later, "the whiskers don't tickle at all, do they?"

"Not a bit," I said, swallowing hard.

She lay on the bench and started to pull me down on top of her. From the other side of the pond came the screech of some wild animal. Startled, I sat up and stared at her.

"Moira, we can't do this! Why did you have to start—"

She pushed me back angrily. "Why did I have to . . . so you're Mr. Innocent, is that it? So you were totally uninvolved when we were dancing?"

"All right, maybe I—"

"There's somebody else, isn't there." She stood up and sighed deeply. "That phone call you got when I was at your place . . . I could hear it was a woman . . ."

I looked her in the eye. "Moira, the point is, you're my student. It would be unethical for me to—"

"Drop the bullshit, all right?"

"Bullshit? People lose their jobs over stuff like this!"

"Well, we wouldn't want that to happen, would we." She looked away into the darkness. "Let's go," she said. "While the rain's still off."

We followed the narrow path back to the main trail, then walked single file, saying nothing. I wiped off the occasional drops of water that fell from the canopy of trees above. The rumble of thunder sounded from time to time.

"I know of a shortcut a little ways along," Moira said. "It'll get us out of the woods faster."

"Let's take it. This isn't the best place to be in a thunderstorm."

Another hundred feet along the trail Moira slowed down. "It's around here someplace," she said, looking intently to her right.

"Good thing you have cat vision," I said.

"This is even better," she said, pulling a small flashlight out of her bag. The beam cast ghostly shadows as we walked on. "Okay, here it is."

She shone the light on a large pine tree marked with an 'X.' An overgrown path that most hikers would have overlooked cut off at an angle just before the giant tree. I tromped along after Moira, my legs brushing against the wet underbrush on either side.

"Where does this take us?" I asked.

"You'll see in a minute."

The path came to an abrupt end at a broad expanse of lawn dotted with trees.

"Is this someone's backyard, or what?" I said.

"You know, I think it is."

"Well, we can't go traipsing across someone's yard in the middle of the night."

"Why not?" she said. "That's your house straight ahead."

"What? But how in the—"

"Professor Seifert made the path. He wanted a quick way to get into the woods from his house. That time he invited our class over he marched us out to the Yellow Trail and showed us the mark on the tree. Said he needed to have the path trampled down every so often."

A sudden clap of thunder boomed directly overhead and it began to pour again. Moira and I broke into a run toward the house. We were soaking wet by the time we reached the porch.

"Inside, quick!" I said as I pulled the screen door open. We rushed in and stood next to the wrought-iron table, dripping water onto the carpet. Moira wiped her face with one hand.

"You shouldn't have done that," I said, "you just lost half your whiskers."

"You're looking a little bedraggled yourself, Mr. Fool."

"All right, I deserved that. Let's go in and dry off."

We walked through the kitchen and up the stairway to the second floor. I reached into the linen closet in the hallway, took out two towels, and handed one to Moira. Juniper appeared out of nowhere and sidled up to her.

"She remembers me," she said, crouching down to stroke the back of her neck.

"I guess so. Or maybe she's mistaken you for some slightly oversize cat friend of hers."

Moira stood up, frowning. "I'll try to take that as a compliment."

"Which is exactly how I meant it."

She shivered and wrapped the towel around her shoulders. "Can I take a shower, Colin? I'm starting to feel chilled to the bone. Or are you still pissed off?"

"I thought *you* were the one who was pissed off. Go ahead and take your shower. There's another one in the basement, I'll go down there."

I tiptoed up the stairs a few minutes later wearing only a towel; the shower was still going and I could hear Moira humming a tune. I finished drying myself off in the bedroom and put on a shirt and jeans. I looked out the window and saw that the rain hadn't let up. Moira emerged from the bathroom in a T-shirt and shorts. She looked down at herself self-consciously.

"Sorry. This is all I had in my bag."

"I can give you a sweater if you're still cold."

"No, I'll be fine. It's not but a few minutes' run to my dorm. I'll go the way we came in, back through the woods."

"It's still pouring out there, Moira. Let's have a look at the radar and see when it's going to let up."

We went into my study and I turned the computer on. A moment later the weather site came up. The front looked virtually stationary and the indication was that heavy rain would continue for several hours.

Moira gave me a questioning look. "All right if I stay here?"

"Of course. I'll give you some flannel pajamas and you can use my bed. I'll sleep downstairs on the sofa."

"No way, Colin, I'm not going to take your bed."

I held up a hand. "It's not a problem, I can sleep anywhere. You're the guest, so you get the bed." I glanced at her skimpy clothing. "I don't think it would be a good idea for us to be in the same room together, and especially not in the same bed."

Moira smiled. "Well, that helps soothe my wounded pride some, at least."

I put my hand on her shoulder. "Wounded pride! Moira, you're one hell of a good-looking woman. If you weren't my student—"

She glanced at me, then looked away. "I know you're right, if I look at it rationally. It's just that I wasn't my usual rational self tonight. I hope you don't think that I had everything all planned out, Colin. It just kind of . . . happened."

"The thought never crossed my mind. I was flirting as much as you were. Both of us set ourselves up for what happened in the woods. It's not always easy to be vigilant about what's going on inside of us, or where things can lead. We should be, but we can't always."

"Is that your final philosophical statement of the evening, Professor?"

I laughed. "I suppose it did sound like I was pontificating. Yes, that was my final statement. I'll see if I can find those pajamas."

We walked into the bedroom and I rummaged in a dresser drawer.

"Gray flannel, not terribly feminine, I'm afraid."

"Hey, I don't care, as long as they're warm."

Juniper was lying at the foot of the bed and meowed softly at the intrusion.

"You may have to share the bed with her," I said.

"Good. It'll be just like when I'm home."

"See you in the morning, then?"

"Right. See you in the morning."

I awoke with a start. In the semi-darkness I could see Moira descending the stairs, her bag over one shoulder and a piece of paper in one hand.

"Sorry I woke you," she said, "it's hard not to make those stairs creak." She held up the sheet of paper. "I snitched this from your printer. I was going to leave you a note."

I swung myself out of the sofa and rubbed my eyes. "How can it be morning already? Feels like I just lay down a couple of minutes ago."

"It's six-thirty and the rain's off. I thought I should head back before it got light outside."

"Okay. You have your cat outfit?"

"Yes, it's in my bag. I hung it over the shower rod to dry last night."

We walked through the kitchen and stood by the door to the porch.

"Are you sure you'll be able to find your way?"

"Sure. Don't forget I have cat vision—and my flashlight." She turned and grasped the door handle.

"Well—" we said simultaneously, then laughed.

"Thanks for being my dance partner last night," Moira said.

"Thanks for being mine. I don't know when I've had a better one. Seriously." I came close to stroking her cheek, but stopped myself. I noticed that all traces of her cat's whiskers had disappeared.

"You know what?" I said. "I think you've turned back into a human being again."

"I'll tell you a secret, Colin—I was a human being the whole time."

I nodded slowly. "You okay?"

"Yeah, I'm okay." She touched me on the arm, then walked

through the porch to the outside door. I followed her down the steps and watched as she set out toward the woods.

"See you in class on Monday," she said, glancing over her shoulder.

"Right. See you then."

I stood there until she disappeared among the trees, thinking back to what had happened at the pond. Moira had been right about the phone call, of course. Was it true that I had held back because she was my student, or was it because of Annika? My mind in a muddle, I went back into the house and got a pot of coffee going.

Chapter 26

I felt nervous as I walked along the hall to class on Monday morning. Had Moira truly been as calm and collected as she appeared when she left the house? What if our encounter in the woods had affected her more than she had let on? She had never missed a class yet, and if she wasn't there today it would be partly my fault. True, she had made the first move, but I could hardly consider myself blameless.

I breathed a sigh of relief as I entered the classroom. There she was, occupying her usual seat in the first row and smiling up at me. As I warmed the students up with a few routine questions, I noted to my consternation that Jason, whose attendance had been sporadic over the past two weeks, was absent once again.

After class, Moira lingered until all the other students had left, then walked toward the door with me.

"Have you given any thought to weapons lately?" she asked.

It took me a moment to make the connection. "Only in passing, if that," I said. "How about you?"

"Well, I did check out the St. Eustace reproduction in the entrance tower before class. His sword is pointing to a huge stone at the base of the wall. What are you supposed to do, go hacking away with a hammer and chisel out there with people marching in and out? I don't think so. And you'd have another impossible situation with the original in the museum."

"Right. Maybe St. Eustace is the wrong saint after all, just like the lindens in the library courtyard were the wrong trees."

"You said there was a statue of him in the chapel. Isn't that still a possibility?"

"I suppose so. We can go over there now if you have time. I'll pass you off to the custodian as an art student who's fascinated by neo-Gothic architecture."

"Well . . . I'm still wondering about that signature business. Like maybe it would be in one of the diary volumes after all. We could check in the library."

"Okay, can't hurt to look."

I pulled Volume I off the shelf and handed it to Moira.

"The master's voice," I said.

"Let's hope he speaks to us." She slowly paged through to the end of the book.

"No master's signature, as far as I can see."

"Okay. Let's try the other two."

We looked through Volumes II and III with the same results.

"Check the first one again," I said. "Maybe we missed a signature at the end of the introduction."

Moira started leafing through the book again.

"Just his initials," she said, then turned back to the title page and pointed to a shield containing a falcon and fleur-de-lys. "Is this his coat of arms?"

"Yes. There's a stained-glass version of it in the private chapel. It was part of the word game I had to figure out to find where the first clue was hidden."

"Wait a minute, Colin." Moira stared up at me. "Isn't a coat-of-arms a kind of signature?"

"You know, you could be on to something. If what we need is a depiction of the coat-of-arms with a saint nearby. . . . Here, I brought a copy of the poem along. Let's have a look at it again."

"Hold on," Moira said, her voice a whisper, "I thought I heard something."

She tiptoed out to the aisle and disappeared around the corner. A moment later she came back, looking relieved.

"Guess I'm hearing things. Or getting paranoid."

"Look, why don't we go down to the courtyard. No one's going to sneak up on us there. And it's too nice a day to be inside."

We sat down on a bench in one corner, far away from anyone else, and studied the poem for a few minutes.

"All right," I said, "on the assumption that the chapel's the place . . ."

"Could you sketch it out for me? I need to be able to visualize where things are."

I drew the floor plan in the margin next to the poem, then marked the left side of the apse with an "X."

"Here's where I dug around the stone below Luke's coat-of-arms to find the first clue. There's an aisle down the center and three rows of pews on either side. The first thing you see when you step in is the statue of St. Eustace, to the left of the doorway. Oh, another thing—there're a couple of niches in the back wall that have bas-relief statues of Biblical figures in them. They're based on Dürer's *Four Apostles* painting."

"So they're saints too."

"Now that you mention it, yes."

"Any of them have swords or anything?"

I thought for a moment. "Paul does. He's almost always depicted with a sword."

"Hmm. So we've got the signature—the coat-of-arms, in other words—and more saints than we need." Moira looked at the poem again. "There's nothing else we've figured out yet, right?"

"I don't think so . . . 'In and out'—whatever that means. . . ." I read the lines out loud: "*In and out, then out and in, / provide a helpful place to begin;/ four is thus part of the recipe, / instead of my usual number three.* Any ideas?"

"Maybe. Look at the next two lines: *Strike this balance, and soon you will be / where once you were on bended knee.* The 'in and out' line is balanced, because the phrase is reversed—and the 'bended knee' bit would make sense if we're right about the private chapel. You were there before and you had to bend down to dig out the mortar, right? And Luke knows that you were, so to speak."

"True. But I was also 'on bended knee' out by the lindens in the North Woods, and in the Garden of Time before that. Which Luke also 'knows.' Three times so far, with one step to go . . . Wait a second, though . . . I found the first clue in the private chapel. *In* the chapel . . . "

"Right. And that led you where?"

"To the *Melencolia* engraving in the museum . . . and then up onto the roof. And from there I looked over to the Garden of Time."

"So you were *in* again—in the museum, I mean—then *up* or *on*. Darn, we don't want any 'ups' or 'ons,' we only want 'ins' and 'outs'!"

"Yes. Maybe if we limit ourselves to the places where I actually found the clues? *In* the chapel, then *in* the Garden of Time—"

"And the third clue was . . . *in* the North Woods, *in* the clearing, *under* the tree . . . the 'under' is useless, but we don't need all those 'ins' either—we need some 'outs'!"

We stared at the poem for several seconds.

"Here's another angle, Moira: If you're *in* a garden, it's not the same as being *in* a building, right?"

"Of course not. Because you're outside . . . you're not in at all— you're *out*. Colin, let's see if we can get this to work. You found the first clue *in* the chapel, the second was *outside* in the Garden of Time, the third was *outside* in the North Woods—"

"And we need four things, and we need to have balance—so the fourth location has to be *in* again."

"Yes! In the chapel!"

"Or in the museum, maybe?"

"No! You weren't there 'on bended knee,' were you? It has to be 'where you once were on bended knee.'"

"Well, I was, actually. But only because of my harebrained idea of trying to figure out where exactly the *Three Lindens* painting was on the wall. Not something Luke could have anticipated."

"Colin, it has to be the chapel—you started there, and you finish there. How much more balanced can you get?"

"It all adds up, doesn't it."

Moira looked at her watch. "I hate to say it, but I have to get going. I'm having lunch with a girlfriend at twelve-thirty."

"And I have my class this afternoon. Should we see if we can get into the chapel after that?"

"Sure."

"How about if we meet by the bench across from the Rapunzel tower—at two-thirty, say? Give or take."

"Perfect, I'll even allow you some leeway." With a smirk, she headed off through the archway.

I had lunch at home, then went to my office to look through the materials for my Beginning German class. Charlotte's door was open as I passed by.

"Hi, Colin," she said. "Any problems with the devil or problematic queens over the weekend?"

I felt my face growing warm. "No, I guess not."

"Good. Well, I have a big favor to ask of you."

"Oh? Sure."

"Klaus's father died yesterday in Argentina. He's already left to catch a flight there. He's going to go on some sort of pilgrimage, too, so he won't be back until two weeks from tomorrow. I was wondering if you'd be willing to take over one of his classes."

"Of course. Which one?"

"Medieval literature. I'm sorry to stick you with that because it'll be a fair amount of preparation, but I remembered from your dossier that you're pretty familiar with the period. The class meets at 10:10 Tuesdays and Thursdays for an hour-and-a-half. So it would be tomorrow's class, this Thursday's, and the two next week."

"No problem. It's been a while since I've read anything in Middle High German. It'll be fun to get back into it."

"Well, good. Klaus's syllabus has two days on Neidhart von Reuental coming up and then he goes on to the courtly epic for the second part of the semester—Hartmann von Aue and so on."

I smiled. Neidhart's poetry was the subject of Annika's dissertation. Too bad she couldn't be here to teach in my place. Too bad she couldn't be here for lots of reasons.

"Fine," I said. "Neidhart was one of my favorite poets in graduate school. And Hartmann von Aue—I have a special relationship with him, of course, if you recall Klaus's reference: 'ein riter der gelêret was . . .'"

Charlotte laughed. "Oh, I remember that well, it was your very first day on campus, and you parried it so nicely! Thanks so much, Colin, Klaus will appreciate your covering for him. He'll probably be totally dragged out by the time he gets back."

"How old was his father? Over ninety, I suppose?"

"I don't rightly know. Klaus hasn't ever said much about him in all the years he's been here."

Looks like I know more about him than you do, I said to myself. I wasn't about to mention the photo I had seen of Klaus's father as an SS officer.

Charlotte handed me a copy of the syllabus, detailing which poems were to be discussed. I stepped into my office with mixed feelings. What I had said about the Middle High German poets was true enough, but the extra class preparations would more than likely mean postponing the final stage of the treasure hunt. And Moira and I were so close now. Ah well, it couldn't be helped. I glanced through the syllabus, glad to see that I recognized several of the poems. Then it was off for my rendezvous.

Moira was sitting on the designated bench as I approached on the Promenade.

"Hi," she said. "Have you heard about Professor Hochstraaten yet?"

"That his father died? Yes, I'll be teaching his literature class until he gets back."

"Oh, he didn't say anything about his father in the email he sent me. All he said was he'd be gone for a while and would I water his plants. He was so precise about it. He wants me to go out there this Saturday and the next, between one and three o'clock. And he said he'd leave a list of the plants and how much water each one needs."

"Precise kind of guy, isn't he." I stroked my chin for a moment. "What does he do, put a key under the doormat?"

"No way, I don't think he'd ever do that. He said he'd leave it with Charlotte. I already asked her if I could get it from her on Friday."

"Well . . . how about if I give you a ride out there on Saturday?"

"Thanks, but I really don't mind biking. I don't do enough of it."

"Wow, can you really make it up that steep gravel road?"

"Oh, that's not how I go. My boyfriend drove me that way once when my bike was being repaired. There's a paved road from the other side that Professor Hochstraaten told me about. Takes longer, but it's flatter and it beats breathing dust."

"Sure . . . well . . . you see, I've sort of been wanting to have another look at his paintings. There's so many of them, and I haven't given them more than a glance. I've only been in his house once."

"He does have quite a few. Some of the saints in his bedroom are interesting—pre-Raphaelites, or something like that."

"Really? I wouldn't mind seeing them, if you think it would be all right. I've always been partial to the pre-Raphaelites."

Moira shrugged. "Fine, if you want to go out there with me. Maybe we could leave around twelve-thirty or so?"

"Great. I'll pick you up at your dorm."

"Okay."

We crossed the footbridge to the Rapunzel tower and stepped inside. Ned was just leaving the utility room with a bucket of water in one hand.

"Hi, Ned," I said, "I hate to interrupt your work again . . ."

He put his bucket down. "No worries. The blackboards can wait a few minutes."

"Well, thanks. Ned, I'd like you to meet Moira MacGregor. She's an art student, and she's always wanted to see inside the private chapel. Moira, this is Ned Avery."

Ned paused for a moment before speaking. "I saw your photographs over in the art building a couple weeks ago. I liked them a lot."

Moira blushed slightly. "Did you? Thanks, I always appreciate hearing that."

She extended a hand in his direction. Ned hesitated, then wiped his on his pants.

"My hand's not the cleanest, ma'am."

"Oh, I'm sure it's good clean dirt, as my mother would say."

Ned smiled, gave her hand a hesitant shake, and stepped back inside the utility room to get the key. Moira and I followed him along the corridor to the private chapel. As before, the key turned in the lock almost noiselessly.

"Thanks, Ned, I don't think we'll be long today."

"Whatever. You can just slide the key under my door if I'm not there."

"Fine, I'll do that."

"It was nice meeting you, Ned," Moira said. "Thanks for letting us in."

"No problem. Nice meetin' you too, ma'am." He touched his hand to his cap with a trace of a smile.

Once we were inside the chapel, Moira looked around in all directions.

"Colin, this is really delightful! Much more to my taste than the college chapel. And here's St. Eustace, right where you said he'd be."

She studied the statue for a moment, then shook her head.

"I don't think this guy's our saint, Colin."

"Why do you say that?"

"Look where his sword is pointing—right to the back of that pew. It's almost touching it, even."

"Unless we're supposed to extend the line of the sword through the pew and see where it hits the floor? Sounds unlikely, though."

"It does. It's too . . . too *messy* a solution, not straightforward enough for someone as precise as Luke Baumgartner."

"Yeah, definitely." I led Moira to the bas-relief statues recessed in the rear wall. "That leaves these four. More specifically, Paul, the one on the right."

"Look at his sword," Moira said, "it's pointing straight down."

"But where to, exactly? There's two rows of stones under him." I bent down and scrutinized the area. "The mortar's all the same color. That's what helped me find the first clue—it was different around the stone the clue sent me to. I wonder if Luke did that on purpose even, to make it a little easier."

"Are you sure there aren't any other saints with weapons here, Colin?"

Moira walked slowly past the statue of St. Eustace toward the windows in the apse. "Oh, that must be Jonah. Don't think I've ever seen such a cheerful whale before."

"And there's Luke's coat-of-arms, in the little window under King David. See where the mortar's missing around the bottom stone?"

"Colin!" Moira pointed to the window at the far right.

"Oh my God, I'd forgotten all about him—St. George!"

"Look at his lance, Colin. Now that's what I call a tool of a violent trade!"

The lance had run the dragon through and was pointing downward and to the right at an angle of about forty-five-degrees. I dropped to my knees and examined the edges of the three rows of stone below the window.

"Guess what? The mortar around the stone at the bottom doesn't match the rest of it."

Moira knelt down. "You're right, it doesn't! Let's look at the poem again—maybe more of it will make sense now."

I laid my copy on the floor. Moira began to read aloud:

"'. . . soon you'll be / where you once were on bended knee. / *From first to last, from left to right* . . .' Yes! You started over there on the left, and now you're going to finish here on the right!"

I got to my feet. "Everything fits! Damn, I wish I'd brought my tools along. But I wouldn't have had time now anyway, with my class coming up. And then I've got those extra course preparations to deal with as well . . ."

"That's not a real problem, though, is it? There'll be time enough later on. I don't suppose that stone's planning on going anywhere."

I smiled. "Right. I started working on this, what, close to two months ago? Guess it won't kill me to wait a little longer."

Chapter 27

That afternoon, as I was preparing for the first of Hochstraaten's classes on Middle High German poetry, my thoughts drifted quite naturally to Annika. Her dissertation defense would be coming up soon. Very soon, as a matter of fact. What had she said? Middle of November, if I remembered correctly. Surely she wouldn't take it amiss if I called her to wish her well. I pulled out my phone and selected her number.

"Hi, Annika, it's Colin."

"Hello, how are you doing?"

"Oh, fine. A little busier than usual. One of our colleagues is out of the country for a couple of weeks and I'll be teaching his class on Middle High German poetry. You'll never guess which poet we're talking about this week."

"Not Neidhart, by any chance?"

"Yes, Neidhart. I feel a little out of my depth."

"I'm sure you'll do fine. You used to say he was one of your favorite poets. And he's one of mine too, of course."

"Even now, after having written however many hundred pages on him?"

"Only two hundred. And yes, even more so. He's become almost like a family member."

"I'm glad to hear it. That's mainly why I'm calling you, actually—to wish you luck on your defense. It must be coming up soon."

"Yes, on the 14th—a week from this Friday."

"The 14th. That's a good number."

"Yes, I remember. It was the number of your favorite baseball player. He played first base, and you said that was the position you liked to play when you were in high school. Not that I even know what first base is." She laughed quietly.

"I'm amazed you still remember that, Annika."

"Oh, I remember a lot of things. And actually I do know what first base is. And second and third base, even. Your instruction finally sank in."

"How about the infield fly rule? Seems to me I tried to teach you what that was once."

"Now *that* I definitely do not remember," she said, laughing again.

"It was crazy back then. I don't know why I felt compelled to explain the rules of baseball—not just to you, to other Germans, too. Usually without success. There seems to be a deep-seated resistance to our national pastime in the Teutonic psyche."

"That may well be true. Our sporting space is very limited. It is taken up by *Fußball*, and not much else."

"Well, that's a great game too."

There was silence for a moment.

"How did we get onto this baseball kick?" I said.

"I was the one who started it, remember? Your favorite baseball player."

"That's right. Well, as I said before I just wanted to wish you the best of luck—not that you'll need it. *Hals- und Beinbruch*, Annika. I'll be thinking of you on Friday."

"Thank you, Colin, that's kind of you. I'm sure all will go fine."

This time I felt buoyed up by the conversation. It had been almost completely trivial, but then, much of what people said to each other in daily life was just that. The situation vis-à-vis Annika no longer seemed quite so bleak to me. I set about preparing the Neidhart poems that Hochstraaten had scheduled for Tuesday, interrupted only by thoughts about another impending event: my invasion of his house on Saturday. How in the world would I ever get into that back room of his? Where would he keep the key, if he hadn't taken it with him to Argentina? . . . His desk drawer seemed the most likely place. And his study would be open because of the potted plants. The drawer, though—the damn drawer would certainly be locked. . . .

Suddenly I thought about Dorothy Sayers' *Strong Poison*, the novel I'd started on the drive down to Kentucky and finished the following week. Toward the end of the story Lord Peter needs one of his female employees to do some lockpicking for him and enlists a reformed burglar to play the role of teacher. Miss Murchison learns how to manipulate the tools remarkably quickly.

I googled "lockpicking" and found more sites than I could have imagined. Several offered detailed instructions, complete with diagrams and videos. The most common types of locks seemed to be pin-and-tumbler and wafer. A so-called tension wrench and the right type of pick would be needed to open either one.

Next I checked Amazon and found a kit for twenty-four dollars that looked reasonably professional. With hardly a second thought, I placed an order for next-day delivery. As I was typing in my personal information I started to wonder: would I be putting myself on some sort of national listing of people who ordered materials that could be used for illegal activities? That was precisely what I had in mind to do, of course. But who would ever know? Plus, it was a worthy cause. I pushed the

"Place Order" button before I had a chance to reconsider.

Hochstraaten's class the next morning had attracted only five students. This was not surprising, since German poetry of the Middle Ages had the added difficulty of being written in a language that had changed considerably over the centuries. Klaus had wisely chosen an edition of poems with modern German translations on the facing pages. The students were alert and focused on the subject matter. What especially engaged them in Neidhart's poems were their strong social distinctions and the irony he often used in characterizing them. I had individual students read several poems out loud in the original, and with some coaching they did a creditable job of producing the unaccustomed sounds of Middle High German. In the end I had to concede, if grudgingly, that Klaus had prepared his students well.

During my German Culture class that afternoon my thoughts kept wandering from the Martin Luther selection I had assigned to the somewhat disreputable order I had placed on Amazon. Still, Luther's polemical notions made for a lively discussion, and the ninety minutes went by quickly enough. Feeling slightly guilty for not having given the class my full attention, I left Riedenburg Hall and hurried home, hoping that my illicit package might have arrived. Miraculously, it lay there on my doorstep, no more than twenty hours after I had placed the order.

I raced up the stairs to my study, tearing the package open as I went. The kit contained a dozen or more tools, mostly picks along with a few tension wrenches. Feeling completely intimidated, I printed out one of the lockpicking guides I had looked at the day before, then went down to the porch and set about working on the deadbolt lock in the kitchen door.

None of the various picks seemed to be getting me anywhere. Had I ended up buying a pile of crap? No, that couldn't be—the selection of tools looked very much like the ones pictured in my guide. I went through the instructions again, wishing that I could find someone like Lord Peter's reformed convict to show me the tricks of the trade. But the time I could expend on this was limited, since I had extra classes to teach. On Thursday morning, after a post-breakfast review of the second set of Neidhart poems, I trotted along to Riedenburg Hall. As an added touch of authenticity, I brought along a CD of German instrumental and vocal music from the medieval period. Middle High German poems had been sung rather than just recited in their day, and many of the melodies associated with Neidhart's poems in particular had been preserved in the extant manuscripts. The biting social commentary of some of his texts led the students to make interesting comparisons with contemporary performers, and a lively discussion ensued on the relative merits of singers like Bob Dylan and Bruce Springsteen.

My continued lock-picking attempts over the next day-and-a-half were at best mixed. At one point I was fairly sure I had successfully raised two of the pins in the kitchen door deadbolt lock above the shear line. How many more were left? Three or four, I assumed. Just as I thought I heard the slight click of the third pin rising into place, the pick slipped out of my hand. Would I ever get the hang of this?

I alternated between the deadbolt and the lock in the middle drawer of my desk. This type had a somewhat different mechanism than pin tumbler locks and could be easier to deal with—or harder, depending on which website you believed. Eking out time between class preparations and paper-grading, I tried using the technique of raking with a ripple-edged pick, but was able to get the lock open only once. The much heavier-duty lock in the kitchen door, however, completely resisted my next attempts, including one in which I ineffectually tried to imitate the techniques I had seen a young man use in a video.

On Friday afternoon I finally succeeded in opening the kitchen door lock, but was unable to replicate the process. And that evening the desk drawer yielded to my efforts again. But here, too, the application of any skills I had developed had been purely hit or miss. As I dragged myself to bed, I began to wonder: was I really prepared to prowl around Hochstraaten's house in what would certainly be a criminal intrusion? What if a neighbor happened to see me turn in at Klaus's driveway and then mentioned it to him later? How sure was I that the van Thielen painting had been acquired by unscrupulous means anyway? And wouldn't I be compromising Moira as well? Maybe it would be better to call her in the morning and tell her she would have to bike out there after all, that I wasn't feeling well.

I lay in bed turning various scenarios over and over in my mind. The last thing I remembered before dropping off to sleep was hearing a distant voice saying: fool if you do, fool if you don't.

Chapter 28

"Should we take the shorter way?" I asked. "I'm pretty sure I remember where the cutoff is."

"Fine by me."

We sped along the highway and turned onto the gravel road marked by the "fresh eggs" sign. I immediately switched to inside air. A few minutes later we turned again and began crunching our way up the steep hill. A metallic-red motorcycle slowed as it passed by, raising a cloud of dust. Moira turned and looked back.

"Looks kind of like Jason's motorcycle," she said. "Same color, at least."

"Really? You know him well enough to know what color his motorcycle is?"

"Only because he tried to get me to go for a ride on it once. I told him I was afraid of motorcycles."

"Really?"

"No, not really. It was more Jason than anything else. I feel sorry for him, but I sure don't want to go tearin' around the countryside on a motorcycle with him."

"You think that really was Jason back there?"

"Oh, I doubt it. There's lots of red motorcycles around."

At the top of the hill, shortly after the paved road began, Moira pointed to the right.

"The next driveway is Professor Hochstraaten's."

I drove between the double row of pine trees and parked in front of the garage. As we walked up the porch steps, Moira took the house key out of her shoulder bag. It was of the old-fashioned variety, with a long shank and a ring-shaped handle.

"Here, can I do that?" I asked, holding out my hand.

"Go ahead." Moira handed me the key.

I turned it in the lock slowly, listening to the loud click as it opened.

"Was that fun?" she asked as I handed the key back to her.

"Loads," I said.

She gave me a puzzled look as we stepped through the entryway into the living room. Hochstraaten had left her a note on the coffee table.

"Can you believe it? He must've listed every one of his plants . . . whether they should be watered today or next Saturday, how much. . . ."

I glanced at the list over her shoulder. "Living room, kitchen, back porch. How about upstairs?"

"Must be on the other side." She turned the sheet over. "Four small plants by the window in his study and two large ones on the floor. A few in his bedroom and tons more on the sleeping porch."

"Amazing. Where are you going to start?"

"I usually do the main floor first. He keeps the watering can in the kitchen."

"And you said he has some interesting renderings of saints in his bedroom?"

"Well, they're a change from the landscapes and still lifes down here, at least. The one of St. Sebastian is kind of sweet."

"Sweet? Not grotesquely bloody?"

"No, not this one. He's kinda dreamy."

I smiled. "I'll go up and have a look."

"Okay. See you in a while."

Hochstraaten's bedroom was on the left at the head of the stairs; the sparse furniture consisted of a large armoire, an upholstered chair, a single bed with an intricately carved headboard, and a night table. A Norfolk Island pine, not quite as large as the one I remembered seeing in the living room, stood in one corner near two hanging plants. Small paintings of saints filled most of the walls. I spotted the *St. Sebastian* that Moira had mentioned next to the door. Her brief characterization of the piece had been accurate; the saint gazed ecstatically heavenwards, apparently unperturbed by the half-dozen arrows piercing his body. Glancing at the other paintings, which had an equally maudlin look about them, I stepped back into the L-shaped hallway and flicked the switch for the overhead lights. At the end of the hall to the right, the door to the study stood wide open. After a moment's indecision, I took the lockpicking kit out of my jacket pocket and turned left toward the back of the house.

The door to the mystery room had no handle. Its deadbolt lock was embossed with the name 'Schlage'—trust Hochstraaten to pick one with a German sound to it.

Here goes nothing, I muttered. I inserted a tension wrench from the kit, applied pressure, and then began working with one of the picks, poking it slowly up and down to manipulate the pins. When that yielded nothing I tried a raking motion, alternating between faster and slower. Listening to the sound of grating metal in itself gave me a satisfying feeling, almost as if I knew what I was doing.

Right, I muttered to myself, "almost as if." I switched to a different pick, then a third, and a fourth and a fifth, but got nowhere. Beads of perspiration were forming on my forehead and I could feel my anxiety level rising. This was not going to work. I had no choice now but to try the desk drawer in the study. Gathering up the tools, I walked around the corner to the other stretch of the hallway.

Just before the bathroom, a door on the left was cracked open; this had to be the spare bedroom that Moira had mentioned. I gave the door a slight nudge and peered inside. An unmade bed stood in one corner; draped over a simple wooden chair was a black T-shirt, imprinted with jagged letters and the logo of what looked to be a heavy-metal band. Good God, that had to have been Jason's motorcycle we saw after all! Did he know what kind of car I drove? Had he recognized either of us? What was he doing at Hochstraaten's house anyway?

On the floor a few feet from the door lay a piece of paper containing a hand-written note. I bent over and picked it up.

Remember that you are not to touch the plants. I have arranged for someone to come and water them on both Saturday afternoons. Since this person may know you, you must leave the house before one o'clock on those days and not return until four o'clock.

Your other responsibilities are as usual. I will expect a full report upon my return.

What in hell? I left the note where I had found it and shut the door. Jason would not be returning for at least two more hours. I continued along the hallway to Hochstraaten's study, stepped inside and sat down in the desk chair. The middle desk drawer was locked, as I had assumed. Feeling my breath coming in starts, I took out one of the picks and a tension wrench and inserted them into the lock. The technique of raking had definitely not worked before, so this time I tried moving slowly from the back of the lock to the front, applying gentle pressure with both tools. A couple of minutes later I was pretty sure that I had eased three, and possibly four of the discs out of their casing. How many more would there be? I worked away, and a few seconds later the lock suddenly clicked and I was able to turn the cylinder with the tension wrench. Good God, it had worked. Exactly *how* it had worked I didn't know, and I cared even less.

Slowly, gingerly, I pulled the drawer out, mildly surprised to see the framed photograph of Klaus's father staring up at me. Of course—my careful colleague wasn't about to display the picture to a college student who might or might not recognize the uniform for what it was. It was also no surprise that the rolled-up painting no longer lay on the desk. I began to explore the contents of the drawer.

A concave receptacle at the front contained a few pens and pencils, a pencil sharpener, and two keys. I picked up the smaller one, scarcely able to believe my eyes. Its bit was in the shape of the number three; I would have sworn that it was identical to the one in the metal box at the law office.

"Where in the hell did he get this?" I said out loud, then turned around nervously and listened. All I could hear were some indistinct sounds from down below.

The larger key bore the name 'Schlage'— but there could be other such locks in the house, of course—maybe to a wine cellar, or even to the garage door. Pushing the desk drawer shut and leaving the room, I listened for a moment at the head of the stairs. From the kitchen I could hear the sound of water flowing into a metal container, as Moira filled the watering can yet again. Satisfied that she would be occupied for some time to come, I walked quickly to the door at the end of the hallway. Taking a deep breath, I inserted the key into the lock and turned it. The bolt moved smoothly with only a slight click, and the door opened on silent hinges. The bright early-afternoon light flooded the room from the two skylights and the narrow windows near the top of the three outer walls.

It was as if I had stepped into a small gallery in a fine arts museum. A three-foot strip of oak wainscoting ran around the room, above which hung a single row of small gilt-framed paintings. A straight-backed wooden chair stood near the door. There was no other furniture.

Crossing over to the opposite wall, I began to examine each of the paintings. They seemed to represent a capsule history of the life and death of Jesus: first the Nativity, then the Flight into Egypt, a Madonna and Child, the young Jesus driving the moneylenders from the temple, the Sermon on the Mount, the Last Supper, and finally a Crucifixion scene. The shorter wall on the left also adhered to Biblical chronology: a painting of Adam and Eve in the Garden of Eden, followed by a depiction of the Expulsion, one of Abraham at the point of sacrificing Isaac, and a fiery scene that apparently represented the destruction of Sodom. Not surprisingly, Klaus had given considerably shorter shrift to the Old Testament.

The paintings on the wall at the opposite end of the room stood in sharp contrast to the others. I recognized the van Thielen bouquet of flowers I had found on the desk in Hochstraaten's study. Next to it were two more flower paintings, both larger than the van Thielen. The final piece was a so-called *vanitas*: a skull lay on a table next to several withered flowers, an extinguished candle, and an hourglass. The collection had begun with the first humans in their perfect state and ended with the death motif that so dominated Hochstraaten's thinking.

I moved the chair to the center of the room and sat down, letting my eyes wander from left to right and back again. These paintings had to be worth millions—just how many I couldn't even begin to guess. I had a sneaking suspicion I knew how the collection had been acquired, almost certainly by Hochstraaten's father.

The wall behind me was empty except for a few tiny engravings by Dürer: five scenes from a Passion series, dated 1511 and 1512; a St. Thomas and a St. Paul, each from 1514; and a St. Christopher from 1521. A space much larger than these miniature pieces separated the Passion scenes from the saints. Could it have been reserved for a certain missing engraving from 1513? But how could Hochstraaten have known?

Suddenly there was a clanking noise from somewhere beyond the hallway. Was Moira coming up the stairs with her watering can already? I ran to the door, pulled it shut, and turned the key in the lock. I called out Moira's name softly, and, hearing no response, headed down the stairs. Moira was on her hands and knees near the kitchen, rubbing the living room carpet with a rag.

"Uh-oh, what happened?"

"Oh, I just bumped the watering can against the door jamb and a little water spilled out. Nothing to worry about." She looked up at me. "You've been upstairs for quite a while. Did you find those saints all that interesting?"

"In a perverse sort of way, yes. You were right about the style. They looked like mediocre imitations of the Nazarenes—German precursors of the pre-Raphaelites. I agree with you about the *St. Sebastian*—he is kind of sweet, in a sickly sort of way."

Moira nodded. "Yeah, definitely not my type."

"So how's the watering going—aside from your little accident."

"Oh, fine. I've probably got about another half-hour left down here. Sorry it's taking so long."

"Not a problem. I'm bound to find some interesting books upstairs. Take your time with the watering."

I returned to the study and put the key back where I had found it. What to do next? Klaus was highly organized; it seemed likely that he would have compiled a list of the artworks in his hidden gallery. A four-drawer filing cabinet stood next to the desk, and I might be able to pick the lock if need be. But first I would have a look in the file drawer in the desk itself. Like my own desk at the house, the locking device engaged all the other drawers as well.

I pulled the heavy drawer open and began flipping through the files one by one, beginning with Auto Papers, Bank Statements, and Computer Information. The file after Credit Cards was labeled Dr. Davies. I had little interest in Hochstraaten's medical history and kept looking: Electric Bills, Homeowner's Insurance. . . .

Wait a minute, Dr. Davies . . . the name sounded vaguely familiar. Had some colleague or other mentioned him? . . . No! Mr. Locke down at the law office had. Dr. Davies had been Luke Baumgartner's personal physician and had later committed suicide. Could this be the same Dr. Davies? Why on earth would Klaus have a file on him? I went back to the front of the drawer, lifted the folder out carefully, and placed it on the desk. It contained a single envelope, inscribed simply with the name 'Mabel.' I pulled out the three pages of stationery inside and began to read.

10 November 1933

My dearest daughter,

It is with the greatest regret that I write this letter. I have insisted that you not open it until fifty years after the above date, since I fear that you would be devastated by its contents at your present tender age of sixteen. When you read it half a century hence, you will have attained the wisdom of old age and will, I trust, be able to accept with greater equanimity what I must write here.

You and many others will have assumed that my suicide, a year after the passing of your dear mother, stemmed from feelings of despondency over her death, and it is true that I have missed her sorely. Yet my awful deed has a cause far less honorable than that: it is the necessary consequence of my breaking an oath which underlies one of the most sacred trusts of my profession, the Hippocratic oath which I took some forty years ago as I was about to assume the responsibilities of my late father's medical practice. At that time I swore not to administer a deadly drug to anyone who asked for it nor to make a suggestion to that effect. I broke this vow a quarter of a century ago. Since then, I have hoped against hope that I would one day feel exonerated, by virtue of continuing to aid the sick, by saving lives, to the extent of my ability. This has proven not to be the case, and I find now, as the twenty-fifth anniversary of my transgression approaches, that I am no longer able to bear its burden.

Though he lived before your time, you will certainly remember a great deal about Luke Baumgartner, my irrepressible friend and patient. It was his life that I took away. Luke was not ill at the time. He was as spry and energetic as men twenty years his junior, and his mind was as alert and inventive as ever. Certainly he had been assailed by frequent emotional fluctuations ever since the death of his beloved wife many years before. And he was clearly in a depressed state when he asked me to "help him cross the bar," as he put it. The only events that cheered him in those last weeks of his life were the elaborate preparations for what he called "the great Dürer's Knight riddle," the solution of which he referred to in his final diary entry. Though Luke did on occasion need my assistance in this undertaking – concerning certain activities in his private chapel, for example, or digging in the Garden of Time – he was able to carry out much of the work alone. These preparations required a high degree of physical and mental dexterity. I mention this because I feel that I must confess fully the extent of my crime. Had Luke been in failing health or in great pain, some might find my deed justified to a degree. But the fact that he was not renders my action the more reprehensible.

Having lived with my guilt all these years, both for your mother's sake and for yours, I can go on no longer. It may be that I am committing another sin equally great in doing away with myself – this will be for the Almighty to decide.

What more can I say? I hope sincerely that my confession will not have inspired in you, my darling daughter, only contempt for me. I do not ask your forgiveness, since I believe what I have done to be unforgivable. Please pray for me.

As always,
Your loving father

P.S. You will be wondering about the small key which you found in the envelope; it was designed to play a significant role in the riddle I mentioned above. Luke had two such keys made and gave me one of them as a memento on the last day of his life. The number three was sacred to him, as it is to all of us of the Christian faith. May this little key bring you many blessings.

J.E.D.

I put the letter down and leaned back. The son of a bitch, so this is how he knows as much as he does. And the key that I've had for a few weeks now—he's had an identical one for thirty years! But so what? There was no way he would have had any idea what to do with it. He wasn't the one who had been solving the clues, after all. . . .

After putting the folder back in the drawer, I continued to pick through the remaining files. Electric Bills, Homeowner's Insurance, a thick file labeled House Plants, . . . *Kunstsammlung*—art collection. Eureka.

The folder contained two sheets of paper, torn here and there at the edges, that had been typed on an ancient typewriter; some of the letters had printed unevenly and an occasional mistake had been typed over. A heading at the top of the first page declared the ownership and provenance of the collection:

SAMMLUNG WILHELM HOCHSTRAATEN, KÖLN
erworben durch gütigste Vermittlung des
Reichsmarschalls Hermann G ö r i n g

I could hardly believe what I was reading. Along with Hitler himself, Göring had been the Third Reich's most avid art collector— though 'art thief' would have been the more appropriate term. In order to have acquired the collection in Klaus's secret room, his father must have been a high-ranking member of the SS indeed, and a personal friend of Göring's to boot.

The first section of the page was headed *Gemälde*—paintings.

     1.   Cornelis de Vos, *Adam und Eva*, 1621, Sammlung Heinrich Blumenstein, München (Juni 1936).

     2.   Michael Willmann, *Vertreibung aus dem Garten Eden*, 1690, Sammlung Heinrich Blumenstein, München (Juni 1936).

     3. Johann Carl Loth, *Abraham und Isaak*, 1677, Sammlung Joseph Mandelbaum, Frankfurt am Main (April 1935).

     4.   Hendrick ter Brugghen, *Die Zerstörung Sodoms*, 1625, Sammlung Samuel Freudenthal, Prag (Februar 1940).

Scanning the rest of the page, I discovered that all fifteen paintings were by seventeenth-century Flemish and Dutch artists. They were listed according to the same Biblical chronology that Hochstraaten had used in hanging the pieces, and each was followed by the name of the collection it had come from; a second date presumably indicated when the work had been confiscated. Eight of the paintings were from Heinrich Blumenstein's collection.

As I turned to the second page, labeled *Kupferstiche*—copper engravings—I heard footsteps coming up the stairs. I stuffed the two pages back in their folder and frantically searched for its place in the file drawer.

"Colin, what in—" Moira set the watering can down hard on the floor. "You're going through Professor Hochstraaten's files?!"

"Moira, I—"

"You told me you wanted to look at his paintings. You lied to me!"

"Not exactly, Moira, I did want to look at his paintings. Look, you're going to have to trust me on this. There's a good reason why I'm doing what I'm doing."

"What reason could there be for you to go through his private stuff?"

I got up out of the desk chair, still holding the art file still in my hand. "Moira, I'm sorry I wasn't completely truthful with you. I didn't tell you what I was planning on doing because I didn't want you to get involved. I'm on to something here, something serious. You'll find out soon enough what it is. Everyone will."

Moira crossed her arms and scowled at me. "So you take that file out of his drawer and I'm supposed to believe it's perfectly harmless? Are you stealing it, or what?"

"No, I'm not stealing anything, I was just looking. I was about to put it back when you came into the room." I sat down again, placed the file where it belonged after the House Plants file, and shut the drawer.

"So now it's like it never happened, is that it?"

"Moira, what I did wasn't exactly legal, but it was necessary. Haven't I always been straight with you before?"

"I'm not sure. Either way, we've never been in a situation remotely like this one. And now I'm an accessory to the fact, or whatever it's called, because I saw what you were doing. Damn it anyway!"

"That's ridiculous, Moira, you had no idea what I was up to here!"

Still glaring at me, she picked up the watering can again. "I have to water the plants up here now," she said quietly. "Then we'd better go."

"Okay. I'll wait for you outside."

I double-checked the file drawer to make sure that everything was in its place again. As I closed it and the main desk drawer, it occurred to me: how am I going to lock this? The websites hadn't said anything about *un*picking a lock. I poked around with the picks for a while before giving up. All I could hope now was that when Klaus turned his key he wouldn't notice that the drawer was already unlocked. I swore under my breath, left the room, and walked downstairs.

Outside, the weather was pleasantly warm. I sat down on the porch steps and cursed again. Why hadn't I been more alert to where Moira was in the house? As for what I had discovered, everything fit. Klaus Hochstraaten had grown up in Argentina and still traveled there every summer. Apparently he had somehow managed to smuggle all that artwork back to the United States over the years. However it had happened was immaterial; what concerned me was the course of action I should take, and whether Moira would say anything. There were no two ways about it, I had broken into parts of a colleague's house, even though I was convinced that the ends justified the means. I continued to brood until Moira came out the front door and locked it behind her. It was two-thirty; the likelihood of our passing Jason on the road on the way back seemed small.

"All finished?" I said, for want of anything better to say.

"Yes. Are you?"

I looked away for a moment. "I know you're still pissed at me, Moira, and I don't blame you. But please don't say anything about this to anyone."

"Let's just go, all right?" She opened the car door and got in. I looked at her out of the corner of my eye as I drove out to the road.

"Look, Moira—"

"Let's not talk, Colin. I need to think."

We were silent during the ten-minute trip. At the St. Eustace sign, I turned onto the curving access road up to campus.

"Should I drop you at your dorm?"

"No, the Student Center."

I took a left at the top of the hill and pulled into the parking lot behind Bamberg Hall.

"Well?" I began.

"I'm still thinking," she said, then got out of the car and slammed the door shut.

Chapter 29

For the rest of Saturday afternoon and on into the evening I tried to work on my classes for the coming week, doing my best not to think about the scene in Hochstraaten's study when Moira had suddenly appeared. Would she tell anyone about what she had seen me doing? Should I call or text her and try to explain myself again? No, that would be tantamount to pouring oil on the flames. Her anger was justified, of course. From the limited information she had—and there was no way I was going to give her any more at this point—it looked as if I had simply played her for a fool. Why should she believe that there was any justification for my rummaging through a colleague's files?

During my hours of essay grading on Sunday, it was Luke Baumgartner who kept interrupting my concentration. At one point I took a break and pored over Luke's last set of clues to make sure that everything still made sense. It did; every line of the poem could be accounted for. This, along with the crucial difference in the color of the mortar, had me convinced that I was on the right track. Maybe I could talk to Moira after class the next day and see if we could arrange a time to visit the chapel again. Or would she still be so angry that she wouldn't even speak to me?

Sunday night brought a series of unpleasant dreams in which faceless people pointed fingers and shouted at me. The bright sun that came pouring in through the bedroom window the next morning did nothing to lessen the dread I felt in anticipation of seeing Moira again. After breakfast I slowly walked to Riedenburg Hall and stepped inside the classroom just as the bell rang. Moira seemed deep in conversation with the student next to her and barely glanced up. Jason was missing from his usual seat in the back row. Was there any particular significance in this, or was it simply one more absence?

I began the hour by handing back the essays I had graded on Sunday. After commenting on a few of the more common errors and taking individual questions, I divided the class into small groups for work on the conversational topics they were to have prepared. As usual, I let the students carry on their conversations on their own and moved around the classroom answering their questions. Moira avoided eye contact with me whenever I approached her group. After class, she slipped out of the room before I even noticed.

Then and there I decided to go ahead with what I assumed would be the final excavation in the chapel without her. At some later point I would of course tell her what I had discovered, if she proved interested. But for now . . .

It was a good hour till my usual lunchtime, and I could eat later if need be. Grabbing my briefcase, I set out at a trot for home to pick up a chisel, a hammer, and a flashlight. As an afterthought, I grabbed my sketch pad with the drawings I had made in the chapel a few weeks before; part of my ploy this time might involve showing them to Ned. I hated to have to make up yet another story, but I couldn't see any way around it. The end of the search seemed imminent now, and I felt a vague, gnawing need to keep everything a secret until the final step was completed.

Ned was walking toward his utility room as I stepped into the corridor from the Rapunzel tower.

"Howdy, Professor."

"Morning, Ned. You'll never guess what I'm here for."

Ned tilted his head and smiled. "No? You sure, now?"

I gave my usual not-terribly-casual laugh. "Looks like you've guessed it already. That other time I got a start on a few drawings, and I'd like to finish them off now. Maybe make a couple more, too."

I pulled the three sketches out of my briefcase and handed them to Ned, who looked at each one carefully.

"You really got the shadin' down," he said. "Used to draw some myself, so I know it's not so easy to do. I like this one, lookin' up to those little windas at the top. And the one of the statue by the door is pretty good, too."

"Nice of you to say so. I wish I could draw people, though. I've never been able to get the hang of it."

"Shucks, I've never even tried it myself." He walked over to his desk and fumbled around in the center drawer. "I'll just give you the key this time. You can bring it back whenever you're through."

"Great, thanks."

The third class period of the day was already underway as I walked into the Rapunzel tower, so there wouldn't be much traffic in and out of the building for another forty-five minutes. Feeling a tingle of excitement, I unlocked the door to the chapel and stepped inside. Without wasting any time I went up to the altar and knelt down in front of the St. George window. I felt slightly foolish, as if I was supposed to start praying.

The inside walls of the chapel were formed out of stones that varied from about six inches across to two feet. The stone that St. George's lance pointed to was less than a foot wide, slightly smaller than the one below Baumgartner's escutcheon. This was good and bad: good, because it wouldn't take as long to chip out the mortar; bad, because the *Knight, Death, and Devil* was too wide to fit past the center pin without being rolled up. What would be the condition of a five-hundred-year-old piece of paper that had been rolled into a cylinder for over a hundred of those years? Couldn't Luke have picked a different hiding place, one with a wider stone, so that the print could have been kept flat? I was dismayed and disappointed; it seemed so uncharacteristic of Luke not to have taken that into consideration.

I began to chip away at the mortar as quietly as possible, starting at the upper left hand corner and working clockwise around the entire stone. The chisel was so much more efficient than my semi-functional Swiss Army knife! Once I had carved out a shallow channel on all four sides, I went back to my starting point and repeated the process. On the third time around, the chisel began to break through the last layer of mortar. Two inches were now free along the top of the stone, leaving a gap wide enough to accommodate the tip of my index finger. As I chipped my way past the midway-point it suddenly occurred to me: there was no center pin. What the hell was going on? Was this the wrong stone after all? Had the color of the mortar really been all that different, or had I simply willed it to be? I considered examining the St. Eustace statue again, or possibly the wall at the rear of the chapel under the bas-relief of Paul . . . No, no, this had to be the right place, everything in the poem fit. Or did it?

With a rising sense of futility, I continued hammering along the top of the stone, faster than before and heedless of the noise I was making. When I reached the right-hand corner, there was a dull ringing sound; the chisel seemed to have hit against metal. I bent over and glared at the stone as if my eyesight had the power to melt away the mortar, then chipped out the last bits—and there was the pin, at the corner of the stone instead of in the center! Luke hadn't let me down after all.

I quickly hammered out the remaining mortar that encased the pin and continued along the floorline. Then, inserting the chisel into the gap on the left side, I tried to pry the stone forward. The chisel was too short to give me any leverage, and the claw of the hammer worked no better. I tried kicking the stone as I had last time, until, with a screech, it finally moved slightly inward. A few more kicks, and I could get my fingers around it and grab hold of the edge. After another dozen pushes and pulls, the stone began to move more easily, though it still made a horrendous grating noise. A few more tugs and it was back in its original position. Now I was able to use the claw of the hammer again to move the stone outward little by little, like a gate on rusty hinges.

In the beam of my flashlight I could make out something flat lying at the back of the cavity. With thoughts of being bitten by a rodent flashing through my mind again, I reached in quickly and pulled the object out. Like the three previous finds, it was wrapped in oilcloth, but this time there were no ribbons. Inside the protective covering was a gray metal case about a foot in length and nine or ten inches wide. Unlike the boxes buried in the Garden of Time and the North Woods, this one had a lock rather than just a simple clasp. And and to my great delight, the keyhole was shaped like a reversed number three. Too bad, Klaus—it will be my key and not yours that will open this.

Hearing the muffled sound of people tramping back and forth through the tower, I cleaned up the mess hurriedly, moved the stone back into place, and remembered this time to brush the bits of mortar off my jacket sleeves. Was it eleven-fifty already? The time had simply flown by. I stashed the metal case and tools in my briefcase, then made two quick sketches of the Four Apostles statuary at the back of the chapel; this would be something else I could flash at Ned to make it look as if I'd spent more time drawing than I actually had.

As the noise outside subsided, I tiptoed to the chapel door and reached for the handle. But what was this? Not only had I forgotten to lock the door, it was actually open a chink. Colin, Colin, you shouldn't have been in such a rush! Not to worry, though; it seemed unlikely that anyone passing through the tower would have noticed anything. And anyway, what did it matter now?

I turned the key in the lock and headed along the corridor toward the utilities room. There was Ned in the distance, walking toward the front entrance tower carrying a bucket of water and a mop. A moment later I caught up with him.

"Here's the key, Ned. I'm pretty sure I won't need to bug you again."

"Not a problem. You get some more drawin' done?"

I pulled the sketches out of my briefcase and waved them in Ned's general direction. "I'm not real satisfied with these—I'll have to put in more time on them before I'm ready to show them to anyone."

Ned smiled and nodded. "I know what you mean. Sorta like when I'm workin' on a new riff and don't quite have it down yet."

"Yeah, I suppose so. Well, I'll be heading on home now. Thanks again for your help."

"Sure thing."

I crossed the huge space of the front entrance tower, thinking once again about the chapel door I had carelessly left open. How could I have been so stupid? The hubbub I had heard outside the chapel, of people passing through the Rapunzel tower, could easily have drowned out the soft padding of someone else's feet—someone who had looked inside out of curiosity—or possibly with some other intention in mind? But wasn't I just being paranoid to even consider this? It wasn't as if I had done anything illegal; I had found what I had come for, and I had done it in a manner sanctioned by Luke Baumgartner, the master of the game.

As I pushed the heavy tower door open to the bright light of midday, my concerns melted away as fast as they had come.

Chapter 30

I walked at a good clip along the Promenade, occasionally greeting a passing student. With less than an hour remaining until my Beginning German class, I would have a quick look at what I had found, lock it away in my office desk, and do a few last-minute preparations. Lunch would have to wait today. At this point I was too excited to even think about eating anyway.

Too bad about Moira, she had given me so much help. If the Hochstraaten matter could ever be resolved, though, she would surely forgive what she had seen as a betrayal of her trust. While we had been at my house working on the third clue, she had idly raised the question as to where I would hang the engraving. I tried to visualize this now as I strode along. I had considered my bedroom, but how about the dining room? It would lend that space, with its cherrywood built-ins, even greater elegance. Every time I considered the possibilities, though, I couldn't help thinking of the blank space with the empty picture hook in the Dürer Museum. How long had it been since the *Knight* had hung there next to its two companion pieces, the *St. Jerome* and the *Melencolia*? Well over a century now. Two companion pieces, missing the third . . .

As I reached Riedenburg Hall, a tall, hunched-over figure came limping down the stairway. It was Klaus Hochstraaten, clutching his forehead and looking distraught. But hadn't he said that he wouldn't be back until the following week?

"Colin—thank God! I was about to attempt to drive home—but I don't know if I would have been able to. I just arrived from the airport and I have been struck with a terrible migraine, one of the worst I have ever known. It grows more unbearable by the minute. And—how stupid of me—I have no more medicine in my office." Hochstraaten slumped against the railing, then let himself down on the stairs. "I beg you, Colin, could you take me home? I really do not think that I am in any condition to drive."

"Well . . . of course—I live just down the street—we can—"

"Thank you, Colin, thank you, you are a true gentleman. May I lean on you as we walk down the stairs?"

Hochstraaten grasped my free arm. "You're back before I expected," I said.

"Yes. I was taken ill, and was able to find an earlier flight. I seemed to be improving, but now . . . "

We slowly made our way around the building to the parking lot.

"Look, Klaus, I'll run on home and get my car. It'll only take me—"

"No, Colin, I beg you, no further delay. My car is just there, not ten paces away. Please drive it for me. My medicine takes effect quickly and I will be able to drive you back to campus." He looked at me like a wounded animal.

"Sure, I can do that. But how about if I just take you to the student infirmary?"

"Yes, but . . . they do not have the medicine I need there. I asked once some time ago. It is not far to my house." Hochstraaten handed me the car keys and we walked the few steps to his black Mercedes. I helped him in on the passenger side, then laid my briefcase on the back seat. Damn, what terrible timing!

As I pulled out of the parking lot I caught sight of Moira biking along Faculty Row, apparently on her way back to her dormitory; I was sure she had seen me and must have wondered why I was driving Hochstraaten's Mercedes. For a moment I considered stopping to tell her what was going on, but given her current mood. . . . I drove on toward the road that led down to the highway. Hochstraaten sat hunched over and massaged his temples.

"Turn right at the bottom of the hill, please," he said. "I do not usually take this route, but it will be faster."

"I might need some help finding the cut-off."

Hochstraaten nodded. A short while later I spotted the "fresh eggs" sign.

"This one. And then follow the gravel road up the hill."

At the crest of the hill Hochstraaten straightened up and gestured to the right.

"We turn in here."

I parked in front of the house, then helped Hochstraaten out of his car and up the porch steps. He handed me the key to the front door, his face twisted in pain. As I turned the key in the lock, I thought: how ironic is this?

"Please take a seat," Hochstraaten said once we were in the living room, "I will be back in a moment." He laboriously walked up the stairs to the second floor.

I crossed the room and sat down on the sofa facing the coffee table and the fireplace. All the potted plants looked fresh and healthy following Moira's ministrations. The stairs creaked and I turned my head as Hochstraaten came back into the room. His posture was poker-straight now.

"What the—?" I started to get up off the sofa.

"Please remain seated." Hochstraaten held a pistol leveled at me, apparently the Luger from the case in his study, and a coil of clothesline in his other hand. I dropped back onto the sofa.

"Enough play-acting," Hochstraaten said, sitting down in the rocking chair next to the fireplace. "You have paid another visit to my house, but I do not believe that you received an invitation."

My mind was racing. So Jason had seen us after all. "All I did was give Moira a ride out here to water your plants, Klaus. I couldn't see the poor kid biking—"

"The drawer to my desk was unlocked. I was careful to lock it when I left the house."

I swallowed hard. "So you're saying that I—"

"I repeat, enough play-acting. You were clearly looking for something."

I could feel sweat forming on the palms of my hands. "What would I be looking for in your—"

"Why do you not tell me instead? That would be simpler, would it not?"

I hesitated. "All right. I . . . I sensed you were on to the Baumgartner thing—what he had hidden. I wanted to see if I could find anything that would tell me how far along you were. Look, Klaus, it just happened. I wasn't planning on snooping around. But once I was out here, with all that time on my hands—"

"Ah yes, idle hands make the devil's work. Is that not the expression?"

Who's the devil here, you bastard, I said to myself.

"And how were you able to get the desk drawer open?"

"With my pocket knife."

Hochstraaten nodded. I wasn't sure if he believed me or not.

"How long did you need to do this?"

"I don't know—five minutes, maybe."

"And Moira? Where was she at the time?"

"Somewhere downstairs. I'd told her I'd sit in your study and read while I waited for her. She came in and watered the plants there first, and she said there were more in one of the bedrooms. Then she went downstairs."

"Very clever, to get her out of the way like that. And yet you had not planned on doing any 'snooping,' so you claim."

"I hadn't! It didn't occur to me until I was sitting there reading. To see what was in your desk drawer, I mean."

"And just what did you find, then?"

"The photo of your father . . . some pens and pencils . . . a few sheets of paper, I think . . ." I shrugged.

"Ah. You overlooked the two keys in the front of the drawer, no doubt. A small one in the shape of the number three, for example?"

"Well, yes, I guess there were some keys there—"

Hochstraaten shook his head. "Colin, Colin, your memory seems to be deficient! We both know very well that you already had the duplicate of that small key in your possession. Where was it you found it? In Baumgartner's chapel, or in the Garden of Time? Or in the forest, perhaps?"

I felt no need to tell him the truth.

"It was in the chapel." So someone—Jason, no doubt—must have been spying on me the whole time.

"And the other key in my desk drawer—the larger key—you did not use it, of course, to unlock a certain door?"

"N-no, how could I have known . . . ?"

"Of course, of course. Well, you have told me quite an entertaining tale. Now, if you will allow me, I will point out two things you neglected to do while you were here." He paused to see what effect this statement would have on me.

"I . . . I don't know what you mean."

"Let me tell you, then. Concerning my *Kunstwerke* file, you placed the list of engravings *in front of* the list of paintings, something I have never done. And, in the art gallery itself, you failed to replace the chair next to the door where you had found it."

As I struggled to come up with a response, Hochstraaten continued.

"Your discovery of my private gallery has created an obvious problem for me. Each item in the collection belonged to my father, may he rest in peace. I brought them here from Argentina over many years under difficult circumstances—secreted in my artificial leg, if you must know. So you will understand that I would not be willing to relinquish even one of them. But now that you and Moira know—"

"Leave Moira out of this. She doesn't know a thing about your art collection."

"You expect me to believe that?"

"It's true. I was careful to check on her whereabouts the whole time we were here. Look, I lied to you about not having seen your back room. But I just happened on it—I've told you already what I came here for, to find out how you were doing with the Baumgartner business—"

Hochstraaten held up a hand. "It matters little what you came here for. The point is, you did discover my art collection. And I cannot believe that you will keep this to yourself. You will eventually tell some organization or other which will have an interest in returning the pieces 'to their rightful owners,' as they would say. If you understood my relationship to those works of art, the immense benefits—solace, even—that I draw from contemplating them, you would understand that I cannot allow this to happen."

The low rumble of a motorcycle engine outside grew gradually louder, then stopped suddenly.

Hochstraaten stood up. "There is no need to continue this discussion," he said, "Jason has arrived. You will come to the front door with me now. And remember, I will have my gun in your back, precisely opposite your heart. I am quite capable of using it, just as my father did whenever it became necessary during the war."

We walked through the entryway and Hochstraaten opened the inside door.

"Face the wall so that Jason will not be able to see you, and remain silent."

I felt the barrel of the Luger prodding my back. Should I make a run for it? I wouldn't have a chance—I'd have to wait for a better opportunity.

"Jason," Hochstraaten called through the screen door, "please go out to my car and fetch the briefcase that is lying on the back seat."

A moment later I heard the car door slam, and then the sound of steps on the porch. Jason flinched when he came through the doorway and saw me and the gun in Hochstraaten's hand.

"What the hell's going on?"

"Be quiet, Jason, this does not concern you. Put the briefcase down, then take Professor Ritter's cell phone out of its holster and turn it off."

Jason did as he was told.

"Now take this rope and tie it around his wrists. Tightly. Colin, put your hands behind your back."

Looking shocked, Jason took the clothesline and tied it in a firm knot.

"All right. Step back and let me check your handiwork." Hochstraaten tugged at the knot and nodded. "Good. Back to the sofa now, Colin. As for you, Jason, your role is over. You will stand to one side and keep out of the way."

Hochstraaten picked up the briefcase and followed us into the living room. I sat down heavily on the sofa and clenched my teeth. All that effort, and Hochstraaten will reap the benefits. And then he'll kill me and bury my body out in the woods. Jesus Christ, I've got to think of something!

"Look, Uncle Klaus," Jason said, "you hired me to look after your house. You didn't say anything about—"

Hochstraaten turned to him furiously. "Shut up, you idiot!" he said, striking him on the side of the head with his Luger. Jason went down in a heap, narrowly missing a hanging plant. He felt gingerly around his bloodied ear and began to moan. Hochstraaten stood over him, glowering. "How many times do I have to tell you that this does not concern you—and that you are not to call me Uncle Klaus"!

He turned to me with a simpering smile on his face.

"Let me explain. Jason is my deceased sister's son. I assure you, I did not support her urgings that he come here, given his mediocre record in high school. He has, however, been useful to me of late. Though that usefuless, I am afraid, is now over."

With a glance at Jason, he placed my briefcase on the coffee table, opened it with his free hand, and removed the metal box.

I struggled to remain calm. Okay, next thing is, he'll make me get up off the sofa and take me out in back of the house. That's when I'll have to make my move. God knows what—trip him? Maybe if I can stall for time . . .

"Whatever happened to Ronald Fleishman, *Herr Professor*? At the Stone Bridge?"

Hochstraaten glared at me. "Fleishman was a fool. If he had not insisted on withholding his information from me . . . . But that is over and done with." He looked down at the metal box on the coffee table. "It is time now for our . . . grand opening, shall we say? I take it you have not had the opportunity yet to look inside yourself?" He stared across at me as if the answer mattered to him.

"Of course not. When could I have done that? I'm sure your spy told you exactly when I found it." I gave Jason a dirty look.

"In that case, then, let us have our little moment of sharing."

He turned the box on its side to examine the lock.

"Ah, what a fortuitous coincidence—the mirror image of the number three we were speaking of a moment ago. The magic three . . . the final step." He stared off into space, his eyes glazed over, then looked at the metal box again. "All I need now is to fetch a certain key. . . ."

Casting another glance at Jason, he shoved the Luger inside the waistband of his pants and headed for the stairway. It's now or never, I thought—God knows he seems distracted enough. Hochstraaten dragged his leg as he clunked his way up to the landing; at that point the stairway reversed directions and he was out of sight from the living room.

"Jason!" I whispered. "Get over here and cut this rope! There's a penknife in my right inside pocket."

Jason looked up and hesitated.

"Move! He'll be back down in a minute!"

With a glance toward the staircase, Jason got to his feet unsteadily, came over to me, and fumbled in my pocket.

"Use the blade with the point broken off, it's the sharpest." I held my bound wrists to one side and up as high as I could. Without a word,

Jason began to saw. In a few seconds he had severed the clothesline completely.

"Get back on the floor," I whispered, "hurry!"

A moment later the dragging noise resumed as Hochstraaten made the turn on the landing; it seemed to take him longer to come down than it had to go up. At the bottom step he glanced at Jason again, then walked over to the rocking chair and sat down with a sigh. Placing his Luger on the coffee table within easy reach, he turned the box sideways so that I would have to look on. After studying the small key in his hand for a moment, he inserted it into the lock and smiled as it clicked open. Inside was a piece of velvety protective material. As he removed it, his expression changed. The box seemed to contain nothing but a sheet of letter paper with writing on it. He picked it up and read through it.

"Ah," he muttered, "Only a slight inconvenience, one that will be easily resolved . . ."

Suddenly the front door slammed and Moira MacGregor strode into the living room.

"Moira!" Hochstraaten exclaimed. "Why have you come here? You mustn't—"

At that moment I lunged toward the coffee table, swinging one arm. Moira took a step back and froze near the foot of the stairs. The Luger went flying across the table and landed a few feet from Jason, who picked it up and slowly rose to his feet. All the color had drained from Hochstraaten's face.

"Don't worry, I won't shoot you," Jason said.

He pulled the magazine out, placed it on one of the plant tables, and proceeded to take the gun apart. A few seconds later he had detached the barrel from the handle.

"It's pretty useless now," he said, dropping the separate parts on the floor.

Moira was still standing near the entryway. "I called 911 a few minutes ago. Somebody should be here soon."

Hochstraaten glanced at Moira, then looked imploringly at me. "But I would not have done anything drastic, it was all a game I was playing."

"A game. Not one that I found very amusing."

"About the Dürer . . . ," Hochstraaten went on. "I lay no claim to it, Colin. It was you who found it after all—or soon would have. But you do realize that my private collection means everything to me, that I—"

"*Your* collection? I think you can guess where I stand on that, Klaus—you said as much yourself before. There'll be more than one art recovery organization, I'm sure, that will be interested in having a look at *your* collection."

Hochstraaten tried weakly to get out of the rocking chair, then sank down again with an expression of utter defeat. Supporting his head in his hands, he stroked his forehead and began mumbling something.

"Werlt, ich hân dînen lôn ersehen—"

"What's he—"

"Hang on, Jason," I said, holding up my hand.

"Swaz dû mir gîst, daz nimest dû mir . . ."

"What was that all about?" Jason said.

"It's part of a very well-known medieval poem. 'World, I've seen your reward. What you give me, you take away from me.'"

How ironic, I said to myself. The poem was by Walther von der Vogelweide, considered to be the greatest lyric poet of the time. Walther was on Klaus's course syllabus, just before Neidhart.

As Hochstraaten was about to speak again, the sound of car doors slamming came in through the screen door. Moira stepped back out into the entryway.

"Yes, I'm the one who called," I heard her say.

A burly black man in a sheriff's uniform came into the living room, followed by two deputies.

"Please stay where you are, folks," the sheriff said, "we'll have to pat each of you down. The caller said there was a gun involved?"

"Yes, it's been disabled," I said, pointing to the parts lying in the corner. "Jason there was able to—"

"You can save the details for later. Is there anybody else in the house?"

"No, this is it."

"Pete, have a look in all the rooms. Now if the four of you would stand against that wall there . . ."

Jason, Moira, and I lined up against the wall next to the entry-way. The pat-down produced only my Swiss Army knife, which the sheriff pocketed.

"You, too, sir," the sheriff said, gesturing toward Hochstraaten, who hadn't stirred. Nodding, he rose slightly from his chair. As he did, he fumbled briefly with his emerald ring and quickly slipped something into his mouth.

"Hold on, what're you doing there?" By the time the sheriff had made his way around the sofa, Hochstraaten had sunk back in his chair; a moment later he began retching and hyperventilating. The sound of another vehicle pulling up in the yard came in through the front door.

"Kevin," the sheriff said to the remaining deputy, "get the para-medic in here quick!"

The deputy ran to the door and shouted. Heavy footfalls resound-ed on the wooden steps to the porch and two blue-uniformed men came rushing into the room.

"He swallowed something before I could stop him," the sheriff said. "Looked like he took it out of his ring."

"The ring used to be his father's," I said. "He was an SS officer in World War II. I wonder—"

"Cyanide?" the paramedic said. "Never saw anybody who took it before. Lyle, run out to the ambulance and bring in that red and white Cyanokit."

By now Hochstraaten's normally pallid face had taken on a pink cast. He seemed to have stopped breathing and sat slumped over to one side, his eyes staring off into space. The paramedic knelt next to him and called out, "Can you hear me, sir? Are you all right?" When there was no answer, he felt for his carotid artery but was unable to find a pulse.

"Let's lay him out on the floor," he said when his EMT partner returned. "Easy, now." He checked Hochstraaten's vital signs again. "No pulse, no breathing. Get the IV ready, while I do compressions. You can hang it from the floor lamp. Sheriff, could you call for a helicopter? We've got to get him to the trauma center in Lexington. They can land in that field across the road. We'll need the stretcher out of the ambulance."

The sheriff made the call and gave the necessary coordinates. "Be here in fifteen-twenty minutes, he said."

The deputy named Pete came down from the second floor and reported that there was no one else in the house.

"There is one locked door up there, though."

"I can tell you about that," I said.

"Save it for later," the sheriff said. "Pete, how about you go out to the ambulance and bring in the stretcher."

In the meantime the EMT had inserted an airway into Hochstraaten's mouth and was forcing air into his lungs with the aid of an Ambu bag. Pete returned with the stretcher and set it on the floor next to the rocking chair.

"It doesn't look good," the paramedic said. "Cyanide acts mighty quick, if that's what it was."

He and the EMT laid Hochstraaten on the stretcher. Pete held up the IV as they walked across the room.

"Keep me informed," the sheriff said.

"Will do."

The front door banged shut, shaking the house to its foundations.

Chapter 31

The sheriff looked over at Jason, who was dabbing his ear with a handkerchief.

"So what happened to you?"

"My uncle hit me with his gun. He's the guy they just hauled out."

Moira looked stunned. "Your uncle?"

"Yeah. It's a long story. Anyway, I think I was in shock for a while, but I'm okay now."

"Maybe you are and maybe you aren't. We'll get you to the hospital in town soon's we leave. First, though, I'd like you all to tell me what exactly happened here. What led up to that man taking whatever it was he swallowed, why he hit this young feller over the head, where everybody was sitting, and so on. Kevin, you can take notes. Pete, how about you make some drawings and take a few photos, and then go outside and cordon off the place." He turned to the others. "I'm Sheriff Baines, by the way, George Baines." He motioned toward the dining room. "Why don't we all go in there and sit at the table."

We filed into the room and sat down. The sheriff began with a pronouncement.

"Now, since I don't have much of an idea to what extent there was criminal activity, I have to inform you that anything you say may be used against you in a court of law. Is that understood?

"Maybe I should start," I said, "I'm the one who's principally involved here. My name's Colin Ritter, and these are two of my students, Moira MacGregor and Jason Miller. The man they carried out is a colleague of mine, Klaus Hochstraaten. We're both professors at St. Eustace College. . . ."

Ten minutes later I had finished telling what had happened since my encounter with Hochstraaten on the steps of Riedenburg Hall. Jason occasionally added a few words to corroborate statements that had involved him.

"How about you, young lady?" the sheriff asked. "What's your part in all this?"

"Well, Professor Hochstraaten was going to be gone for two weeks, so Professor Ritter drove me out here last Saturday to water his plants." She glanced at me before going on. "I got the sense that something fishy was going on, but Professor Ritter wouldn't say what it was. So when I saw him driving Professor Hochstraaten's car on campus with

253

him in it—"

"When would that have been?" the sheriff interrupted.

"Maybe three-quarters of an hour ago? I knew Professor Hoch-straaten wasn't due back for another week, so since I was on my bike already I decided to ride out here and see what was going on. I saw Jason's motorcycle out in front, and then I *really* started to wonder, because he hadn't been in class for a couple days . . . I'm sorry, I'm probably telling you more than you need to know . . ."

"That's all right, you're doing fine."

"So just as I was walking up the front steps, I heard somebody shouting, and when I peeped in through the front window I saw Professor Hochstraaten hit Jason over the head—"

"With the pistol?"

"I couldn't really tell, but it might have been. So then I tiptoed down off the porch around to the side of the house and called 911."

As Moira finished speaking, the clatter of helicopter rotors carried into the house from across the street.

"All right, thank you," the sheriff said. "Back to you for a minute, Professor Ritter. You said that Jason cut the rope when Professor Hochstraaten went upstairs to get the key to the box that's on the coffee table. How was that possible? It can't take but a minute to go up those stairs and come down again."

I shrugged. "We had to risk it. My colleague has an artificial leg. It takes him longer than it would most people."

The sheriff nodded. "I see. And that key he came down with—you say it fits the box. What was that all about? Is it important for the rest of what went on here?"

"Extremely. The box was one of the two reasons he wanted to lure me into coming out here—the other being that he knew I'd discovered his collection of stolen art. That's what's in the locked room upstairs."

"Stolen art. How do you know it's stolen?"

"His father acquired the collection in Germany during the war. He was an officer in the SS. I found a typed list that mentioned who the original owners had been. They were all Jewish collectors, or maybe art dealers."

"But he could have bought them, couldn't he?"

"That's not the way the Nazis did things. They occasionally bought paintings at ridiculously low prices, but mostly they just appropriated them. So—"

"Well, that's neither here nor there for what we're talking about now. How does the box on the coffee table fit in?"

I paused for a moment. "I found it on campus earlier this morning, in the private chapel. By rights it belongs to me—"

"You say you found it?" the sheriff asked. "How was it your colleague had the key?"

"There were duplicate keys, I had the other one, and—"

"Professor Ritter did find the box," Jason said. "The chapel door was open, and I was looking in when he found it."

I gave Jason an angry glance. "I'll spell out all the details when I make my written statement. For what happened here this morning, I think all you have to know is that Hochstraaten had a driving need to possess what he expected to find in the box. But it turned out that all it contained was a note."

"A note. What kind of note?"

"I don't know. He was reading it to himself just as Moira came in."

"Do you think it might shed some light on any of this business?"

"Well, it might."

"Do you know where it is now?"

"It must be somewhere on the coffee table, or maybe on the floor next to it."

"Just hang on a second." Sheriff Baines walked into the living room and returned a moment later with the note in his hand. "Can't say it makes much sense to me," he said. "Here, I'll read it aloud." He sat down at the table and cleared his throat.

"*Never fear, dear friend; though this box does not contain that which you expected, it requires but one additional small step and you will have arrived at your quarry, in a hiding place more suitable than the dank and musty confines of a castle wall. You will find the Knight in the dining room of the house occupied in my day by my loyal friend Dr. Davies – the whereabouts of which you will be able to ascertain without great difficulty, I am sure. The good doctor and I secreted the engraving, by means of a cunning spring device, behind the uppermost shelf in the center of the china closet. You need only press against the panel at just the right spot and . . . Eureka!*

You will note my family crest in miniature in the lower left-hand corner of the engraving as authentication of its having been part of my collection, while present document will grant you, its bearer, the right to claim it as your own. Furthermore, the current owners of the house, whosoever they may be, may claim a reward of $5 000 for any inconvenience caused them, said sum to be drawn on the trust fund *heretofore established in my name. Let me now offer you my heartiest congratulations, my dear friend. May your cleverness and perseverance augur well for your future, and may you, like our undaunted Knight, be inspired to act with self-reliance, hope and faith.*

Yours . . . in perpetuity,
Lukas Baumgartner

Witnessed by J. Earl Davies and Clay Locke, 23 October 1908."

"Lukas Baumgartner . . ." Sheriff Baines said. "Now wasn't he the one who founded the college?"

"That's right," I said. "Over a hundred years ago he hid away the engraving you were just reading about, and I was on the verge of finding it. It's all extremely complicated . . ."

The sheriff sat scratching his head. "I should say so. You can save the details for your written report. About this art collection upstairs, though—if the room was locked, how did you know what was in it?

"I . . . found the key."

"You found the key. Where?

"In Professor Hochstraaten's desk drawer."

Sheriff Baines looked at me hard. "You had access to his desk drawer?"

"Well, to tell you the truth, I picked the lock. I had to be a hundred percent sure what was in the room."

"You realize that was a criminal act?"

"I hardly thought about it at the time. The only thing on my mind was bringing him to justice."

Sheriff Baines nodded. "Well, that matter will have to be dealt with when the time comes. We'll head back to the station now and you can all write out your statements."

"You don't want to have a look at the art collection?" I asked.

"Oh, no, we'll leave that for the experts. Time for us to be on our way."

Outside, the sheriff's deputy had finished cordoning off the house and was sitting on the porch steps waiting.

"That your motorcycle, Jason?" the sheriff asked.

"Yeah. I think I'm okay to ride it."

"With that head wound of yours? Not a good idea. Don't worry, we'll get you a ride out here to pick it up when you're in better shape. And the young lady, too, for her bike."

Jason seemed reluctant, but agreed.

"Kevin, if you want to come with me and Professor Ritter, the two young folks can ride with Pete." He waved to the other deputy. "Pete, stop by the hospital and have Jason's wound checked out, then bring both of them to my office."

I walked with Moira and Jason to the deputy's squad car. Moira looked at the ground. "I blew it. I should have trusted you."

"I didn't give you much reason to. Anyhow, let's talk, the three of us, once we're back on campus. Oh, and by the way—thanks for getting here on time."

She looked up and smiled. "I'm *always* on time."

Smiling back, I headed for the sheriff's squad car.

Chapter 32

The quarter-hour drive to the county seat seemed to take no more than a few minutes. Still feeling dazed, I climbed out of the squad car and walked with Sheriff Baines to his office. It was two-thirty; if it had been a normal day, my Beginning German class would just have let out.

"Can I call the Chair of my department? She'll be wondering why I didn't teach my class this afternoon."

"Go right ahead."

I pulled out my phone and noticed I hadn't turned it back on yet. Had Charlotte been trying to call me? When the screen lit up a moment later, there were no messages, so I punched in her number and after several rings heard her message prompt; I said only that something had come up and that it would be much easier to tell her about it in person.

My stomach was beginning to growl.

"Is there any chance I could get a hamburger or something? I haven't had a bite since breakfast."

"I'll see what I can do," Sheriff Baines said. "Double cheeseburger, maybe?"

"That would be great. And a root beer."

The sheriff got on the intercom with the receptionist and asked her to send someone to the fast-food place across the street.

"It's all right if I call a lawyer, isn't it?"

"Yes, it is. You can use the phone on my desk. Dial 9 first."

"I have the number in my cell phone."

"I'd prefer you to use the landline," the sheriff said. "There's a directory right next to the phone."

I looked up the number and dialed it.

"Hello, Elaine, this is Colin Ritter. Would Mr. Locke be available?"

The sheriff glanced up when he heard the name, but made no comment.

"Hello, Mr. Locke. You're not going to believe what I got involved in today. . . ."

It took several minutes to explain in broad outlines what had happened.

"Yes, Mr. Locke . . . really, could you do that? That would be great. See you then."

"That Clay Locke you were talkin' to?" the sheriff asked.

"Yes. He said he'd pick me up around three-thirty."

I was sitting across from Mr. Locke at a table in a small room that adjoined the sheriff's office. I had talked almost non-stop for forty-five minutes.

"I suppose picking that lock wasn't the brightest idea," I said. "I did consider asking the police to get a search warrant, but I didn't think they'd do it."

"No, they certainly wouldn't have. The rolled-up painting you found wouldn't have been near enough evidence. But we should be able to do a plea bargain and have you plead guilty to civil trespass. You weren't intending on burgling anything, after all. It would help if you could get a couple of affidavits as to your good character, though."

"Okay. I'll ask Charlotte Rossi first thing."

"Yes, she'd be a good one. And maybe the Dean of the college?"

"He doesn't know me from Adam."

"I suppose not, you haven't been there all that long. Would there be anybody back in Minnesota?"

"Oh sure, lots of people—at the college where I taught, and my professors at the university . . ."

"Good. You don't need to go into the specifics of what happened, just say you need a character reference for personal reasons. Charlotte you can tell more, of course."

"Right. Man, will she be shocked when she hears about this!"

"Yes, I'm sure she will be." Mr. Locke got up from the table. "Well, you still have the rest of your report to fill out and I have a couple of errands to run here in town. How about if I pick you up in half an hour or so?"

"Thanks, that would be perfect."

I handed my completed statement to Sheriff Baines. "Any word about Professor Hochstraaten in the meantime?"

"I'm afraid so. He was dead on arrival at the hospital."

"Good God." I stared at the sheriff. "I can hardly believe he killed himself, even though I know he must've felt like he was at the end of his rope. I didn't find him a very likeable person, but still. . . ."

"Yes, it's a terrible thing, any way you look at it. I'll give the college president a call, so that he'll hear about what happened from an official source."

"Could you call the college pastor, too? His name is Martin Roland. He and Hochstraaten were close in an odd sort of way."

"I'll do that."

We were silent for a moment.

"Well, you're free to go, Professor Ritter. You have no plans to leave the area in the near future?"

"No, I'll be at the college till the end of the school year."

"Good. You'll be hearing from the county about the date of your hearing."

"Okay. Looks like Jason and Moira finished their statements a while ago?"

"Yes. I had Kevin take them back to campus." He gestured with his thumb toward the door. "Mr. Locke said he was going to drive you home. He should be waiting out in the hallway."

"Great. Well, thanks for all your help, Sheriff Baines."

"You're welcome, that's what we're here for."

I found Mr. Locke examining several "wanted" posters on the wall outside the sheriff's office.

"Nice of you to wait for me," I said. "You heard that Klaus Hochstraaten died?"

"Yes, the sheriff told me. He must've been suffering somethin' awful to do himself in—mentally, or spiritually, or whatever you like to call it. I hate to sound callous, but it's lucky for you that the sheriff actually saw him take the poison. Makes everything a lot more clear-cut."

"That hadn't even occurred to me. When you think about it, though, I'm the one who drove him to do it."

"I wouldn't look at it that way. We're each of us responsible for our own actions. You did what you had to do, and for good reason. And he did what he had to do. No doubt you'll brood about it for a while, but I hope you'll come to see it that way."

I nodded. "I hope so too."

"Well, shall we be on our way?"

"Fine with me. To tell you the truth, I was almost expecting they would keep me here overnight."

Mr. Locke laughed. "Oh, no, I was able to persuade the sheriff that you weren't a serious danger to society."

The road wound around, uphill and down, through the yellows, reds, and russets of the autumn landscape.

"You seem to be bearin' up right well, Professor Ritter," Mr. Locke said.

"Really? I'll probably just collapse as soon as I walk in my front door. I do have to see if I can locate Charlotte right away, though. If you could drop me at Riedenburg Hall, there's some chance she might still be in the building. If not, she lives right across the street."

We turned off the highway at the granite St. Eustace marker and headed up the hill to campus. I got out of Mr. Locke's car a few feet away from where Hochstraaten's Mercedes had been parked. Good God, I said to myself, a few hours ago. . . .

"The sheriff will be faxing me a copy of your report," Mr. Locke said. "Once I've studied it I'll give you a ring."

"Very good. Thanks for all you've done. I really appreciate it."

As I walked across the parking lot, Charlotte and Michael Rossi were leaving the building by the back door.

"Boy, do you look bushed," Charlotte said. "Where've you been? A couple of your students stopped by wondering why you hadn't shown up for class. Did you get hit by some kind of bug or something?"

"No, nothing like that. Look, just so you're prepared, I've got some pretty awful things to tell you."

"Colin, what is it?" she asked, looking alarmed.

"I'll start with the most shocking thing of all: Klaus Hochstraaten is dead. He committed suicide."

She and Michael stared at me, stunned. "I've often wondered what it must be like living in his skin," Michael said. "He always struck me as seriously depressed."

"Yes," Charlotte said, "and those terrible migraines of his. How did you find out? Did somebody send word from Argentina?"

"No, no, it happened here, out at his house, he'd come back earlier than he'd said he would. Jason and Moira were there too. He'd pulled a gun on me, and my hands were tied—"

"Colin," she interrupted, "sounds like you've got a long story to tell. Let's go over to our place."

We crossed the road to the Rossis' house and went inside.

"I'll bet you wouldn't mind a drink," Charlotte said.

I slumped down in an easy chair. "Thanks, a beer would be great."

Michael went into the kitchen and came back with three full mugs on a tray.

"Hope you don't mind Guinness," he said. "That's all we have in the house at the moment."

"Perfect. Guinness is good for you, my maternal grandmother used to say."

The Rossis sat down on the sofa and I recounted all that had happened in recent weeks, from my work on the Lessing paper and figuring out Luke Baumgartner's last words, to Klaus's faked migraine, the ordeal at his house, and, finally, his suicide.

Charlotte and Michael sat spellbound as I attempted to thread the various occurrences together. When I came to the end of the story, I felt my entire body relaxing for the first time that day.

"You know," I said, "this all started with Luke Baumgartner's diaries. Those last words of his . . ."

Charlotte patted her husband on the knee. "So you were right all along about that final entry."

"It was just a feeling I had. I can't imagine how you ever figured it all out, Colin. I wouldn't have known where to begin."

"I didn't either. A lot of it was pure luck. And Moira was a big help, too. But if I hadn't been working on good old Gotthold Ephraim Lessing, I'd still be on square one."

Charlotte smiled. "Lessing, the man of the Enlightenment. The bringer of light."

"Exactly." I stretched and yawned. "But I don't think I need any more of that at the moment. In fact I'm ready for a serious nap."

Charlotte and Michael got up and saw me to the door.

"As bad as those things were that Klaus did," Charlotte said, "I can't help feeling sorry for him. He was an immensely talented man, and a good colleague in most ways. Worked hard all the years he was here, and there were a lot of students who respected him. Now, I know you're not feeling too charitable toward him at the moment . . ."

I was tempted to bring up Ronald Fleishman. No, not now; later on, when things had settled down, I'd tell the little that I knew. It would be good for the community to hear that the case was closed.

"I can't say I even begin to understand him, Charlotte. In a sense, I suppose he couldn't help being who he was, and part of that was his obsession. And the thing that he obsessed about was art, something that's good and beautiful in itself."

"Ironic, isn't it?" Michael said. "The appropriation and misuse of beauty for one's own purposes."

We grew silent for a moment, then Charlotte sighed.

"Life goes on, as they say. And I hate to be crass, but we're going to have to deal with Klaus's classes. There's, what, almost two weeks left until Thanksgiving break, and another week and a half in the semester after that . . ."

"Well, I can certainly keep on with the Middle High German class."

"That would be great. And I'll cover his other two. How about tomorrow, though? Why don't we cancel that class, and your own, too, so that you'll have a chance to recover."

"No, I think I'll be fine. A good night's sleep should be all I'll need."

"You're a real trooper, Colin," Charlotte said as she and Michael stepped outside with me. "And now we have another position to fill all of a sudden. We'll have to do a national search for both, of course, but I do hope you'll be among the applicants."

"Well, thanks, Charlotte, I appreciate that."

"I imagine a medievalist will be harder to find. Not so many of those birds around. Lord, we've never *ever* had such an upheaval in our department!"

"A medievalist . . . Do you remember the woman I mentioned when you were reading my Tarot cards? That's her field, and she's just now finished her dissertation. There may be a chance . . . well, I don't know, I could call her if you like. I know she's a great teacher."

"Sure, go right ahead. Have her send a resumé if she's at all interested."

"Okay, I'll do that."

"Sleep well, Colin," Michael said. "I'm glad your ordeal is over."

I walked out to the street and stood there for a moment looking across to the campus. Such an idyllic place, and I had been within a hair's breadth of never seeing it again. Feeling exhausted from head to toe, I slowly continued along the road. Upstairs, I collapsed on my bed next to Juniper and savored the softness of the pillow. The metal box with Luke's note . . . I hadn't thought to ask Mr. Locke where Dr. Davies's house was . . . he would know, since he'd talked about hanging out with the doctor's daughter there. . . .

I slept without dreaming until early the next morning.

Chapter 33

It was November 13th, the day before Annika's dissertation defense. I would make a point of calling her the following evening to see how it had gone and to tell her about the job opening at St. Eustace. Whether she would be interested or not was another matter. I had made it through my own classes this week and Klaus Hochstraaten's with a surprising burst of energy. Introducing Klaus's class to the genre of the German epic and its French influences had gone well, and the students seemed able to relate to the need of finding a balance between love and chivalry as exemplified in Hartmann von Aue's *Erec*, a knight who errs too much to the side of love. It appeared that no one in the class had any inkling as to what had become of Klaus Hochstraaten, and the college president still had not made an announcement.

Late that afternoon I drove down to Clyde's on the town square to pick up a few groceries. On my way past the law office, I stopped in to see if Mr. Locke might be available. The secretary greeted me like an old friend and buzzed her boss on the intercom.

"He'll be glad to see you, sir."

I walked along the hallway, knocked lightly on the door, and stepped inside.

"Well, good day," Mr. Locke said as he got up from his chair to shake my hand. "I was going to call you later today. I have some news, and I think it's pretty good."

"Oh? What would that be?"

"I heard this mornin' who your prosecuting attorney is going to be. His name is Clarence Warren, and he's one of the most reasonable men I know. I talked with him on the phone about your case, and it looks like things will develop pretty much as I outlined them to you. Not sure about the date of the hearing yet, but it could be as early as the middle of December."

"Fine, the sooner the better. Actually, I stopped by to ask you about something else—where Dr. Davies's house is located. I need to know—"

"Of course, because of what Luke Baumgartner said in that note he left. I had the sheriff make me a copy. Well, Dr. Davies's house was a cute little bungalow, up there in your neck of the woods on the St. Eustace campus."

"No kidding? On Faculty Row?"

"That's right. Pretty much across from the library."

I leaned forward. "Do you happen to remember the number?"

"Sure do—I was there often enough. It's number eleven."

I must have grinned like a blithering idiot.

"Find that amusin', do you?" Mr. Locke smiled back.

"That's the house I'm renting," I said.

"Well, I'll be doggoned! So you rented it from . . . what was their name again?"

"Seifert. Professor Seifert died while he was on sabbatical leave at Princeton."

"Yes, terrible, just terrible. He was supposed to have been a nice feller. It was he and his wife bought the house from Mabel Davies's executor when she died. I haven't been in the place for well over twenty years, I reckon."

I shook my head. "This is amazing—I've literally been a few feet away from the engraving ever since I moved in! Maybe you'd like to be there when I unearth it?"

"I'd be absolutely delighted. And I'd make a fairly reliable witness that everythin' was done on the up-and-up. I suppose you'll want to do the unearthing, as you put it, as soon as possible?"

"Yes, whenever you have time. I'd like my student Moira MacGregor to be there too; she was in on a good bit of the puzzle-solving. Would sometime tomorrow work for you?"

Mr. Locke studied his daily calendar. "I've got a few clients comin' in . . . how about later in the afternoon—around four, say?"

"Sure. I'm hoping that Moira will be free then, and I'll check with Charlotte and Michael Rossi too. And the college pastor, I know he'd be interested."

"Dandy, I'll come to the house at four."

"Terrific, see you then."

That evening I called the Rossis, and then Pastor Roland, who had of course been horrified to hear about Hochstraaten's death and how it had come about. It seemed to cheer him up when I told him that I would be hosting an 'artistic occasion' at my house the following afternoon, and that Moira MacGregor would likely be there. The pastor was of course completely in the dark, and Charlotte seemed equally puzzled.

Later on I sat at the dining room table staring at the built-in china cabinet. It filled the entire rear wall and contained linen drawers in the lower sections and glassed-in shelves above. Elegant cups and saucers filled the shelves on the left and right, and matching plates leaned against the back of the center section. As far as I recalled, that was where I would have to look. I walked over to the cabinet, but resisted opening the glass door; anticipating the event made it all the more exciting. There was less than a day to go now, always assuming that Luke had no further tricks up his sleeve. . . .

But no, he wouldn't have; his note made it clear that this was the final step. In a way I was sorry—what a challenge the whole process had been. And at the same time it had been both a pleasure and a privilege to get to know so many intimate details of this fascinating man's life . . . and death.

Giving the china cabinet one last look, I left the dining room and went upstairs. I remembered that I had a yet unread Dorothy Sayers mystery, *Unnatural Death*, on a shelf in the study. That would be enough to keep me occupied for the rest of the evening.

Jason and Moira had been in class on Wednesday, though both, not surprisingly, had seemed subdued. On Friday, as the remaining class members left the room at the end of the hour, they both looked at me expectantly.

"Time for a conference," I said. Moira nodded and Jason shrugged. We walked down the two flights of stairs and out the front door. A gentle breeze was blowing and flecks of light glinted off the surface of the moat in the distance. Jason and Moira sat down on the top step and I leaned against the balustrade.

"What's the latest on Professor Hochstraaten?" Moira asked.

I shook my head. "He didn't make it."

"Oh Lord, that's what I assumed. For all the trouble he caused, it's still a shame. He was a human being."

Jason frowned, but said nothing.

"Keep it to yourselves, though, until some kind of official announcement comes out."

"About that other business," Moira said, "I'm sorry for the way I acted on Saturday. I just couldn't imagine that anything could warrant your going through a colleague's desk like that. I mean, I knew he was kind of odd and all . . . "

"Never mind, Moira. You acted the way you had to, knowing as little as you did at the time."

She smiled ruefully. "I just wanted to make sure there weren't any bad feelings."

"None whatsoever."

Jason cleared his throat before speaking. "I've been a real shit to you all semester. It was my uncle who made me do it, you know, all that spying."

"*Made* you do it? Like you had no choice?"

"He said he'd have me kicked out if I didn't. I was doing crap in all my courses anyway."

I turned to Moira. "Maybe you'd better wait inside while Jason and I talk."

Jason shook his head. "I don't care. I haven't got anything to hide now."

"It's up to you, Moira."

"I'd like to stay."

"Okay. So why'd you come to St. Eustace, Jason? I'm guessing you didn't have a great relationship with your uncle to begin with."

"I hardly even knew him. My mother was a lot like him, tough as nails. She idolized him. She was the little sister; he was the older brother, the smart one, the college professor. I knew from day one what college I'd be going to."

"So they both grew up in Argentina?"

"Yes. My father, too. Him and my mother got married there, and they all ended up in the United States. The first thing I remember when I met Uncle Klaus was that he acted disgusted. Said I'd mutilated my body."

"The tattoos, you mean?"

"Yeah, it was that stupid gang I belonged to for a while. I wish I'd never had it done."

"Tattoos can be removed," Moira said. "It's supposed to be pretty painful, though."

Jason shrugged.

"Okay," I said. "So how about the art collection in his back room—did you know about that?"

"No, I had no idea what was in that room. I'd never even set foot in his house till he left for Argentina—I was supposed to keep an eye on things. I basically just slept there. All the time I was at St. Eustace, he never had me over, not for dinner, not for anything. Some uncle, huh?"

"So where do we go from here? You're pretty far behind in our German class."

"All of my classes are a disaster. I'm going to quit school. Should never have come here in the first place. My mother will raise holy hell, but I don't care."

"So then what?"

"I dunno. Might sign up for a motorcycle maintenance program. There's a good one in Daytona Beach." He looked away for a moment. "There's something else, though."

"What's that?"

"Are you going to press charges?"

I was taken aback. "For what?"

"For what I did. Tying you up and everything."

"You also cut the rope. Saved my life, you and Moira."

He gave a half-smile. "I guess."

"So good luck, with whatever you decide to do."

He nodded, glanced at Moira, and walked down the stairs.

She frowned as he disappeared around the corner. "He might have said thank you."

"Not his style."

Moira laughed. "Like he has any style?"

"He's confused, obviously."

We sat for a moment in silence.

"So how are you doing, Moira?"

"Oh, fine. Slowly coming back to normal, I think."

"Good, me too. By the way, I'm having a little get-together at my place this afternoon. Pastor Roland will be there, and both the Rossis. Thought you might want to join us."

"Sure. What's the occasion?"

"Not telling, it's a surprise."

She squinted at me. "Something to do with Dürer, maybe? Ever since the sheriff read us that letter, I've been wondering . . ."

"You'll find out soon enough. Just come by at four o'clock."

"Okay, I'll be there!"

Chapter 34

There was one more person on campus I wanted to talk to. As soon as Moira left, I walked over to the castle to see if Ned was there. His door was open, and he was sitting at his desk studying a page of sheet music.

"Excuse me, Ned," I called out.

"Oh, howdy, Professor," he said, getting out of his chair.

"No, no, don't get up. Looks like I won't be needing to borrow that key anymore. I just wanted to talk to you for a few minutes, if you have time."

"Sure, I'm on my break now, come on in and have a seat."

I walked to the end of the narrow room and sat down in a straight chair next to the desk.

"It's about all those visits I made to the private chapel, Ned. I wasn't quite straight with you about why I was doing that."

"Is that right?" he said, smiling. "I sorta thought you might be up to somethin' else."

I gave a thumbnail sketch of my convoluted search and what I had discovered each step of the way. I decided not to mention either of my trips to Klaus Hochstraaten's house.

"Well, the whole thing sounds pretty amazin', Professor, congratulations."

"Thanks. Actually, there's more to the whole story, a lot of nasty stuff along the way, too. It'll all be in the newspapers and on TV in the next few days. I'm not trying to be mysterious or anything, it would just take too long to tell."

"That's fine, I like a little mystery now and then."

I glanced at Ned's pile of sheet music as I got up to go.

"Looks like you might be having another concert coming up?"

"That's right, a week from today. With that same bunch of students."

"Terrific, I'll be there."

"Okay, see you then."

The Rossis and Pastor Roland arrived at four on the dot, following on the heels of Mr. Locke. When Moira rang the bell at five after, I considered chastising her for being late, but decided not to. Once she had stepped inside I made the introductions.

"Delighted to meet you, Ms. MacGregor." Mr. Locke said, "I understand that you've been helping in this search Professor Ritter got himself entangled in."

"Well, a little, I suppose. But Colin is the one who had the patience to see it through to the end."

Pastor Roland gave me a puzzled look. "May I ask what it was you were searching for, Professor Ritter?"

"For the moment I'll just say it was for a missing *objet d'art* that wasn't missing at all."

"No—you can't mean—"

Michael chuckled. "I think you're on to something, Martin!"

I'd never known the pastor to stutter before. "But . . . but how ... how can that be? And how did you ever find it?"

"It's a long, convoluted story. Suffice it to say for now that Luke Baumgartner inadvertantly got himself into a situation that he found difficult to get out of again. Or maybe it wasn't inadvertant at all."

"Colin, you're not making sense," Charlotte said.

Michael smiled at her. "I think maybe he is."

Moira gave me a sly look. "For a Lessing expert, you're not shedding much light on the situation."

Before I could respond, Mr. Locke spoke up. "I've brought along a brief document written by Lukas Baumgartner which should help to do that."

"Good," I said. "Why don't we all sit around the dining room table and you can read it to us."

"Fine. If I'm not mistaken, only Professor Ritter and Ms. Mac-Gregor have knowledge of this at the moment."

As we each took a seat at the table, Mr. Locke pulled a sheet of paper out of his inside pocket.

"Let me read the most essential portion: *'You will find the Knight in the dining room of the house occupied in my day by my loyal friend Dr. Davies . . . The good doctor and I secreted the engraving, by means of a cunning spring device, behind the uppermost shelf in the center of the china closet. You need only press against the panel at just the right spot and . . . Eureka!'"*

He folded the piece of paper again and put it back in his pocket. "So now all we have to know is . . ."

". . . where the doctor lived," Moira said. "And you know where that was, I suppose?"

"As a matter of fact, I do."

She looked from Mr. Locke to me and back again as we stared at the built-in china cabinet in the rear wall of the dining room.

"No! Don't tell me—"

"You got it," I said. "Luke and his doctor friend hid the engraving behind that cabinet, so by the time the Seiferts bought the house it had already been there for seventy years or more. Assuming it really is, and I'm willing to bet on it."

Moira shook her head in amazement.

"To borrow a phrase," I went on, "'what goes around, comes around.' Not terribly original . . ."

"But appropriate," Mr. Locke added.

"Before we start," I said, "I think the occasion calls for a drink. What would you like, Mr. Locke?"

"Well, a drop of good old bourbon would be appreciated, if you happen to have any in the house."

I opened the liquor cabinet and held up an almost full bottle that dated from Walter Seifert's day. "Will this do?"

"Mmm, Russell's Reserve," Mr. Locke said. "Couldn't be better in my book."

"That okay with you, Moira?"

"Absolutely. The genuine article from Kentucky."

"That goes for Michael and me, too," Charlotte said, "as naturalized Kentuckians."

"Pastor Roland?"

"Quite definitely. The equal of a good French brandy, in my opinion."

I took six glasses off the shelf above the liquor bottles and poured a couple of ounces into each.

"To Luke Baumgartner," I said.

Mr. Locke raised his glass. "May his memory live on."

"To Luke Baumgartner," everyone repeated in chorus.

We each savored the bourbon and put our glasses down.

"Here we go," I said. "If you'll just set these plates on the table, Moira . . ."

I opened the center door of the cabinet, lifted them out one-by-one and handed them to her.

"I wish Luke's instructions had been a little more precise," I said as I removed the glass shelf.

"I reckon you'll just have to experiment," Mr. Locke said. "Press in at the bottom of the panel, maybe, around the middle? I think that's the way I'd have rigged it if it had been me."

I pressed gingerly with the fingers of both hands. "I think it might have given slightly."

"Maybe push a little harder?" Moira suggested.

"Right."

I moved my hands farther apart and tried again.

"Ouch!" I pulled one hand away quickly and sucked on my finger.

"No harm done, just pinched it a little." Moira suppressed a snicker as I gave her a warning glance.

"I'll get it this time." I pressed again, and, with a click, the panel sprang open an inch or two at the bottom. It lifted out easily, revealing a recess in the wall that continued below the level of the shelf. An object wrapped in heavy woolen cloth filled almost the entire space. I pulled it out and laid it on the dining room table.

"Your turn," I said to Moira. "I'm afraid of spiders."

"I bet you're not," she said, "but thanks." She took a deep breath and gingerly unwound the layers of cloth. There it was, in what appeared to be its original gilt frame and looking as if it had been printed the day before: Dürer's *Knight, Death, and Devil*. In the lower left-hand corner was a tiny version of Luke Baumgartner's family crest flanked by his initials. A small envelope lay underneath the engraving.

"Should I open it?" Moira asked.

"Sure, here's my knife. And read what it says."

"Okay." She unfolded the two sheets of letter paper.

'Congratulations, my dear friend and quester! There remains but one small mystery to be elucidated, to wit: How did it come about that I once again had possession of the Ritter, Tod und Teufel engraving? Let me explain the sequence of events in reverse order:

When officers of the police arrived on the day after the purported theft and questioned me, I was scrupulously truthful in each of my responses – yet perhaps I could have said a bit more. And to my loyal servant Joseph, who was in charge of the nightly inspection of the museum, I could have mentioned earlier that I myself had opened one of the windows for a breath of fresh air, and that it was quite possible that I had forgotten to shut it; perhaps I should even have told him that I had removed the engraving myself and taken it to my private quarters. But the good fellow had gone to considerable trouble on my behalf! No longer the youngest of men, he had ridden through the night in order to inform the police of what had happened. What, should I then have made a fool of him, should I have made his valiant efforts seem utterly pointless? No, I could not bring myself to do that.

But why, you may be wondering, did I remove the "Ritter" in the first place? It was because I had grown immensely attached to that particular work of

Dürer's, and all the more so since the passing of my beloved Catharine, to the point that I wanted to have it at my side, so to speak, at all times. I cannot begin to tell you how much comfort and resolution I drew from contemplating that inspiring piece.

And now the time has come for my glorious knight to ride on into a new decade, into a new century, perhaps, and make the acquaintance of someone who will revere him as I have. What will you decide to do with your new acquisition? This, my dear friend, is for you to decide.

Lukas Baumgartner'''

"That devil of a trickster," I said.

Mr. Locke held his glass high. "Once again, to his eternal memory."

"And to Dürer's," I added.

Michael and Pastor Roland clinked glasses. "To Albrecht Dürer!" they intoned.

The ceremonies finished, Mr. Locke took a pen and a small notepad out of his jacket pocket. "Let me just jot down the exact time of this event, then I'll be getting back to the office. I'll draw up a document describing the whole process—the directives in Luke's will, what he says in his note, and so forth."

"Excellent, thanks for acting as official witness."

"Not at all, it was my pleasure. Being present on this occasion was a wonderful way to put the capstone on my acquaintance with Luke Baumgartner. I've always felt like I knew the man personally, and now more than ever." Mr. Locke tipped his glass back and drained it. "Lovely flavor," he said, "just lovely."

"I have a question," Moira said. "What will happen to all the paintings Professor Hochstraaten kept hidden away?"

I looked at Mr. Locke. "What do you think about that, sir? I've read about organizations that try to find relatives of the original owners of stolen works of art."

Mr. Locke nodded. "Yes, that's bound to happen one way or the other. I expect the court will consult with some authorities on art—at the University of Kentucky, for instance—and decide who should be contacted. It's bound to be a long and arduous process, given all the time that's gone by since the collection was put together."

After seeing him to the door, I joined the others at the dining room table and leaned over the engraving for several minutes, marveling at its detail.

"Good Lord, Colin," Moira exclaimed, "You own a Dürer!"

I was silent for a moment. "Yeah, I guess I do."

"You *guess* you do?" Michael said.

"See, I've been thinking about this a lot. I remember the good pastor here once saying that museums were 'public treasures,' and he was absolutely right. And then, if you remember, Moira, there was that little poem at the end of Luke's third set of clues—we said at the time that it didn't look like a clue at all."

"Right. But I have no idea anymore what it was about."

"Well, it was definitely not a clue—it amounted to a piece of advice. It made a very simple point: that a fool thinks only about worldly possessions and doesn't know what has real value."

"Yes, I remember now. So in the context of your search for the engraving . . ."

". . . it tells me that the *Knight* should go back to the Dürer museum where it belongs. What was fun and interesting for me about this whole enterprise was the process more than the result. Different from any other puzzle I've ever tried to solve."

Charlotte looked at me and shook her head. "So you're willing to give up an amazing piece of art that I would say you have every right to keep. Looks like you're going for the proverbial noble gesture?"

"That's not it at all, it's just the right thing to do."

"I agree with Charlotte," Pastor Roland said, "it truly is a noble gesture."

Moira gazed at the *Knight* again. "Whatever you want to call it, there'll be some celebration when that empty space gets filled again. I definitely want to be here for that."

I gave her a skeptical look. "I'm afraid you'll be in Savannah by then. I still have some legal business to take care of here, not the least of which will be my day in court. By the time I'm granted legal possession of the engraving it might be springtime."

"Hey, do you think a mere five hundred miles will keep me away? I wouldn't miss it for the world!"

I nodded. "Now that I think about it, you'll *have* to be here, as one of the parties instrumental in finding the engraving. Without you, would I ever have come upon the three lindens out in the North Woods? I can't imagine how."

Moira smiled. "So I have co-conspirator's rights?"

"Definitely."

"And what are you going to do with Mr. Knight in the meantime?"

"Good question. Come to think of it, I should have had Mr. Locke take him down to his office for safekeeping. In fact, I'll do that this afternoon yet. But first, I'm just going to stare at him for a while. Thank you all for coming. It wouldn't have been nearly as much fun without you."

That evening I waited until eight o'clock—seven, Minnesota time—before calling Annika.

"Hello, Colin," she said brightly, "by now I recognize your number."

"Hi, Annika. You can probably guess why I'm calling. How did it go?"

"Very well, the committee members gave me lots of compliments afterwards."

"Well, congratulations. I was afraid you might be out somewhere living it up."

"Oh no, I just wanted to relax tonight. We had a little celebration in the German offices this afternoon."

"Good. That's what we did after my defense, too. Nothing big, just a few close friends."

"Yes. I remember that very well."

"You know, I actually have a second reason for calling you. St. Eustace suddenly has another job opening—for a medievalist, no less."

"A medievalist? Really?"

"Yes, it came about rather suddenly. One of our colleagues died— killed himself, as a matter of fact."

"Oh no, that's terrible!"

"Well, it's a very long and complicated story."

"Suicides always are, I think. So the college would want someone for next semester already?"

"That's right. I thought you'd want to know about the possibility. I hope you'll apply, Annika."

"Do you? Well, I certainly will consider it. When did the . . . death come about?"

"The day before yesterday."

"My God! So recently?"

"Yes. Otherwise I would have let you know sooner. As it is, I'm sure you're the only one who's heard about the position so far. I doubt that Charlotte has mentioned it to anyone else yet."

"Charlotte . . . ?"

"Charlotte Rossi, she's our Chair. The college is very small, so we're only a three-person department: Charlotte, me—at least for the moment—and . . . maybe you?"

"Hmm, so small. That might be a bit awkward, Colin."

I took a deep breath. "I'm sure it would be at first. But maybe with time . . . and talk . . ."

"Yes, that can help. For better or for worse."

I winced as I thought back to the last days of my relationship with Annika.

"It must be meaningful talk, Colin, not just platitudes, not promises that turn into betrayals."

"That's exactly what I have in mind, Annika. For better or for worse."

She was silent for a moment.

"Charlotte Rossi, you said. And what is the address?"

"It's simply: German Department, St. Eustace College, Arcadia, Kentucky 40304."

"Arcadia. That sounds very hopeful. But there are no guarantees."

"No, there are no guarantees."

Norman Watt taught German language and literature courses at St. Olaf College from 1966 to 2000 and was part of the college's "Great Conversation" program. Since retiring, he has translated numerous historical and family documents from German to English. His novel Fanatic is currently being translated into German.